Remember Who You Are!

Remember Who You Are!

The Story of a Son of the Manse

David Findlay Clark

Cualann Press

ISBN: 978-0-9554273-1-2

First published in 2007

British Library Cataloguing in Publication Data. A catalogue record of this
book is available at the British Library.

Printed by Bell & Bain, Glasgow

Published by:
Cualann Press, 6 Corpach Drive, Dunfermline, KY12 7XG, Scotland
Tel/Fax +44 (0)1383 733724
Email: info@cualann.com
Website: www.cualann.com

Yes, I know what Larkin said,
but in spite of all that this book is

dedicated to the memory of my parents

By the author

Stand By Your Beds! A Wry Look at National Service

Help, Hospitals and the Handicapped

One Boy's War

Biographical Note

Dr David Findlay Clark OBE DL MA PhD CPsychol FBPsS ARPS

Retired from working as a consultant clinical psychologist in the NHS and in private practice, Dr Clark is a son of the manse who was brought up in Banff and educated at Banff Academy and Aberdeen University. He is still a Clinical Senior Lecturer in the Department of Mental Health there though no longer active in teaching. After a period of National Service in the RAF (from AC2 to Flying Officer) he worked first as an industrial psychologist at Leicester Industrial Rehabilitation Unit of the then Ministry of Labour before becoming a clinical psychologist in the NHS. He has taught and researched at the Universities of Leicester and Aberdeen in the course of his work within a number of hospitals in the NHS, eventually retiring from the NHS in 1990 as Director of the Grampian Health Board's Area Clinical Psychology Services. For his work in that context he was awarded an OBE in 1989 and, having been active in one or another form of public service for most of his life, became Deputy Lieutenant of Banffshire in 1992.

For over twenty-five years he has been an Honorary Sheriff in the Sheriffdom of Grampian, Highlands and Islands at Banff. He has been a Consultant for the WHO in Sri Lanka and has also been invited to lecture on his research in India, Canada and the USA. A new edition of his popular book on National Service, *Stand By Your Beds! A Wry Look at National Service* was published in 2006. He is the author of a textbook, *Help, Hospitals and the Handicapped* as well as a contributor of chapters in several other major texts and over thirty professional research papers in learned and technical journals.

Latterly he has taken to less academic forms of journalism by writing magazine articles and a book, *One Boy's War*. He writes now as an additional activity to his pervasive hobby interests in photography, painting and drawing, music and golf. He lives with his wife, Janet, in Banff, and has two married daughters and four grandchildren.

Contents

List of Plates

Acknowledgements

In spite of the restraints which were imposed on my brother and me as sons of the manse – and which were common, I think, to almost all the children of clergymen in those early days of the twentieth century, there is no doubt that I owe it to my mother for teaching me about being diligent, and generous to others, as she was. My father created an atmosphere of learned application and the value of books and ideas and my late younger brother showed me a way of adapting to all the family pressures rather differently, and probably better.

At school, two teachers enriched my life. Mrs Kelly in Primary 6, who was humane, thoughtful and, exceptionally at that time, seemed to like children. George A. Scott, who taught me up to Higher English, was a gifted teacher who never used the belt but who could be stimulating, witty and interesting even in his *obiter dicta*.

The Milne family at Paddocklaw farm, in the course of only several weeks each year, played a larger part than ever they knew in forming my adult attitudes and values. They made the vernacular agricultural background within which I was brought up real and taught me to value those who endlessly toiled on the land amid the exigencies of weather and the economy. They made me strong physically and taught me about practicality and cooperation.

Professor Rex Knight and his wife, Margaret, opened up new intellectual vistas for me, provided me with superb models of how to think analytically, logically and accurately and were instrumental in setting me on the right path for my life's work.

Finally, my fellow students, Ralph Dutch and his late wife, Mary, to say nothing of my own dear wife Janet, gave me life-long love and friendship, sharpened up my thinking, were genially tolerant of my weaknesses, shared many of my pleasures and anxieties and were endlessly stimulating as company.

These were the influences that made me what I am and I am deeply grateful to them all.

Coming to the more contemporary scene, I am, of course, much indebted to Professor Alexander Fenton, CBE, for writing such a charming and thoughtful Foreword and I am, too, enormously grateful to Lord Steel for being willing, in a very busy life, to find time to write an Epilogue.

I should also like to express my warm thanks to Rainbow Books and especially to Mrs N. Morrice for allowing me to quote in full her late and charming husband's poem, 'I Remember Sunday' and to Hodder and Stoughton for permission to quote from Joan Bakewell's autobiography, *The Centre of the Bed*.

Foreword

Prof. Alexander Fenton
CBE MA BA DLitt HonDLitt (Abd.) FRSE FRSGS HRSA FSA
FSAScot.

This is an unusual book. It is an autobiographical account of the writer's first twenty one years, but it does not simply relate a series of events in chronological sequence. It amounts also, as David Clark himself says, to a psychological report on himself written by himself, and as such, it incorporates a rare depth of thought and self-analysis into its pages. The strong influence of family background and of the educational system is made plain, and the growing boy's reactions to them make at times compulsive reading.

The title of the book, *Remember Who You Are!*, aptly symbolises the atmosphere of an upbringing in a large, sometimes cold, manse, where the minister and his wife were heavily engaged in parochial affairs, and a maid saw to the everyday needs of the two children. The parents had little time or even inclination to be demonstratively affectionate, but nevertheless had high expectations which put a considerable strain on the boys, who were expected to maintain patterns of perfect behaviour and set an example to their carefully selected playmates and other youth of the parish. Little wonder that David can use words like 'prisoner' and 'deprived' in relation to his childhood, and indeed the whole book is a review of the steps that marked a gradual sloughing of the shackles of the manse and eventually of religion.

Parental expectations were extended to school achievement also. The educational system of the time predisposed pupils to follow certain expected lines, such as – for gifted youngsters like David – the ministry or teaching or the medical or perhaps legal profession. Even a lang-heidit lad o' pairts should conform. In this regard, it is interesting to compare the stories recorded by a number of north-easters of roughly contemporary vintage and with a range of types of ability, reproduced in David Northcroft's *North-East Identities and Scottish Schooling* (Aberdeen, 2005, p. 111-49). Though these are confined largely to reminiscences of school-days, they include people whose occupation as adults included farmer, fisherman, policeman, housewife, car salesman, teacher, journalist and one Director of Education. It is a pity that there is no attempt to analyse the effect that school years and home circumstances had on the course of later life of each individual. This, however, is something that David does admirably, and his book is in many ways a thoughtful extension to the contents of Northcroft's publication. He broke away from a system that conditioned pupils to become servants of the parish at various levels, and in so doing demonstrates that native ability can overcome convention. Encouragement from wise individuals is also a matter of some importance and sometimes of good luck, and in Professor Rex Knight, the well-known psychologist, David found an adviser and friend who set him on his real path in life, that of a clinical psychologist.

David Clark writes with clinical observation, yet also with passion and humour, creating a very human story marked by the series of turning points in his life, not forgetting the epic solo cycle tour that took him round Britain. This is a story of achievement, and not least of the sometimes hard won establishment of self-identity.

Chapter I

RUDE AWAKENINGS

'A child is not frightened at the thought of being patiently transmuted into an old man.' (Saint-Exupéry *Flight to Arras* 1942)

My father staggered out of the bedroom at the top of the stair. I had never seen him like this. His eyes glistened with silent tears. He reached blindly for the banister and hung on to it for a moment, white-knuckled, before he saw me. At that, he quickly reached for a handkerchief, gathered his composure and asked me with gentle urgency to go downstairs and speak to the maid for a while. Something about the intensity of the episode led to my instant and unquestioning obedience.

As I went, I dropped the favourite green Dinky toy racing car I had been playing with on the elegantly carpeted manse staircase. For once, I had, perhaps intuitively, omitted to supply the usual sound effects, knowing that my father was in the bedroom with mother. She had been in bed a lot recently but, wrapped in the innocence of childhood, it never occurred to me to wonder why. During these recent days usually there had been a rather austere nurse, whom I had never taken to, in the room with her. There was a brief hiatus. Something about the situation made a profound impression on me and it held a suddenness and drama which few children, even as young as I then was, would be likely to forget.

Much later, I was to learn that my father had just visited my mother who was then due to give birth, at home, to a new baby to replace a little sister of mine who had died of pneumonia in infancy. Father had hired, on his doctor's advice and at a cost he could ill afford, a midwife to tend to my mother's needs and ensure that all went well with the birth. The explanation of his deep emotion was that he had just entered the bedroom to find my mother in distress, the baby born, a longed-for girl, beside her, still-born, strangled by the cord around her neck. Meanwhile, the midwife remained slumped, asleep, in a chair in the bedroom. It was very quiet. To me, it was, in retrospect, rather like watching a film with no sound track.

I was too young to grasp, even imagine, the mental turmoil, rage and distress my father must then have experienced. In adulthood I was to hear about the episode from both of my parents, though never from both of them at

13

one time. It was as if the one feared for the effect on the other of telling the story with the other present. Indeed my mother, herself a midwife, very seldom said anything about it all her life, though I know she was deeply scarred by it. Looking back, I imagine that that midwife might have committed some sort of professional, even criminal, offence, but all that transpired, as far as I know, was that she was immediately sacked and I never saw her again.

Shortly afterwards, after various comings and goings, there was a quiet private funeral. Again, I spent time with the maid in the kitchen while my parents shared their private grief.

For many years as children, my brother and I visited, on a Sunday afternoon, the cemetery at the top of the town while my mother placed flowers on the little unmarked grave. The wind murmured its condolences in the fir wood over the dyke as I speculated about what my two little sisters might have been like at my age. In these days of low birth and neonatal mortality it is a reminder of just what hazards lay in store for parents in all social circumstances six or seven decades ago. For my brother Tom and me these little sisters were never as real as they were to our parents. I would stand by my mother's side at the cemetery with due solemnity week after week. Little was ever said.

'This is where your little sisters are buried, David. You mustn't ever forget them,' was as much as ever was uttered. So we remembered the fact of these brief lives but never really experienced the reality of any relationship or bonding with them. Only with adulthood came the realisation of what a loss, so deeply felt, that was for my parents.

Memory is a fickle jade. It captures our identity. Our egos would disintegrate but for the sustaining continuities of experience it affords us. Even when later discontinuities become too painfully obvious, we depend on this subtle and capricious storage system, whatever its lapses, its confabulations and its treasures without price, to maintain this identity. In childhood one hardly even recognises it as a faculty at all. Memory writes easily on the clean slate and we take it for granted, storing our impressions without effort.

We are, in due course, taught to make strange and often false distinctions between remembering, which in so many cases we did without consciously trying, and learning, which later became a business, formalised by schooling and structured by the disciplines of needing to know things, about things and how to do things. But all too early, the slate is overwritten, palimpsested and crammed to the corners with time's scribbles. Reference to it becomes more sporadic, the trace has become confused, elaborated sometimes by random decorations and effaced by the schoolboy's damp sleeve of repression, or by more deliberate attempts to make space for more recent messages by rubbing out the old and little read.

Can psychological science therefore tell us anything about how those memories available to the autobiographer might be retrieved and organised? In 1991 there was a study by Holland and Rabbitt in the *British Journal of Psychology* in which they compared the recall of autobiographical events by two groups of elderly volunteers matched for intelligence. One group lived in residential care and the members of the other group lived independent lives. The researchers found that the group in residential care actually recalled and spontaneously rehearsed more memories from their early than from their recent lives, whereas the reverse was true for the independent elderly. A subgroup of cognitively impaired subjects was also investigated to look at the effects of senile confusional states. Although the unimpaired elderly in care produced more early than recent memories, they were still able to produce substantial numbers of recent memories. Impaired subjects produced very few memories at all and those they did produce tended to be early ones. Holland and Rabbitt concluded that the frequency of rehearsal (or reminiscence) seemed to affect the likelihood that a memory could be recalled. People in institutions more often spend conversational or even rumination time in rehearsal of the memories of early events. People in the community with active and perhaps more varied lives are more likely to use their memories for everyday purposes and therefore to store recent events better. They are also less likely to have time to spend simply rehearsing the details of the distant past. Frequency of rehearsal is thus a function of the use which people in different situations make of their memories.

It is, of course, common knowledge among those who study such things that cognitive impairment due to organic neurological changes in the elderly does deplete recall from recent life. However, where such changes have not so far made too many inroads, and where there is enough of interest in the quotidien round, then some sort of even balance is possible between recall of the long gone and perhaps more detailed and unembellished memories of more recent origin. Hopefully, this autobiographer sits, at the time of writing at least, more as one of those active elderly going about the community than as one of the institutionalised or impaired.

Each of us does well nevertheless not to place too much trust in the accuracy, in any objective sense, of our recall system. Quite apart from those memories which have inexorably and unwittingly slipped beyond all recall, there are others which are so private (if not shared by some 'significant others') that even the most blatant exhibitionist would be reluctant to set them before the public gaze. All of us select our memories, consciously or unconsciously, some for reasons we understand well enough and some for reasons we never will. Few people can fail to recognise, even as they experience them, events, feelings or situations which they know immediately they will remember for the rest of their lives (short of suffering brain damage).

Equally, there are millions of other memories which are shot through with an inherent transience such that they do not even register as discriminable events having a beginning and an end. Somewhere among the latter there may be a wealth of explanatory data which fits into the former with the compelling neatness of a complex and well made jigsaw puzzle. We are able to use, however, only the pieces that have not been lost to give some acceptable semblance of the whole completed picture. This forms an approximation in which the frame, the straight edged pieces at the sides of the puzzle, is usually the easiest part to complete. But there will be sections of the picture within the frame well enough completed, because the pieces give good clues, together with other more fragmentary details and perhaps part-pictures running out into blank space, some even without any links to the rest, though clearly within the frame and apparently belonging to that particular puzzle, which give some coherence until missing pieces can be found.

Such metaphor is especially apt in the case of the memories of one's very early life. Events then cannot be placed, as they are experienced, against the framework which review of one's later life supplies. Then, they are stored more effectively probably because of the rich or strong emotional overtones they then carried.

My own first actively recalled memory is of lying in a cot with thin, turned wood vertical bars at the sides. I was looking at a pattern of flowery blue wallpaper in a room I later identified as the large south-facing bedroom in the manse at Banff. Much more vaguely, I remember some interaction involving adults looking down at me, although whether these were my parents or not I could never tell. In early adulthood I remembered enough of the detail of this to describe it to my mother who validated the accuracy of the situation, though not the event nor the exact time. It was concluded that I must have been just under the age of two at the time. The emotional tone of the memory, in spite of the thesis I have just presented, is utterly lost to me.

It has always been quite hard for me to get to grips with the fact that between the birth of my grandfather and of myself just under a century passed. Old James Clark, market and jobbing gardener and son of Hugh Clark, ploughman, was born in 1839. My father, David (Alexander) Findlay Clark was born on 6 June 1882, and I myself first saw light of day on 30 May 1930. For reasons lost in time my father and his family dropped the middle name, Alexander, early in his life.

For most families, an interval of over 90 years might be expected to span three rather than two generations, but the Clarks seem to have delayed their procreative activities till they were nearly half a century old! In that activity I was happy to break the mould. It did mean, however, that my brother Tom, two years my junior, and I grew up with a head of the house who seemed more like the grandfathers of our contemporaries than a father – more patriarch than pater. With the benefit of hindsight, it is easy to see that this played a large part in forming aspects of my adulthood.

My mother, Annie Whyte McKenzie, was born on 10 January 1896. She was therefore some fourteen years my father's junior. She was the daughter of James McKenzie and Annie Whyte. The latter died the year before I was born. My paternal grandmother, Helen Findlay, died in in the same year, 1929, aged eighty-three and paternal grandfather, James Clark, died in 1921, aged eighty. The result of all that was that my brother and I only ever knew one grandparent and even he was visited only once a year at his miner's cottage in Fife. Curiously, from all that I ever heard my parents talk about their own parents, it seemed that of the three grandparents we never saw, old James Clark especially, was easily the most interesting of our immediate forebears. Time, of course, and their absence, may have lent enchantment to the view. James McKenzie, or Grandpa as we knew him, had been a regular soldier, and Regimental Sergeant Major in the Militia until his honourable discharge after more than twenty years' service. He then worked at the coal face as a ripper in various coal mines in and

Plate 1: My maternal grandparents, James and Annie McKenzie

around Lochgelly in Fife. He was a powerfully built man, broad shouldered and well muscled, not unduly tall but with a presence which was unmistakable. At heart he was probably more soldier than miner and to his dying day wore a waxed and curled moustache which fascinated me as a child. I abhorred to be kissed by him because of its spikiness, but was at the same time intrigued to examine the traces of his previous meal which seemed always to have been strained through it.

He smelled strongly of old tobacco which he both chewed and smoked (though happily not the same tobacco) in a number of pipes of various shapes and sizes. His much deplored but persistent habit of spitting, with challenging accuracy, into a spittoon which sat just inside the brass hearth rail, from his favourite chair four or five feet away, was something which I, at the age of three or four, viewed with what I now know as ambivalence. My mother especially, proud of her training as a nurse and midwife, would berate him long and loudly for this unendearing habit. He remained unmoved and unrepentant. The subtle skills he exercised in being so often noisily on target and also of seeming to be able to suck soup from his spoon at a spoon-to-mouth range of about half an inch filled me with admiration. The business of emptying the spittoon and of watching the soup disappear through the wiry portcullis of the brown stained moustache was, however, much less savoury.

Both my parents struggled and strove in their early lives to free themselves from the shackles of a poverty-stricken and harsh working class life. My father was, on the whole, more inclined to reminisce on some of the incidents of his youth and early manhood, perhaps because he, being so much older than my mother, was already approaching his 'anecdotage' at a time when she was still heavily preoccupied with the business of organising his, her and our daily lives. Some of the motivation for his indulgence in this derived from a measure of pride in achievement – something which, in later life, I thought was in fact well merited – but also it sprang from a more typically ingrained attitude, out of Samuel Smiles, by John Calvin (as the horse breeders say) by which he would present his ways of coping with his early vicissitudes as a model for weaker spirits, such as my brother and myself, to aspire to.

At the public school in Girvan in these latter days of the 19th century, the brighter pupils could, on reaching the age of fifteen, be appointed by the dominie to act as pupil teachers, thus easing for him the load of dragging an unwilling squad of younger pupils through the syllabus of the so-called three R's, along with Bible Study, Singing and Penmanship! Thus my father earned a pittance which afforded him the luxury (for a jobbing gardener's lad) of staying on long enough at school to study for his Prelims, examinations which would, in due course, allow him to matriculate at Glasgow University. In the interim he had also worked as a labourer at a nearby farm along with his brothers and cousins.

His only sports at that time seem to have been walking (the only means of travel), Cumberland wrestling and smoking (then thought, as it was in my own youth, to be a manly pursuit). One impediment to his progress to university was that there had been no facilities at the Girvan school for pupils to study any language other than Latin. A further language was necessary for university admission. Undaunted, my father then went out, bought a German grammar and a German dictionary, and set about teaching himself that language. This he did with enough success and fluency, both to pass the necessary examinations, to enjoy a stay in Germany in 1922 and, much later to communicate with German prisoners of war in Banff in 1940–41.

The protracted 1922 holiday in Germany was embarked upon with a friend from theological college called Coulter, though whether they returned together has never been clarified. They certainly met again many years later in Banff, because I remember much friendly banter and even uproarious reminiscing (not in my mother's presence, as I remember) between the men. It seems that a sail down the Rhine had flung together my German speaking father and a certain Gräfin, whether a self-appointed countess or not, and they had disembarked for a stay in Wiesbaden for high jinks on their own.

Needless to say my father was holidaying in what he liked to describe as 'mufti'. The only relic of this brief romance is a solitary fond postcard in old German script to my father. He only once spoke to me of this episode, quite wistfully, not long before he died. He told me that he could have decided to stay in Germany then but would have had to work, probably as a teacher again, although he thought that the countess was quite wealthy. In the event, he had already formed a relationship with my mother, though they were not engaged, so he returned (I fancy rather reluctantly) to this country overloaded with Deutschmarks, literally in the millions, because at that time there was roaring inflation, increasing by the day in Germany between the wars, and tourists from this country needed to buy suitcases simply to carry unspent notes back home. 'Tempora mutantur ... !' Unfortunately, the barrowload of Deutschmarks then converted in Scotland to a small envelope of pounds sterling.

None of the family, other than a cousin of my father's, a George Clark who had, according to my father, been an engineer who designed the original Hampden Park football ground, had ever before aspired to any sort of higher education. In consequence, father's achievement in taking even an Ordinary degree at Glasgow University and funding himself throughout on what he could earn from his uncertificated teaching and farm work was initially lauded, though with prudent parsimony lest he get swelled headed.

Both his parents, relatively uneducated but both well-read seemed to have been reasonably proud of the lad. He wished later that he had had the courage to take an Honours degree (though he went on later to take a higher degree which he felt himself was a near equivalent). Perhaps it was something of that early frustration which was to lead him to urge me to aspire a little higher when my own time came to wander in the groves of Academe. An MA on its own, however, put never 'a penny in his pooch'. He then had to attend Moray House Teacher Training College in Edinburgh for a further year in order to gain his teacher's Certificate. By that time, however, he had, with growing sophistication, learned of sources of bursaries for young men of limited means. So, with his farm earnings as well, the business of sustaining himself in 'digs' and attending the course in Edinburgh became less of a hardship.

His first proper job was as a teacher at Hillhead Academy in Glasgow and for a long time I kept the silver fob watch which he had bought with his first pay there. For a number of years he seems to have worked away quite happily in school, apart from when he had to take a music class, something which, for no good reason I could ever divine, he was most uncomfortable about. At weekends and holidays, however, he commuted to see his parents and siblings in Girvan and to work at the farm of Pinmill, near Girvan, during the holidays.

Old James Clark, my grandfather, when he was not market gardening or odd-jobbing, had apparently been addicted to the Rationalist Press and had been something of a scourge of the landed gentry around Ayrshire, for some of whom he worked. He was wont to anathematise them in speech, both privately and in public meetings, and to argue vigorously for greater recognition of the primary producers and for the improvement of the conditions of work for the ordinary man. A socialist before his time, he became a strong supporter of Keir Hardie, wrote leftist political pamphlets and joined the Fabians. In fact he eventually engaged in a spirited correspondence with George Bernard Shaw following one of the latter's newspaper articles. My father often told of how proud his father was about this but, to the family's huge regret, every bit of that correspondence was lost in a fire at home some time before his death.

Grandfather had left school at eleven years of age. Reports show, however, that he had clearly been one of those intelligent but formally uneducated men of the 19th century who took every opportunity to read widely, to argue and to discuss anything and everything under the sun. *Man and Superman* and *The Black Girl in Search of God* had been among his standard texts. Old Jimmie was known locally as a freethinker and atheist – much to the chagrin of his wife, Helen, who seems to have been altogether a gentler soul, less astringent in both manner and ideas. I often felt my father respected my grandfather but was not as close to him as he was to my grandmother. On the occasions when he would take me as a small boy to see the house at 20 Montgomery Street in Girvan in which he had been brought up, there was always a greater warmth in his voice and style when he talked of his mother.

Old James Clark's wrath against the gentry was not lessened by the loss, in her early adulthood, of his youngest daughter, Susan, my father's favourite sister. She was described as attractive and, in my father's view, the most intelligent of the family by far. As was the case for so many working class girls of that era, she worked 'in service' in a posh home near Girvan. My father's view of her was that she could, more easily than he, have prospered in a university environment.

'Aye, boy', he would say to me, 'it was a real tragedy. Susan could have gone far enough, but girls were just not encouraged to aspire beyond their station in those days. She was far too good for what she was doing.' Even allowing for the golden glow of long remembered hindsight on my father's part, it was clear to me from the sort of comments I used to hear from my other less well-endowed aunts that Susan must have had exceptional qualities.

One terrible night there was a fire at the house of her employers while she was helping with the children. Having managed first to get the children safely ushered out of the burning house, she was sent in again, on her master's orders to retrieve some of the fittings and furniture. While trying to do so part of the roof fell in and she was trapped inside and was burned to death. Old Jimmie could see evidence neither of a benevolent God nor of a benevolent employer in that.

What was originally quite a large family of Clarks was gradually whittled away by disease (TB in at least one case), accidents such as Susan's and the 1914–1918 war. By the time my parents and I were to visit Girvan, in the 1930s and '40s, only my father, his younger brother, Hugh, a bachelor tiler, slater and chimney sweep, and three aunts, all unmarried also, were alive. Maggie, Nellie and Jessie were 'characters' each with markedly individual styles and Hugh and the three of them were eventually persuaded by my father, after the death of both their parents, to pool their resources and buy a pleasant bungalow, 'Kerlaw', in Roodlands Road, Girvan. Many years later, when none of the other siblings survived, that house was to become my parents' retirement home and, only a short time later, the home in which my father lived out his lonely last few years.

Plate 2: My paternal grandparents, James and Helen Clark

My paternal grandmother was buried in the silver sand of the seaside graveyard in Girvan but old James, who worked until the day he died, had always made it clear that he had never in his life sought the services of any clergy nor had he any need for 'hallowed ground'. So he was simply buried in a field at Pinmill, with no burial service. Later, my father, by then a minister of the Church of Scotland, arranged for his re-interment in the family lair in Girvan with my grandmother, and, eventually, my own parents to hold him down! Amid my sorrow, the situation afforded me a wry smile when I scattered the handful of sand over his last remains on the day of my father's funeral in 1966.

That smile was occasioned by the memory of the fact that my grandfather would have nothing more to do with my father from the day when the latter announced that he was to give up his perfectly respectable job as a teacher in Glasgow in order to study for the ministry – not of Education, but of religion! My father was always rather secretive about his motivation for such a swing in his life's pattern at nearly the age of thirty. Whether he had been disappointed in love, or simply disillusioned by teaching, or whether what he had seen of the deprivations of inner city life in Glasgow had left him with a feeling that other kinds of support for the people there might be better given by him in another kind of role will never be known. He would only say that he 'got the call' to devote his life to others in this rather different way and to undertake a Bachelor of Divinity degree at Edinburgh University forthwith.

He had even resigned his job before telling his parents. His mother, being a devout woman, and, as a midwife, well aware of the miracles of life and the tragedies of infant and maternal death had apparently been understanding and tolerant. His father, however, had been overcome with rage and frustration. There and then he forswore my father from ever darkening his door again.

'Ye come in here – nivver a word to us about leavin' yer job – a decent, worthwhile job amang the best o' bairns – an' tell us that you're going to be hoodwinked by a' that superstition an' mumbo jumbo religious twaddle – the opium o' the masses – at least for them that canna think for themsel's.'

My father had been firm in his decision in the face of all this, but aul' Jimmie was unrelenting.

'If ye dinna change yer min' an' settle for a decent, sensible job like the school teachin' ye've worked sae hard for, then ye needna darken this door again! There's naethin' for ye here so dinna let me see ye in this hoose again until ye get rid o' that daft dog's collar.'

Protest with all the reasonableness that he could muster or not, thus was my father summarily disinherited and banished from the family home. Not that his father had any worldly goods whatsoever anyway with which to endow him, but there is no doubt in my mind from his talking to me as a young lad that he greatly missed going back to Montgomery Street at weekends and holiday times. In fact, he did, after some time, work out stratagems whereby he might surreptitiously visit my grandmother, but only when it was known that Aul' Jimmie would not be around for a few hours. My father used to take a quiet pleasure in showing my brother, Tom, and me the Montgomery Street house and the back lanes he had used to visit his mother.

It was about this time in 1907 or 1908 that he again found hmself set to studying other languages, and, even more difficult, scripts. Both ancient Greek and Hebrew were then set subjects for the degree of Bachelor of Divinity (a postgraduate degree). Undaunted, my father tackled both with enthusiasm and no little skill. Later, in talking to him, I got the impression that, although he had studied them primarily to pass the set examinations and perhaps also to be able to base his studies of Comparative Religion and Biblical Criticism on a first-hand knowledge of the primary sources and of the complications of multiple translations and interpretations of ancient scripts, he was basically more invested in using Latin and German in his everyday life.

Again, during the Second World War, he set about learning Norwegian, the better to understand and relate to the soldiers of the 42nd Norwegian Mountain brigade who came to be stationed in Banff. Many of them had escaped from their Nazi-occupied homeland by means of the so-called Shetland Bus. Indeed, he never tired of looking for roots and derivations from other languages when he used and read English and he was always a stickler for correct word usage and the use of a wide and subtly differentiated vocabulary. His repeated adjurations to me as a boy to check word usage by reference to Fowler's *English Usage* or the Chambers' dictionary when either he or I was uncertain of syntax or semantics bordered on pedantry.

Nevertheless, I have often been aware subsequently that a capacity to discern such nuances of language usage and meaning and to select terms with exactitude, relevance and sometimes originality plays a large part in the capacity to order, categorise and select in one's thinking generally – something certainly akin to what we like to call intelligence. Confusions between 'militate' and 'mitigate', 'continual' and 'continuous', 'solipsism' and 'solecism' would have been anathema to him and, subsequently, to me. I owe him that debt, as well as his reverence for books, not as objects but as repositories of knowledge and wisdom and as a route to the vicarious extension of experience and ideas.

My father's first jobs in the ministry of the Auld Kirk of Scotland took him to St Matthew's Parish Church, Edinburgh, as assistant minister, with a brief period of detachment, as a *locum tenens* at the church of St Mary's Hope, Orkney. He used to tell a story of how he was awakened one dark night in his 'digs' on that island (for there were no Churchill Barriers or causeways between the islands in those days) to see a flickering light under his door, deep moaning noises and a slow and deliberate step mounting the stair to the attic bedroom he rented. Wind and rain howled and rattled against the skylight and pitch darkness lent an eerie ghostliness to the scene. Torn between prayer (orthodox) and the need to grab a big stick from the corner (unorthodox), he was saved by the eldritch bawling of his landlady.

'Donald! Come doon aff that stair an' nae fleg (frighten) the meenister!'

Donald was the mildly psychotic but powerfully built six-foot mentally handicapped son of the household and he was given to walking in his sleep by candlelight.

Almost incredibly, an episode of exactly the same kind was to befall me some time about sixty years later when I was marooned by gales on the island of Stronsay in Orkney. In the course of my work as a consultant clinical psychologist, I used to do clinics every three months or so in the Northern Isles. One late autumn, the boat got me to Stronsay where I had several domiciliary visits to do. The gale rose to hurricane force, however, and there was no way the little 'flit-boat' which ferried me to and from the bigger steamer anchored offshore could survive in the raging seas. I was put up for a night in a sturdy stone built house near the shore – again in an upstairs room with only a lifting latch to secure the door and no electric light. The generator went off after supper! Some time in the dead of night I was awakened by the whole house shaking and shuddering in the 100 mph gale – and something else! There was flickering light showing under my door and the sound of footsteps deliberately but steadily coming up the wooden stair. The steps would stop for some minutes. Only the howling of the gale. Then the steps again and the light flickering, sometimes almost seeming to go out. I heard heavy breathing. I was quite undecided how to tackle this unexpected and creepy experience since I was reluctant to raise my hosts. It was just after 4 a.m. by the luminous hands of my watch. Then the footsteps started up again – only to recede downstairs, to be followed by a bang as the outside door slammed shut. I relaxed and tried to regain a fitful sleep.

In the morning at breakfast, my host asked if I'd been disturbed by the door banging. I said nothing about the heavy breathing and the footsteps on the stair. By now I was not even sure I hadn't been dreaming.

'You see, it's just Ronnie,' (we'll call him) his father said. 'He's mildly schizophrenic and often just gets up in the night and goes away out on his bike for a run. He can see in the dark like an owl and there's only the one road on the island anyway. He'll likely be back later on.'

The parents were remarkably insouciant. They knew the island people would recognise the lad and ensure that no harm came to him. How he stayed upright on a bike in the dark and in the storm force winds, however, baffled me. I told them nothing of my anxious fantasies of ghosts and ghoulies. The parallel between that story and my father's of so long ago was nevertheless quite fascinating – even unnerving.

Perhaps my father's greatest claim to fame, however, while he was in Edinburgh, arose from the mischance that he was on duty for his senior minister one weekend in 1911 when the famous illusionist and showman, the Great Lafayette, died in Edinburgh. He had asked that his body be laid to rest with his dog buried alongside him. The Jewish Rabbi who would normally have officiated refused to accommodate this wish.

The Reverend Mr Clark had no such scruples, especially since a fee of £5 had been mentioned – a princely sum in 1911! – and he promptly joined the cortège of horse drawn carriages as it wound its way through Edinburgh. Later the remains of both man and dog were buried with dignity and circumspection.

The Scotsman of 15 May 1911 published an extensive three column report of the funeral commenting that along the entire funeral route of some two to three miles 'large masses' of people were assembled. 'The tragic death of the victim, his mistaken identification leading to the cremation of two persons instead of one, and the mystery surrounding the personality of Lafayette were sufficient of themselves to account for the deep interest evinced by the public.' I myself have been unable to trace any further details about the mysterious cremation of two persons instead of one – perhaps he was an illusionist to the last!

I now quote from a typescript found among my father's papers. This is probably a transcript of the original *Scotsman* article of Monday 15 May 1911. The content is, however, so fascinating that I include it here.

Straight in from the cemetery gates is a broad carriageway, which at a distance of 30 or 40 yards divides into two and circles round a large ornamental mound filled with trees and shrubs. This probably would not, in ordinary circumstances, have been used for interments for another 50 years. Beyond it the cemetery proper opens up. This circular mound is about 50 feet in diameter; it rises with a gentle slope to a height of about nine feet, and on the crown of it is a weeping elm tree. It was on the top of this mound, under the weeping elm tree, that Lafayette had caused a vault to be built for his dog, and it was there where his own cremated remains were deposited. The vault, which is five feet in length by four feet in depth and four feet in width, is lined with white tiles. On the top is a heavy iron-framed lid with a padlock, and over all was placed, after the burial of the dog, a marble slab with this inscription:– 'Dedicated to the loving memory of my dearest Beauty' and in the lower corner on the right were the words, in smaller letters, 'The Great Lafayette'. This slab, removed of course in order that the vault might be opened, was lying this day on the side of the mound fronting the cemetery. While on this subject, it may be said that Lafayette had given orders before his death that there should be reared over the grave of the dog a large monument of Carrara marble of Grecian design and that will still be gone on with though the inscription will now be altered.

In preparation, however, for the interment of the ashes of Lafayette, the coffin in which the dog had been interred had been lifted, and was laid on trestles across the opening of the vault. The coffin is of oak, with silver handles. It has a double lid. The inner, of glass, and the outer of polished oak. The dog had been embalmed, and on the outer and inner lids being taken off, there was the creature couchant, sitting in state as it were, in the attitude of one of the Trafalgar Square lions. It was, it must be said, a curious sight. The two lids, the glass and the oak, having been removed, a silk cushion was placed over the coffin pending the arrival of Lafayette's own ashes, for it had been resolved that the casket with the remains of the dead man should be placed in the same coffin as that of the dog – another of the eccentricities connected with this extraordinary funeral.

It was not until about four o'clock that the funeral procession reached the cemetery. The band could be heard playing the Chopin Funeral March, and immediately a calm fell upon the dense crowd at the gates; the discordant noises ceased; the male portion of the audience with one accord uncovered their heads and stood mute while the black hearse with the casket and its pall, the open carriages resplendent with flowers, Lafayette's blue-grey motor car, with two negroes behind it, and the line of mourning coaches passed them. Nothing could have been more respectful.

As the bandsmen entered the cemetery they opened out into two lines and allowed the hearse and the two coaches to pass between them. These, taking a sharp turn to the left, came by two paths to encircle the mound where the interment was to take place. A narrow path had been opened on the side of the mound farthest away from the gates, and here the hearse halted. The mourners left the coaches. The undertaker took the oaken casket containing Lafayette's ashes from the hearse and, carrying it breast high, walked at the head of the procession of mourners along a narrow turfed path which had been formed to the graveside. The mourners walked in single file and made a circle round the vault. Mr Lafayette's brother headed them, and several ladies in deep mourning were of the party, which also included the chauffeur leading a black and white dog belonging to the deceased, the animal being adorned with black crape (sic) bows.

Then followed what may probably be regarded as one of the most extraordinary interments of modern times. What was done was done because it was supposed to be giving effect to Lafayette's wishes, frequently expressed on this subject. The cushion already referred to was slipped off the coffin, the undertaker, stooping down, placed the casket between the forepaws of the dog.

Plate 3: The cortège procession for the Great Lafayette through Edinburgh in 1911

It was a weird spectacle all the same, recalling rather some old pagan rite than anything within the domain of modern experience. Lafayette was a Jew, and it was thought at first that a religious ceremony according to the rites of the Jewish Church would be performed at the grave. A Hebrew merchant of the Edinburgh Synagogue, who had accompanied the remains of his co-religionist to the cemetery, said to a reporter: 'It could not be. It would have been profanation, as anything pertaining to a dog is to a Jew accursed.' Yielding to the earnest wish of some of the mourners that a religious service should be conducted at the grave, a Presbyterian clergyman kindly came to the rescue. This was the Rev. D. Findlay Clark, assistant in St. Matthew's Parish Church; and nothing could have been more appropriate or consoling to the mourners than the committal service, which was commenced after the casket was placed in the coffin. Part of it was liturgical, part of it extempore, but all of it was solemn and appropriate to the tragic circumstances in which Lafayette met his death. After the prayer by the minister, the band played a verse of the well-known hymn 'Days and moments swiftly flying'. The service was punctuated by the sobbing of several of the ladies round the grave, who seemed quite overcome with grief. The mourners left the cemetery immediately, and as they drove back to the city they would have seen that the great crowds on the streets had for the most part dispersed.

I was later to find an old cutting from the *Carrick Herald* of September 1963 which contained an article written by my father (one of a series, but the others seem to have disappeared) entitled 'Peeps into The Past'. It went:

Having graduated MA at Glasgow and BD at Edinburgh Universities, I attached myself to St Matthew's Parish Church, Morningside, as a student Assistant to the Rev. Norman McLeod Caie BD, a very popular preacher who was filling the church to its utmost capacity. My duties were to read the 'Lessons' and occasionally to conduct a service. It is not regarded as quite orthodox that an Assistant should conduct a funeral service. Circumstances, however, alter cases, and those I am about to relate were, and I venture to think, will continue for a very long time to be regarded as unique, if not positively weird.

On 9 May 1911, fire broke out in the Empire Palace of Varieties. It was on the stage, shortly before 11 p.m., minutes before the end of the performance of the famous illusionist T. G. Lafayette (Sigmund Neuburger). His cremated remains were interred in Piershill Cemetery, Edinburgh, on Sunday 14 May.

As well as being an illusionist, he was passionately fond of his dog, which had died, and for which he caused a vault to be built. On the top and over the urn containing the ashes of himself and the dog was a marble slab with this inscription: 'Dedicated to the loving memory of my dearest Beauty', and in the lower corner were the words, in smaller letters, 'The Great Lafayette'. Altogether it was regarded as one of the most extraordinary interments of modern times.

Moreover, Lafayette was a Jew, and it was thought at first that a religious ceremony according to the rites of the Jewish Church would be performed at the grave. And this is how the Assistant at St Matthew's Church became involved. The best known undertaker in Edinburgh at that time was Messrs W. T. Dunbar & Sons, Morrison Street. They were chosen by Lafayette's brother who first approached the minister of St Matthew's Church to conduct the Funeral Service. Being Communion Sunday, that was impossible. However, as a special favour, he allowed the undertaker to apply to myself. Accordingly, Dunbar drove me to the West End Station Hotel, where Lafayette's brother was in close conclave with the Jewish Rabbi about the burial of the dog in the same coffin as the ashes of Lafayette. After a prolonged argument the Jewish Rabbi declined to take any part in the service on the ground that the dog, according to the Jew, is an 'unclean animal inasmuch as it neither chews the cud nor has a divided hoof'.

Plate 4: Portrait of my father shortly after gaining his BD degree at Edinburgh University, c. 1910

However, yielding to the earnest desire of some of the mourners that religious sevice should be conducted at the grave, Lafayette's brother finally gave his consent. After 52 years it is quite interesting to read in the Press of that time, 'A Presbyterian clergyman kindly came to the rescue. This was the Rev. D. Findlay Clark, Assistant at St Matthew's Parish Church, and nothing could have been more appropriate or consoling to the mourners than the committal service which began after the casket was placed in the coffin. Part of it was liturgical, part of it extempore, but all of it was solemn and appropriate to the tragic circumstances in which Lafayette met his death.'

In due course I was seeking pastures new. Accordingly, on the advice of one of the most influential ministers of the Church of Scotland, whose name was a household word throughout the Church, I submitted an application for Lochgelly. At that time, exactly 50 years ago (from the time of writing) Fife was suffering from a wave of so-called heathenism, including dog racing and other forms of betting and gambling. According to the members of the Home Mission Committee it was a tremendous undertaking for a young and inexperienced man to take upon him. Apparently the members of the congregation thought differently, for as a result of a vote, I was appointed as Minister of the Church and Parish of Lochgelly. I'm afraid the worthy Beadle of St Matthew's Church was not greatly taken with the appointment. In his Irish brogue he said to me, 'Sure now, Mr Clark, you would never think of going over to Fife!' 'Why not?' I said.

He replied, 'Don't you know the people in Fife are very fly, so fly that the very cows come out of the field backwards?' Personally, I found them to be quite generous and friendly disposed to the church – even those who were said to be opposed to it.

That little article went on to describe the early days of my father's time as a Parish Minister in Lochgelly, the town in which he found his wife, my mother. Curiously, another cutting, this time much more recent, and from the letter columns of *The Scotsman* of 8 December 1992 quotes a Betty Robertson, onetime resident and schoolteacher in Banff but now writing from an address in Edinburgh, in the following terms:

Sir, – The recent publicity surrounding the death of the Great Lafayette reminds me of the tale told by the late Rev. Dr D. Findlay Clark, minister for many years of St Mary's Church, Banff.

He it was who, as a young assistant minister in Edinburgh, conducted the funeral service. The tale was told by him to fellow members of the education committee – one of whom was my father – on the way from Banff to Keith to attend a meeting, and took the whole 20 miles in telling.

He told how he had been approached out of the blue by a man asking if he would take Lafayette's funeral service, explaining that the priest they would have expected to take the service had refused to bury him with his dog. Dr Clark had no such scruples, especially when he was informed that the fee would be £5. That very day he had seen an advertisement for a trip to St Kilda costing £5. He had ruled this out as being well beyond the reach of an assistant minister's stipend.

So the service was conducted, the cheque received, the trip to St Kilda enjoyed. But the tale, unfortunately did not have a happy ending. The cheque bounced!

It is informative to compare the two reports. My father did indeed tell us the essence of this tale, adding that the dog had apparently been very much part of Lafayette's act. The bit about the £5 fee I had not heard, but I became aware in later life that my father had been wont to walk a lot, mostly in the Scottish Lowlands, and he was something of an explorer to boot. He was a frugal man and had always worked hard for his pennies so it would not then have been surprising had he taken the chance to visit, free of charge, a remote island. In fact, he was later to spend his honeymoon walking with my mother on the Isle of Man, on Arran and in the Lake District.

As my father noted in his own little piece quoted on the previous page, he completed his apprenticeship in Edinburgh and was then inducted to his first charge, Lochgelly Parish Church, in the mining heartlands of Fife. On leaving

St Matthew's in 1913, my father was presented by his congregation with a magnificent mahogany roll-top desk and matching swivel chair. This I have inherited, and often, as I write at it, I let my eye catch the brass plate on the top commemorating the occasion and I allow myself a wry smile. The desk has 'good vibes' for me, in spite of my agnosticism, and I can well imagine how the old man had bent over his manuscripts as many a rousing sermon had been penned. So different from those of the son who, philosophically nearer to his grandfather, was more likely to be writing psychological case notes and other secular pieces.

It was a common view at the time that father's particular brand of liberal or even mildly socialist personal philosophy, linked to a stirring and dramatic preaching style was tailor-made for a parish like Lochgelly. Communism was rife among the miners and it was thought that, if nothing was done about it, there was likely to be an imminent rebellion of the Godless, the workless and the hopeless. A single man of conviction, ability and a background of a working-class home and a deprived inner city teaching post, coming into a new charge at the age of thirty-one was thought to be the means of settling down and civilising the unruly mob. It seems to have worked.

Even allowing for the exaggeration of friendly relatives, it seems that my father developed a style of preaching more related to his penchant for teaching and the drama. He quickly filled the church, Sunday after Sunday, with a congregation of all ages and types eager to hear his expositions of classical literature, critical studies of different religions (including his own) and pastoral psychology. He seemed to succeed in being populist without trivialising his material and to have the knack of introducing complex ideas without talking down to his audience.

That early setting of his style in the pulpit was clearly reinforced by his congregation's response – something that eventually led to his being called in 1918 to the larger and urban charge of John Knox's Church, Mounthooly, in Aberdeen. In no time there he was reputedly not only filling the church twice on Sundays but was preaching to overflow congregations listening through loudspeakers set up in the street outside the church because the latter was full.

At that time he had lit upon the stratagem of lecturing rather than preaching. He would make the study of some literary work the subject of his sermon – *Nicholas Nickleby* or *Tess of the D'Urbervilles* – and would expound the theme and purpose of the book, its message to a Christian, or to others, and only obliquely introduce the specifically theological interpretation of life as depicted in the novel or play. All this was not to say that he was not fully concerned with the more serious theological and philosophical issues facing his religion and his practices as a pastor. He was, in fact, a highly cultured, compendiously well-read man with a good sense of humour, a high level of social skill, compassion and intelligence.

These qualities were eventually recognised by the award to him in 1951 of an Honorary Doctor of Divinity by his *alma mater*, Edinburgh University. It gave him enormous pride that day to sit alongside his fellow Honorary Graduands amongst whom were Sir Edward Appleton and Dame Edith Evans. It may be too that he took some pleasure, within a few days of his Honorary degree, of attending my own graduation at Aberdeen University where I was capped with a First in Psychology and English.

Before heading for Aberdeen and his city ministry, however, my father had met in the course of his pastoral visiting, something by which he always set great store throughout his ministry, the McKenzie family of 45 Grainger Street, Lochgelly, including one of the daughters, Annie. She was at home some weekends from her work as a nurse and midwife, later as a Sister, at Dundee Royal Infirmary. My other aunts, when they were alive, had often hinted at the fact that Annie set her cap at the new minister in no uncertain fashion since they saw her as a born social climber. In the light of my mother's later attitudes, this would not surprise me. Whether that was true or not, there seems then to have developed a deep and lasting affection between the two naturally rather undemonstrative and possibly inhibited mature adults, both, in the style of these days, relatively inexperienced in the company and ways of the opposite sex. Suffice it to say that they eventually married in 1927 after a relatively protracted courtship extending over my father's years at both Lochgelly and Aberdeen, and even to the time of his new post at the Parish Church of Banff.

My father's call to St Mary's Parish Church in Banff came simultaneously with a similar call from the Parish Church of Cardenden in Fife. In the light of his courtship experience in Fife it is not clear what my father's motivation might have been for choosing Banff, away in the north. He told me much later that he had liked the look of Banff as a town and that he thought it would be a better place in which to rear children. He had felt, though, that he might have been removing himself from the busy hubs of cities like Aberdeen and Edinburgh and that his career within the church might suffer somewhat with his being out 'in the sticks'. He was ambitious to be well thought of in the ministry and may even have harboured notions of the Moderatorship in the fullness of time. In the end, he took the view that my brother, Tom and myself, then no more than twinkles in his eye, would enjoy a better life in a rural, seaside parish like Banff rather than among the smoking coal bings and political unrest of West Fife. Even at his age then, he must have been confident of his procreative skills in spite of his limited experience (or perhaps I underestimated him) for he came to Banff before he was married, no less thinking of raising a family, and even lived, yet again, in 'digs'.

'Broadcroft', in Bellevue Road, was run by an old maiden lady called Miss Mann. She let my father a room, gave him his meals, and was later to become a regular babysitter for Tom and me on the many, many occasions when our parents were not at home in the manse of an evening. My father left there after his marriage to my mother in 1927 and took up residence in a house called 'Dunard' on Seafield Street, Banff, where the family stayed until, on the death of Rev. Dr W. S. Bruce, the Senior Minister at Banff, when we all moved into the manse on Sandyhill Road.

My mother was never inclined to say much about her earlier life other than that there seemed to have been a lot of mutual support among her sisters especially. Her brothers she talked about rather less. Again, as in my father's case, they were a large family of eleven in all, and the pressure to get the boys into jobs and the girls married off must have been extreme. How they all lived together in the tiny miner's terraced cottage in Grainger Street, Lochgelly, must have been a miracle of confusion, compression and compassion. There were two rooms, one a bedroom, and the living room had a box-bed on one side separated from the seating area only by a curtain. There was a tiny kitchen just inside the door with no hot water and there was a lavatory, shared by the next house, across a coal dust covered unmade road at the back.

Most of her brothers started life as miners though they went on to other jobs, including a jute factory worker in Dundee and a publican away in Lincolnshire (the only two I ever knew) and her sisters, with the exception of herself and her youngest sister, Helen (Nell), were all early school leavers who found what jobs they could until they married. Nell learned bookkeeping and accounting and Annie, my mother, having been reasonably good at school, went to Dundee Royal Infirmary to train as a nurse and midwife. There, as in all student groups, she had a small self-sustaining cicle of friends in what must also have been a very tough and poverty-ridden regime of nurse training under God-like consultants who terrorised even the trained staff, and harridans of Ward Sisters and Matrons who oversaw their long hours and ludicrously low pay with harshness rather than sympathy or co-professionalism. Nevertheless, my mother was intensely proud of her calling and more often recalled the rewards (in human terms) of her hospital experience than the disappointments and travails.

For many years after we came to live in Banff we visited and were visited by one of my mother's nursing colleagues of yesteryear, a Mary Duthie, known to us boys as 'Auntie' Mary – although her husband, so-called 'Uncle' Jimmie Duthie, was of more interest to us because he was the Sales and later General Manager of Aberdeen Motors and always had interesting things to tell us about cars and could also take us for runs – usually up Deeside.

Throughout his life, my father never had a car. He would walk up to twelve or fourteen miles a day visiting country parishioners and think nothing of it. Even in the 1930s few people, other than the solicitors, the doctors and the better-off farmers, had a car. The tiny stipend of the minister was never likely to make that affordable. By the time the war was over in 1945, my father, then 63, probably felt he was too old to learn to drive, and in any case he was not a terribly mechanically-minded man. Even mending a bicycle or changing a gas mantle was taxing for him.

For all that, the fact that both my parents had committed themselves to 'helping professions', concerned with people more than with things or processes, played a large part, I am sure, in determining my own later occupational predilections. Models are models, and I sensed, even as a child, that both my parents not only took pride in what they did but also that they seemed to do it quite well.

Chapter II

CHILDHOOD SUMMERS

'If all the year were playing holidays,
To sport would be as tedious as to work.'
(Shakespeare *Henry IV*, 1.2.201)

The years between infancy and schooldays were filled with fragments. The dramas of birth and death such as I recounted in the previous chapter always cut deep scores on the wax of our early memories. Other episodes represent more superficial scratches on the *tabula rasa* with a few only unsmoothed by time. It is hard to separate what one often thinks are true recollections from stories later told to one by parents and others.

The comings and goings associated with the birth of my younger brother, Thomas, I can just grasp. These were, however, largely submerged by often unhappy memories of the travails of growing up under the spartan and somewhat harsh disciplines imposed on me by my parents, and sometimes by some of the servant girls in the manse. Neither the latter nor my parents were averse to doling out vigorous slaps when something about my behaviour displeased them.

If the psychoanalysts are right, something of the mildly obsessional traits I have from time to time been accused of in my subsequent life may well stem from the many violent thrashings I was subjected to when, in the course of my toilet training, accidents inevitably happened. I can remember the fear and apprehension I felt when, not long out of nappies, my sphincter muscles would lapse. I remember crying, not because of my incontinence, but in anticipation of the formal thrashing that both my father and my mother would administer in the bathroom after I had been changed. These were always several blows with the hands or a slipper on my bare bottom and attended by many adjurations to control myself and stop being 'a horrible, dirty boy' in future. They were very painful and I stung both with pain and resentment for longer than one might expect in a tiny lad. I am sure I must have been over three before these became less frequent. Once, after one of those thrashings, dizzy with fear and misery, I stumbled and fell down the main staicase of the manse, rolling over and over until I came up hard against an old oak settle which lay in the hall at the foot of the stairs. My bleeding head was patched up but no sympathy came my way because of my earlier iniquity.

It may well have simply been the climate in which my own parents grew up – or the notion that they could not tolerate any deviations from what they understood as perfect child behaviour – but both my parents were inclined to resort to slaps and kicks when I needed to be 'disciplined' for transgressions less severe than many for which my own children would only have had adverse, if firm, comment. It was to become what I later saw as a defect in their parenting style that both, my mother especially, could never bring themselves to praise explicitly any of my accomplishments, whether in the home, at school, on the sports field or even university. I am sure they talked proudly of these to others from time to time. As far as I was concerned, however, my classmates' accomplishments and skills were always held up as something which I should aim to equal or better, even when I knew perfectly well that theirs were, in fact, lesser accomplishments. It is highly likely that these pressures led to my life-long drive to master a variety of skills and perhaps not to veil sufficiently a deep strain of competitiveness. Indeed I could see the same process operating in brother Tom. In the sense that our later achievements were probably a bit above average, the technique may have worked, but it did not conduce to what many would describe as a happy childhood.

Later in our pre-school and school years our parents would occasionally try to express, usually rather indirectly, some genuine affection but it was seldom verbal or associated with cuddles or bodily contact. Indeed they seemed to be anxious about that sort of thing, even between themselves. What they replaced that with was always gifts at Christmas and birthdays and, when we were young, parties to which they, rather than we, would invite 'suitable' boys and girls to attend. In a big house like the manse, with a big garden, these were high points of the year, although I am told I could be rather detached from the other participants at times.

In consequence, the times that stand out in memory largely comprise holidays when we would be taken away for a month each year when my father was relieved by another minister taking his services alternately in July or August each year. Tom and I grew up to look forward to a summer holiday in Lochgelly one year and in Girvan the next.

These were, to me, even in my tenderer years, patently different in style and activities. Each was, no doubt, formative enough in the varying impressions they made on me.

At Lochgelly, we stayed in the cramped but comfortable terraced miner's cottage in Grainger Street which was the home of my Grandad – still working down the mine. These cottages were in blocks of four. They were single storey, brick-built (and unusual for this reason to one brought up among the stone-built houses of the North) with an area of concrete about 10 feet square in the 'L' shape formed at the back of the house by the wall with the living room window and that containing the back door (always used) and the tiny kitchen window. This pad of concrete became a blissfully smooth area to me when, in attempting to match the machismo (or, more likely, poverty) of the kids in the neighbourhood, Tom, my brother, and I would try running around at play with them in our bare feet. The proper road outside the house was, of course,

tarmac, but the lane along the back of these miners' houses was the place we played and it was hard-packed coal dust, earth and stones. Such activities would have been frowned upon in our middle-class environment of the manse at home in Banff, but our need to identify with the kids we were to accompany to the playpark near the pits was then more pressing. There, there were at least some swings, a big chute and

Plate 5: The first (totally unrecognisable) photograph of the author, summer 1930, at Banff Links

a roundabout with which there was nothing to compare at home.

The slight rise on which this playpark was situated overlooked a coal mine which memory tells me was called the Nellie Gray. For some obscure reason, most of the mines were named after what were to me equally obscure women. All day and all night the great spoked wheels of the winding gear would turn and appear to contrarotate as they hauled to the surface cages of coal, slag and, occasionally, men. Three shifts a day were worked, day shift (6 a.m. to 2 p.m.); back shift (2 p.m. to 10 p.m.) or night shift (10 p.m. to 8 a.m.). At the end of whatever shift my grandfather happened to be on, there was a sacrosanct hour after he had wearily trodden the half mile or so from the pit when we were all banished from the main room. The exception was my aunt Nell who fetched and poured the hot water into the zinc bath in front of the fire. None of us would even have considered breaching the privacy of the living room while Grandpa divested himself of his helmet, Davy lamp, steel toe-capped boots, leather kneepads and sweat and coal dust-blackened clothing. If it was not raining, the latter was hung up on a hook just outside the back door. Grandpa would then begin to soak away the dust, bruises and scars of eight hours of endlessly swinging a pick or shovel in the narrow black seam of the wretched carbon eighteen inches wide and perhaps a couple of feet deep, over 1,000 feet down in the bowels of the earth.

Impressionable child that I was, there has remained with me the sight, the sound and the smell of those days. Perhaps I sensed, even then, the iniquitous exploitation of the labour of these tough, friendly, coarse, often intelligent and

Above: Plate 6: 'I could be rather detached from other participants at times.'
Below: Plate 7: Tom (left) and myself with birthday and/or Xmas presents in the manse garden – probably summer 1934

thinking men. They risked, and often lost, their lives in the hot, dark, wet and methane-ridden caverns. And all that for trivial rewards and the 'privilege' of living in a low-rent miner's cottage – from which they might be summarily ejected should the coal dust bring pneumoconiosis or a roof-fall a fractured spine or thigh. They clumped and shuffled up the road from the pit after the hooter had signalled the end of the shift, red-rimmed eyes glistening like navigation lights in the glow of the street lights on black-stained faces. Conversation was desultory. Sweat channels traced a topography of their own on features drawn with fatigue and only occasionally animated. Among demonstrators of the latter would be a few who had won a pound or two at the then illegal pitch and toss games sneaked in secret hollows among the bings of slag or where they were screened by wagons shunted by the pit. Some may have had high hopes of a win from a carefully trained and nurtured greyhound on the track at Cowdenbeath on a Saturday.

Inevitably, there was a knapsack from which jutted the top of a Thermos flask at one side and the top of a brass Davy lamp at the other. A few would keep their helmet lamps there too after their 'piece' had been eaten. Most, however, kept them clipped to their helmets with the tube which fed them acetylene looping over the back of their shoulders to the small tin reservoir of water and carbide clipped to their belts. Only later was I to discover the joys, and the risks, of playing with carbide 'bombs'. But that is another story.

The smell when my grandfather entered the door was pungent. To me it was unique, evocative, even romantic, but perhaps fortunately, transient. After his bath a hairy, powerful and pink man emerged in thick worsted trousers, a rough woollen shirt with no collar so that his yellowish vest or combination top just showed above the top button hole. His outer working clothes were then removed entirely from the house either to the hook at the back door, or, more often to the shed in the yard across the dirt road. His shirt and underclothes were taken by aunt Nell or one of the neighbours. A lot of the washing was shared – largely through goodwill and neighbourliness, but partly because there was only one washhouse in the yard across the way for every four houses – and one 'lavvy', also across the road, for every two.

The smell of these outer clothes, magnified it seemed by the contact with the warm, soapy water, evoked a mixture of coal dust, oil, smoke, carbide and pipe tobacco in proportions which varied with the shift and the predominant activity of the day. Occasionally, the sweet, clean smell of pine resin superimposed upon the other more usual odours would signal that new 'roads' had had to be cut down the pit and props had had to be set up before any more serious coal cutting could safely be done. Not that it was ever very safe in these mines. The womenfolk lived in dread of the sound of the hooter blowing repeatedly between shift times – the signal that there had been an accident or emergency for which the Mine Rescue Squad had to be called out from Cowdenbeath. When it did, several times during the course of my holidays in

Plate 8: Grandpa McKenzie (right) at the pit

Lochgelly, people would come out of doors and gaze anxiously towards the pit until someone could be seen who might know what had happened. Gas or a roof fall was the commonest explanation, but the scale of the event was never really clear until some of the men got to the surface with the news. Inevitably, a bobby and some of the women would gather near the pithead. Talk was desultory and faces were drawn. Some would look back along the road to see whether an ambulance was coming. That was always a bad sign. Others would gaze up at the great winding wheels to see whether the cages were still running. That was usually a good sign.

Grandpa would often regale my brother and me with stories of the pit ponies and the canaries which lived most of their lives down the pits. To me, then, they became more like animal heroes than exploited species. There was always the illusion that these merry songbirds would somehow signal the presence of the deadly methane by an appropriate whistle rather than by the more drastic expedient of actually passing out, often fatally. With the animism of childhood, or of George Orwell, I somehow felt also that the ponies were hauling the heavy steel skips as an act of sheer altruism in the interests of us humans. The noise and the heat of the pit 'roads', cages and apparatus, the darkness, the dust and the blown foetid air were their natural environment. The fresh green of spring grass, the sweet smell of new-mown hay, daisies or clover and the changing patterns of cloud, rain and sun were willingly foregone by them.

Perhaps the miners knew how much they owed them for it was common for the animals to be named and talked to as companions – certainly to be sworn at fractionally less than their fellow men. On the one occasion when Grandpa was able to take me down the pit in the cage (when he was off shift, naturally) I was not sure whether to be terrified by the deathly rattling plunge into the dark abyss or to be proud of the status such a 'Descensus in Averno' would inevitably bestow. At least I would see the ponies when we ended our hectic plunge, should we be lucky enough to come to a planned stop at the bottom, and no doubt the canaries would be perkily singing away in their cages. I never knew whether they were or not. The noise of the cage gates, of skips rattling their way along the narrow gauge rails heaped with steaming and fuming slag or coal, the beams from the miners' lamps probing the dust clouds till they disappeared into blackness captured my attention enough to exclude any confirmation of such romantic nonsense.

Struggling up to the coal face on hands and knees in the wake of a recumbent, crawling Grandpa and being shown where to hack out a great lump of gleaming black coal was nevertheless a consummation as fulfilling as the experience was formative. The yellow beam from my borrowed head lamp kept wandering wildly from track because the borrowed helmet was several sizes too big for my juvenile head and wobbled from side to side as I struggled along. The leather kneepads were equally autonomous in their attempts to dislodge themselves from my aching patellae, so it was not an easy progress. Several times I was unnerved by spontaneous cracks from strained pit props on either side of me in the Stygian, hot darkness. As we came up to the point where other 'on shift' miners were hacking at the seam with short handled picks and others were shovelling away the broken coal behind them – none able to stand up or even achieve a cramped crouching position, there was some brief conversation.

'Hey, Jimmie, (to my Grandpa) diz the foreman ken ye've a bairn doon wi' ye? He's gey wee fur this sort o' caper.'

'Dinna fash yersel', Russell, I squared it wi' the Manager last week. We're jist bidin' lang eneuch for him tae hack oot a bit o' coal fur a souvenir.' Then, the whites of Russell's eyes amid a face pouring with sweat which cut deep channels through black dust were caught briefly in the wandering beam of my light.

'Here ye are, boy. Come in atween me an' yer granda. There's a fine sheeny bit here jist waitin' tae be howkit.' I was handed his short pick to have a swing at the promising protruberance from the face of the seam and after a few false starts when I couldn't get any purchase on the pick, I eventually dislodged a lump of about a cubic foot which Grandpa expertly broke in two, handed me one and kept the other in his piece-bag.

'That's your bit, Davie. Ah'll tak this yin for Thomas.' Then we laboriously turned around and began the crawl back to the 'roads' and later, the return to the surface.

From that day on, though I did not recognise it then, and young though I was, my political leanings were from then on well left of centre. The lump of coal was cosseted like a baby, all the way back along the prop-lined seam. It was probably easier for a slight eight-year-old than for the broad-shouldered grown man with the short-handled pick who brought up the rear. Once at the 'roads' we got a lift back to the cage on a train of loaded skips.

The coal was borne in triumph up the street to Grainger Street where my story, somewhat embellished, was told to relieved parents and aunts. Later still, wrapped in newspaper and in one of our holiday cases, it found its way with us in the train to Banff. In the manse, it eventually lay by the fireside in the parlour, soaking in a dish of chemical solutions which were, by regular basting, soon to transform it into a 'coal plant'.

These novelties were fashionable at the time. The chemicals, such as saltpetre, copper filings and alum interacted with the carbon to produce intricate patterns of crystals in shades of blue, green, pink and white to produce a fragile but intriguing effect like coral growth. By the time the 'plant' was started, of course, several surreptitious chips, even chunks, of the lump of coal had been spirited away by myself: one into my pocket 'for luck', and some smaller pieces to be passed to my school friends, with the even more embellished story of their origin. The current exchange rate allowed of a few marbles, some catapult elastic, a bit of candle, or even a very small and significantly old Dinky toy aeroplane.

Old James MacKenzie's two great recreations were his pipes and his 'bools'. The former hung on a wooden rack by the side of the fireplace and included long and short stemmed clays, a couple of briars and an elaborate Meerschaum. Several had metal caps which he would flip up with near sleight of hand in order to check the condition of the combustion or to light up. Some were never smoked outside, whereas a favourite would accompany him everywhere. I never discovered what his favourite tobacco was. My father, however, a smoker himself, would always take down some relatively expensive tobacco for Grandpa when we went on holiday.

Grandpa's prowess with the spittoon has already been drawn to your attention. His prowess at the 'bools' I have heard was also redoubtable and he was not immune to accepting a challenge for a bob or two.When he was on day shift in the summer, there was light enough in the evenings for him to go through the washing and feeding rituals after work and still find time to wander up to the green. Many a time did I hear his pipe being tapped out on the arm of his chair by the fire before he slipped out of the kitchen door with the familiar muttered, 'Ah'm awa' tae the bools then, Nell.' No doubt this was his opportunity for a blether with his pals as much as a chance of a rink or two. Whether he drank or not I was never sure. I never saw him drink alcohol nor saw him suffer from the after effects thereof. Nor did I ever see alcohol in the house. Probably he did not. Both pride and poverty would have dictated sobriety.

There was, of course, in these days of the early 1930s no such thing as television. Even radio (or 'the wireless' as it was called) was not all that common in working class folks' houses. I had already spent one or two holidays at Grainger Street before the familiar tones telling us that 'This is Henry Hall speaking' or the swinging cadences of Geraldo and his orchestra enlivened the air waves. One consequence of that was that most entertainment was self-made. Singing, story telling, Ludo, cards and, more frequently than now perhaps, piano playing, were the home activities for the leisure hours. Grandpa would take Tom, my younger brother, and me on his knee of an evening, between high tea and bedtime, and bump us up and down in time to his only moderately tuneful renditions of military marching songs, or scraps of verse from the contemporary music hall. If I was taught the words, then I have forgotten them.

What I have not forgotten was the awful sense of conflict I felt about remaining on his knee. My parents were obviously pleased that the old patriarch was willing to put off time with us (because he was a man of fairly inflexible habits and routines) and he did seem to take pleasure in the proximity, on his terms, of his grandchildren. However, the hard waxed ends of his full moustache kept scraping my cheek and the periodic deep intrathoracic rumblings and wheezes which presaged another attack on the spittoon vied with the smoke from his pipe to promote my increasing nausea. I well remember watching the process repeated with my year-old cousin Billy a year or so later with something approaching relief that I had by now assumed the role of interested spectator rather than participant.

At the same time, my admiration for my grandfather's resonant snoring was unbounded. He slept in a large box bed built into the side of the living room, achieving visual, if not olfactory or auditory privacy, by means of a curtain pulled across the length of the bed and hung on a rail behind an embroidered valance. Nothing subsequently has matched the surrealism of the chatter of my parents and aunts round the fire in that room set against the constant, if intermittent, gulps, snorts, snores, rustlings and, dare I say it, farts, constantly there as background 'noise' against which the 'signal' of meaning had to be deciphered. In these circumstances, night shift came as something of a relief to all of us – especially to my mother, whose aspirations to middle-class habits and sentiments were more than a little dented by the coarser realities of an old miner in a box bed.

As for my brother and myself, we were accommodated in 'the room', that is, the front bedroom, facing on to the proper street (with tarmac) where we shared a small bed (with much squabbling about our respective rights to a fair half of it) at the other end of the room from the double bed shared by our parents. Aunt Nell, whose room this was, and our wee cousins, Anne and Billy were boarded out for the duration of our holiday with aunt Janet, along the street. She was another of my mother's sisters whose husband, Duncan Thorburn, was also a miner in the same pit as Grandpa. He was later to die, prematurely, his lungs riddled with pneumoconiosis. I remember, guiltily in retrospect, his long suffering explanations to us when we asked him why he did not speak properly. Even then his voice was reduced to a near whisper – and still he went down the mine, only later getting a job on the surface.

It may simply have been that for both my aunt and my parents, cleanliness was next to godliness or it may have derived from my boyish coprophilia. Be that as it may, the other well embedded memories of those summer fortnights of the years between 1934 and 1938 were of the 'lavvies' and of the 'washhouse'. Of the former, there were two, one for every two houses, built side by side of yellowing brick right across the dust road behind the house. They were scrupulously maintained. Daily cleaning by alternate housewives was both a matter of honour and of expertise. For the residents, however, it became important to 'perform' every night before stripping for bed because otherwise one might be compelled to go through a fearsome and desperate rigmarole before relieving stressed innards in the middle of the night. That would have involved finding a torch, usually with a fading battery; finding shoes and a coat or dressing gown; trying to unlatch the 'room' door without waking one or more of our parents (usually impossible), then traversing the living room from the box bed of which came the obligato of the orifices already described; then finding the key of the back door, turning it – and it was very stiff – and finally a dash across the unlit dirt road in the wind and rain with the great key of the 'lavvy' clutched in a white-knuckled hand. The knob of the 'lavvy' door had long since been replaced by a pirn (an old empty spool of sewing thread) so at least it didn't have to be turned. At last, comfortably slumped on the seat, you could then bolt the door, forget the wind and the rain – for these privies were substantially constructed with a thick concrete roof and floor in addition to their brick walls – and regale yourself with a torchlight read of an old copy of *The Broons* or the football scores in the *Daily Record*. For some reason, there were never squares of Arthur Mee's priggish *Children's Newspaper* nor of *The Scotsman*, which might have been available at home, hanging from the nail in the wall.

The washhouse was another sixty or seventy yards away, down the gardens and to the left of the back of 'our house'. It was shared on a fairly inflexible rota by four households. For some reason, so far unexplained by horticulturalists, rich, red, arm-thick, jungle-deep stalks of rhubarb seemed to burgeon around the 'lavvies' and the washhouses. Nobody boasted about it. It was taken for granted, and since rhubarb and ginger has always been one of my favourite jams, I was never going to complain.

In each washhouse – each even cleaner than the lavvy – was a large cast iron, hemispherical bricked-in tub over a fireplace with an iron door held by a heavy iron latch. The tub had a circular zinc lid hinged near its rear edge. When blankets or sheets were 'hottering' in the tub the lid was down and steam and suds would jet and bubble round the edges as if it were the edge of hell's entrance. Meanwhile, the womenfolk, for washing was a hard, tiresome and highly social activity, would be scrubbing away on corrugated zinc scrubbing boards, the short legs of which rested on the bottoms of wooden tubs about 30 inches in diameter which sat on trestles near the boiler. Big spurtles were always at hand with which to test the sheets for readiness to be removed from the hellish soapy brew in the boiler and transferred to the tubs or to the one big enamel sink against the wall for rinsing. The washing yet to be tackled was contained in wickerwork baskets with handles at each end. The window sills were the repositories of thick sticks of hard soap. This was cut as required with an old carving knife from a two foot long block of two-and-a-half inch square section soap. There was also a miscellany of clothes pegs, some up to 9 inches long with the ideal shape and rounded head for making dollies and wee mannies. There were also some of the more modern spring-loaded ones – 'affa tooters o' things – if ye ask me', as one of my aunts declaimed, although I never did ask her.

Against the other wall stood the mangle – a machine which seemed to me to be ideal for the tasks of Procrustes, and certainly big-rollered, be-cogged and structured as if it had been built for such a giant rather than for the fairly well-muscled but smallish women whose task it was to work it. Tom and I would mess about with it and wind it round without too much difficulty so long as it was doing no work, but as soon as a sheet or blanket was bitten between the rollers, our bravado evaporated and we quickly became little more than nuisance value to the women in their urgency to get on with it and get the clothes out on to the lines outside.

Other tools of almost surgical interest to be found around the washhouse included galvanised scoops with turned wooden handles for emptying out the boiler and tubs. Their handles, like the wooden tongs used for retrieving articles from the tubs and boiler, and, of course, the spurtles, were intriguingly clean – pale creamy white and silky smooth with constant use and immersion in the boiling hot soapy water. Useful as the scoops might have been to make excellent holes for marble playing, we would never have dared to remove them from the washhouse. The dishonour which would almost certainly have befallen aunt Nell had Mrs Macdonald, Mrs Thorburn or the other user whose name escapes me, discovered that her nephews had been the criminals to commit such an offence with the sacred items would, we were assured, have been unspeakable.

Why should the details of a washhouse in west Fife have preoccupied me so much? Our presence on such occasions was due to the fact that my mother took it as a part of her duty to help with the washing while we stayed there and while we were in her sight, then at least we were not getting up to mischief. Secondly, and only fractionally more importantly, the only way we could get a bath was to be immersed in the residual soapy water in the boiler after the fire had gone down and the clothes washing (transitive) had been finished. Seated in the round-bottomed boiler tub it was expected that our own washing would have been intransitive. I doubt if we were trusted to do a proper job, however, so it also became a transitive verb as soon as my mother and aunt took to my back with an old bit of loofah which felt like it was going to lift the skin from my back rather than just cleanse it. Grandfather's zinc hip bath in the living room was exclusively for his use. To this day, I never quite worked out how my mother and father got their baths. Perhaps they were so close to godliness that their cleanliness was never in question.

At Lochgelly too, there were occasional visits to the sweetie shop for 'penny lines' or a bottle of a sweet and somewhat laxative mixture called 'sugar ellie'. The latter was a liquorice-based drink on which many of the local kids seemed largely to subsist. It was cheap, but I was not much enamoured of it myself. However, in the interests of corporate unity, I pretended enjoyment. There was no need for such stratagems when the ice cream man with his big tub of Italian ice cream rolled up. This tub was in a gaily painted box on the carrier at the front of his bicycle. Though the bicycle bell signalled his presence more than it gave a warning to imprudent or unwary pedestrians, it was little needed. His daily, and occasionally, twice-daily visit to the street was never missed. My parents made great play of treating the extended family to cones or sliders as a gesture of recompense for the hospitality we were receiving. It was excellent ice cream! Nobody could believe it when the poor 'Eye-tie' as he was called in these old politically incorrect days was interned under Article 18B in 1939. He was not the sort to spread sedition and violence, nor did we see him as the type to signal frenziedly to Heinkels or to sabotage factories. The nearest to sedition came possibly when he muttered things like 'Ah no tink that-a Cowdenbeath play any good-a footaball. Raith ees better!' and the nearest to violence was demonstrated as he thrust his scoop deep into the frozen vanilla mass before loading our cones.

As well as buying the ice cream, my parents would, with the same principle in mind, sometimes visit 'the Store', as the local Cooperative shop was called. They would bring in meat, vegetables and bakeries for high tea in the evening or for lunch at the weekend. Tom and I, at the initial instigation, I think, of our cousin Annie, who was then in her early teens, nevertheless savoured traditional chip-shop fish and chips, or pie and chips for the first time. We were for ever converts to that lamented Scottish unhealthy food habit – in spite of my mother's sniffy disapproval when we were again back at home.

Whether going home or setting out, these summer holidays were always a fiasco of ill-planning, confusion, irritability and luck. My mother's ingrained habit of trying to pluck a chicken, telephone the secretary of the Women's Guild, iron a shirt, and shout instructions at Tom and me at the same time (always too late) as she was packing the cases got well in the way of a decent, rational and controlled departure, whether Home or Away. Many years later, I discovered, not in any way to my surprise, that she had been known locally as 'the late Mrs Clark'! Her furious, lasting and largely futile conflict with the inexorable passage of time was eventually to kill her of a stroke – although, to her credit, she did often perform near miracles in a remarkably short space of time.

Ofttimes, as the minute hand on the parlour clock approached midday – the departure time of the train for Aberdeen from the Banff Bridge station, on the hillside about three quarters of a mile away – she would cry out from the bedroom upstairs where she would be changing into her finery, 'David, phone Old Smith for his taxi to take us to the station!'

It is my secret belief that 'Old Smith' had already sussed out from the local gossip that the meenister's family would be wanting a taxi for that train, for no sooner was the phone back on the hook than the big, black taxi, steaming gently from the round glass temperature gauge on the bonnet, would draw up at the door. 'Old Smith' would begin loading the cases and breathlessly, to the perpetual and thinly disguised irritation of my long-suffering father, we all would pile into the car and head for the station. Usually it would become a desperate chase as we watched the train leave Macduff and chug its measured way round the half mile or so of hillside toward Banff as we wheezed and rattled, flat out at twenty miles an hour, down the road to make the necessary interception.

Much as my father enjoyed his month in the summer 'in mufti' as he was wont to put it, he tended to wear his black Homburg and dog-collar for the train. It afforded him the authority of the cloth (greater in these days than now) sufficient to hold the train in the station, some minutes past its scheduled departure time. While we bought the tickets, the luggage was loaded in the guard's van and we, the boys, shrank, as do all small boys whose parents unnecessarily draw attention to themselves, from the notoriety thus engendered.

It happened at both ends of a trip. I have even noticed solicitous relatives conspire to get us to a railway station in good time by ordering the taxi for a suitably early time and by helping with the packing – even the night before. That I could understand – especially on our departure. But still, in spite of all those noble efforts, the redoubtable lady would find a wealth of delaying gambits or trivial diversions to haul us once again to the brink of disaster, coming as close as possible to snatching defeat from the jaws of victory. Many times, in my adulthood, when times have been unusually stressed, I have displaced my ancient anxieties into dreams recapitulating in some lightly distorted form these panic-ridden holiday preliminaries.

Holidays in Girvan carried a rather different stamp, not in the manner of their beginnings and endings, for these were typical and perennial, but in their general atmosphere. We were visiting the douce and gentle southwest Clyde coast where my father's remaining unmarried brother and sisters had collaboratively set up home together in a pleasant detached bungalow in Roodlands Road. That was a quiet street with pavements on both sides of the road in a middle class area of the town. There was, it is true, a playpark very near, but it was the kind with lots of neat flowerbeds, specimen trees and small fences to get in the way of footballs. The nearest playpark to be properly comparable with the Lochgelly one was nearly a mile away by the seaside where the Glasgow daytrippers descended at the weekends. My aunts were not so keen on it. What Girvan did have over Lochgelly, however, was a pond on which one could both sail model yachts and hire small 'speed!' boats barely large enough to hold a parent and child. Sharing one of these with a brother was entirely feasible so far as space on board was concerned, but utterly futile if sibling harmony were to prevail during the holidays. The controls consisted only of an accelerator pedal and a steering wheel and only one person could be the master of the ship. Real sharing was impossible and any attempt by our parents to fob us off with a shared boat led inexorably to surreptitious violence.

What my aunts did excel at was making potato scones and rock cakes. All the way down in the trains (and it took all day) I salivated over the prospect of almost unlimited helpings of both. It became something of a tradition that plates heaped with freshly baked potato scones and with rock cakes would greet us at our evening meal on arrival.

That arrival was the culmination of a long day's travel. There would have been an earlier departure (though just as hectic) from Banff, since we had to change trains at Aberdeen and again at Glasgow where we boarded the 'boat train' destined for Stranraer and the ferry to Ireland. This last carried an air of adventure and some mystery, for it conjured up to me stories of spies, romance and mayhem reminiscent of other, more glamorous 'boat trains' to the Continent and even of the Orient Express of the adventure stories I was already addicted to. On board the train from Glasgow to Stranraer must have been a fairly high ratio of people actually leaving Scotland to cross the Irish Sea. Some, to my child's mind, were sure to be spies, criminals, double dealers, Moriarties not just hounded by Holmes, but agents, not for linen sheets or racehorses, but for foreign powers and the forces of evil. No wonder then that I would scan the faces in the carriage for the slightest sign of a malign facies. Lombroso would have been proud of me.

But we would all be weary by the time that Girvan hove in sight in the gathering summer twilight. The trunk and cases would be dragged on to a taxi (if one was available) and if not, the trunk, at least, would be left in left luggage to be collected on the morrow. We then walked the mile or thereabouts to Roodlands Road.

As we finally approached the house, the beaming faces of aunts Maggie, Nellie and Jessie could often be seen peering from the bay window of the front room. Uncle Hugh, a naturally shy man, observed more reticence and appeared from the kitchen or back garden as we entered. It was clear that my father was seen as the local boy who had made good and that they were all inordinately proud of him. In spite of the fact that he never actually said anything to give that impression, I think he rather liked that. Curiously, his siblings' adulation never surprised me, partly because of the reputation my father enjoyed as a parish minister in Banff, and partly because the near half century of age difference between us left him, as far as I was concerned, a rather remote, austere and quite powerful figure with a 'hot line' to God – to whom he talked at least weekly. Equally curiously, the relaxed, if admiring relationship between him and his maiden sisters seemed to encourage an almost youthful interest in us and our doings, wishes and enthusiasms while we were there.

He had always been a keen walker, in the hills and elsewhere, so we roamed the hills behind the town, tried golf for the first time on the links, fished at the harbour point and sailed our model yachts on the boating pond. At home in Banff, he was always 'engaged', was writing his sermon, or had a funeral, baptism or marriage to see to, so we were largely monitored rather than played with, and that mostly from the study window.

As boys we had a lot of time for uncle Hugh. He was a slater and chimney sweep and he kept homing pigeons in a loft above his workshop at the bottom of the garden. For one thing, he was often fascinatingly black and carried a rich sooty smell – quite different from the methane and coal dust aroma which surrounded the Lochgelly miners. For another, he taught us to enjoy sandwiches made with butter and castor sugar – his staple diet or 'piece' to sustain him each working day. He left each day, pushing a large hand cart with all his tools before him and returned only in the evening for a proper meal. People then had no idea that a diet such as bread, sugar and fat might be damaging to health and we little realised then that his pigeons were fed on much safer victuals. They enjoyed a mix of maize, barley and lentils as well as vegetable scraps and seemed content to home in on that indefinitely. Helping uncle Hugh to feed the pigeons, each of which he seemed to know almost personally, was a high point of the day.

Tending the birds seemed to have imbued Hugh Clark with a placidity and natural quietude which permeated his being generally. I used to watch him pick up a pigeon from the loft floor with a firm but gentle hold that left the bird entirely secure and unalarmed in his gnarled and black ingrained fist. He would mutter to it like a child, stretch its wings to examine the pinions, show me the details of its eyes, and let it fly off to a perch. I later discovered that racing pigeon fanciers set some store by the eyes of a pigeon. Apparently they can see there the genetic correlates of high flight performance.

Hugh was well known as a man who would mend a roof or sweep a chimney for a pensioner or invalid as a 'love darg', muttering only about maybe sending in a bill if he ever fell short of feed for his pigeons. He never did. As a result, the old aunts and he lived a very frugal life of total decency. For them, being 'respectable' as well as being respected in the town was an overweening goal.

It was easy even for a brash young boy to see that having a parish minister as a brother was, for them, something of an accolade. That he had a wife and children as well only added to this. Although my father was one of a large family, nine in all, I think, none married but he. Several died young, some by natural causes (of which there were many in those days). One brother was killed in the Great War of 1914–18 and a sister, Susan, my father's favourite ('the finest of all the Clarks', he would often say) was tragically killed as described earlier.

It always surprised me that my aunt Maggie never married. She was a nurse, privately employed most of her life, and perhaps her concept of service was such that time off to meet others of either sex was just not available to her. To me, she was a kindly, unassuming and intelligent woman from whose neat small features shone eyes bright with understanding and gentle humour. She was better read than the other sisters or Hugh. Nellie was the housekeeper and baker, more plain of feature and style and of far fewer words than Jessie, the youngest of them, whose tongue never rested. Jessie was a hectically jolly if somewhat overactive woman who made something of a virtue of not being quite as bright as the others. She wasn't, but she was a happy soul and just as kindly as her siblings, even if at times she did seem to be the butt for some of Nellie's more snide remarks.

Our visits were the occasion for the dining room rather than the kitchen to be laid out for meals and for the best front bedroom to be offered to my parents and for two of the sisters to 'double up' so that 'the boys' could have one of the back bedrooms to themselves. They all hung on the middle class image of the time, with 'good' furniture in the bedrooms and living/dining room. The house was in a quiet middle class street and they prized the fact that their neighbours were bank cashiers, shop owners and schoolteachers. Uncle Hugh did come and go by the front door when he was 'dressed', but he slipped out the back from his workshop when in his working clothes. It was quite different from Lochgelly.

At that time my father had a number of contemporaries from his earlier years in Girvan minding their shops, visiting the library or beleaguering the golf course. On our way to the beach or to the boating pond we would from time to time have to put off valuable playing time while he reminisced with one or another of these 'worthies'. What a tragedy it was that, by the time my father eventually retired (in his eighties!) he returned to a town of strangers. By then, looking forward to a renewal of these meetings, he returned to his 'calf grund' only to find that it was peopled by ghosts. He had outlived his friends and relatives and had to settle for solitary walks over long-trodden memories, watching the skeleton trees of his autumn cast their leaves in silent requiem for brothers, sisters, and, all too soon, a wife. However, the Girvan of the late '30s and early '40s offered some special treats and experiences for a couple of pre-adolescent boys. Not the least of these was the opportunity to be introduced, though with little success then, to golf. Father had a regular playing partner in the form of a cousin by marriage who was a schoolteacher and not averse to

Plate 9: Uncle Hugh, my father, brother Tom and myself in the garden at Roodlands Road in Girvan, 1935

Plate 10: Aunt Maggie in Girvan in the 1930s

tolerating our violent, if often misdirected, or even vain, lunges at the ball. He had a daughter, Morag, to whom I paid, at first, little attention. By the time my voice had broken, however, I had taken quite a shine to Morag Williamson in spite of her being a few years my senior. For a time I remember getting quite anxious lest she marry before I could sort of 'catch up with her' in age. Curiously, she never did marry – nor did I catch up with her. By then I had other fish to fry. Nevertheless, that introduction to golf was later pursued with more application, and success, and the game has afforded me much pleasure, much frustration and much companionship since.

The boating pond was a feature of many seaside towns in those days. Girvan in particular was one of the Clyde towns which was descended upon in July by hundreds, perhaps even thousands, of Glasgow people and their children for the 'Glasgow Fair', the two weeks of merrymaking and mayhem for which their long days in the shipyards, mines and factories had prepared them. Pennies had been saved and anticipation and thirsts whetted for eleven long hard months prior to hitting the beach, the 'amusement arcades', the 'shows', the dance halls and the boating pond. 'Clydebuilt' was a phrase to conjure with whether it applied to the *Queen Mary*, or the Clyde steamers that plied between Ardrossan or Ayr and Cumbrae, Arran and Ailsa Craig, or to the 18-inches-long racing model yachts we were bought on one of our very first visits to Girvan. They may not have been as large as some of the superbly crafted models to be seen tacking across the pond, nor had they the complicated rigging or steering linkages of those possessed by the real afficionados to be found gazing critically at their pride and joy as they dipped and surged across the waves – all to scale, of course. For all that, it was easy to forget the time of day in our competitive enthusiasm and brotherly rivalry. It was also easy, unfortunately, to forget about the edge of the pond. We used a stick to catch and turn our yachts when they reached the side of the pond and we then sprinted across to the other side to await their arrival and ascertain the winner – and to make sure there was no cheating.

On one such occasion, my reach failed to match my enthusiasm at a time when my father had unfortunately wandered off to the knoll at one end of the pond to check that Ailsa Craig was still firmly in position. I remember the shock of the cold water seeping through my clothes and the mild surprise that I had my eyes open and could see the brown side of the pond slide past my face as I sank to the bottom. I must have flailed with my arms though I could not then swim, but then – blackness! The next thing I remember was lying on the concrete floor of the adjacent shelter/lavatory and retching violently as I spewed up several pints of Girvan boating pond. Then followed the usual admixture of chastisement and relief from the adults around. The ultimate indignity to me, however, was the fact that I was still lying on a lavatory floor with my good holiday shirt, trousers and pullover sodden and muddy, feeling cold and miserable, expecting the most awful tirade from my mother on what would be a very prompt return to Roodlands Road, and worse still – no sign of my yacht! No wonder then that I was inhibited from learning to swim until perhaps some seven or eight years later when I was a student at university.

That little trauma, however, was not to put me off either the rowing boats which were for hire on the river where it ran into the sea via the harbour, or the traditional trip on a fishing boat out to and around the Ailsa Craig. There was a measure of ambivalence about the sail to Ailsa Craig. On the one hand, I was fascinated by the prospect of close-ups of gannets diving for fish, watching the puffins juggle even more sand eels into their colourful and chunky beaks. There were also the granite quarries to see. I had been assured that that was where most, if not all, the curling stones in Scotland were cut. On the other, as a non-swimmer rescued from recent near-drowning, I was distinctly chary of venturing out over twelve miles or so of the rolling swells of the lower Clyde estuary. The sturdy handrails on the gunwales of the boat, the numerous lifebelts and life rafts and the obvious insouciance of the cheery Glaswegians who comprised the bulk of the passengers were greatly reassuring.

'See yon burds, hen! The fishers nails herrin' tae bits o' boords an' the puir brutes braks their necks whan they hit the boords. Is that nae awfae!'

So it seemed to me as I watched these beautiful Solan Geese circle and dive, circle and dive, as they hunted a meal for late chicks. Happily, I never saw the practice referred to in action, though there were, here and there,

Plate 11: Tom and I in the sea at Girvan beach

dead gannets with obviously broken necks. Some were also culled for food, perhaps using the same technique, by the few then residents of the rock, just as they were on St Kilda and occasionally in the Northern Isles. Many, many more, however, have met their end less suddenly and decisively in recent years through pollution by oil on the sea.

Plate 12: Father takes us to the beach at Girvan – but Tom has his admirers (probably summer 1937)

Paddy's Milestone, as Ailsa Craig was called, held something of a fascination for me, so much so that on one occasion, scorning the trippers' day 'doon the watter' from the main pier in Girvan on the paddle steamer *Jeannie Deans*, (which we had done the year before) Tom and I set out in one of the rowing boats for hire from the harbour determined to make our own way to the rock. It looked big enough not to tax our navigational skills and had we not already explored the rather boring River Girvan as far up its length as was reasonably navigable? So we sneakily paddled our way quietly past the boat hirer and the other rowers heading upstream and settled into an easy stroke in the opposite direction, heading for the harbour mouth and the West. Beyond the harbour mouth was not permitted – but we fancied our chances.

Once past the harbour entrance we found it curious that the selfsame rock that had looked so immovable and permanent from the vantage point of the lighthouse pier, tended to wander across our horizon, and to sway up and down a lot more than we had expected. A mile out, with the blisters already burgeoning on our hands, and the realisation dawning that not only had we slaved and sweated to cover less than a tenth of the way there, but we were faced with the hard fact that we also had to row back to a shore that now looked too far distant for comfort.

Arthur Ransome might well have scripted the story rather differently, but the fact that we might have to pay a double charge for overstaying our hire of the boat frightened me more than the incipient thought that the turn of the tide might make a landfall in Girvan – or a landfall anywhere, for that matter – unlikely. However, the weakening afternoon sunshine gave me an excuse for the beads of sweat forming on my brow. The long swell made itself more felt as our fatiguing muscles slowed the boat's way, but early nausea was fought back. My wee brother would never have let pass an opportunity to crow if I had as much as burped, no less vomited. And he was showing no sign of doing so. Consequently, a reluctant decision was made to postpone the row to the Craig for another day and we pulled, it seemed endlessly, for the shore.

The mannie at the landing stage had just begun to berate us for being late back, and, worse still, to count the shillings now due. Little of his vituperation seemed to penetrate my dulled and totally exhausted body, when father suddenly appeared at the steps, paid the excess and brusquely adjured us to get home at once.

It seems that cousin John Williamson, who, when he was not golfing or walking, scanned the sea endlessly with his binoculars. His front bay window, high over the golf course, afforded him the ideal vantage point to do so. He had spotted two stupid boys rowing far too far out to sea. Little did he appreciate who these errant Magellans were till he met our father passing his house and discovered that we had, in fact, hired a rowing boat that afternoon. My father had apparently walked the length of the navigable river to meet us – without success – when the dread thought occurred to him that deeper waters might have called us. We were therefore deprived that evening of both potato scones and rock cakes. We dared not complain about our blisters.

Uncle Hugh and the aunts were distinctly subdued at teatime. Even before we were allowed to take our places at the table, there had been some 'very serious talking' to us in the back bedroom. The hazards of disobeying rules, of going to sea in a small boat not intended for that purpose, and, worst of all, not saying where we were going were recapitulated in some detail. At home we would have been thrashed and sent to bed without supper. At Girvan, however, my parents had thought it better to temper their wrath with mercy. Partly, I think, that was because they did not wish to seem harsh parents in front of the extended family, and partly too because, remembering the boating pond episode the year before, they were aware that, but for a certain amount of good fortune, they might have lost one or both of us for ever.

On the whole, the Girvan holidays were better because my father in particular was more relaxed than we usually saw him, and that seemed to convey itself to our mother. In Lochgelly, father could settle with a book, walk round the Loch or do little jobs in the patch of garden. Mother, by contrast was always, it seemed, a bit too aware that she had 'made it' by comparison with her sisters and spent a lot of time organising them. She was prone to organising us boys with equal vigour. Of the two of us, I think Tom was the more adept at adjusting to the change in circumstances and found it easier too to adapt to different playmates. I was not averse to football, the playpark and the beach but whereas I could spend hours with my nose in a book, Tom was disinclined – partly because he was, of course, younger, but partly too because he more readily took people at face value. I suppose I was quite a quiet boy, rather uncertain of myself, but inclined surreptitiously to observe, and later, analyse in my simple way, others.

The contrast between the two cultures of Girvan and Lochgelly as evidenced by Grainger Street and Roodlands Road taught me much about how people saw their origins and much too about the substantial differences in the way people had to live out their lives. None of them, though in different ways, had much opportunity for self determination. They were all hard up financially and lived from day to day. Control over the circumstances of their lives was a luxury they could not depend on and their aspirations were simple and restricted. My parents were the only members of their large respective families who had broken away from these restraining attitudes and background by dint of education and profession. Only later in my life did I recognise that I suppose I admired them for it. There were times though, especially on holiday, when I guessed that they too were aware that they had lost a little of the spontaneity and warmth that characterised the lives of my grandpa and my aunts and uncles. And how I wished I had known my paternal grandparents, especially Aul' Jimmie, jobbing gardener, Fabian pamphleteer and atheist!

Chapter III

LIFE IN THE MANSE

'Unto whomsoever much is given, of him shall much be required.'
(*Holy Bible*, Luke 12:48)

Being born into a Scottish Presbyterian manse carries with it a few privileges but many burdens. Most of these, I have subsequently discovered, seem to have been shared by all whose lot it has been to have experienced a similar accident of birth. Most of all, one became quickly aware, first, of the lack of privacy, and soon after, the frequently spoken, and always tacit, demand that one's behaviour had to be exemplary. Not only would the 'All-seeing Eye' in the sky be observing, satellite-like, your every action, but so would the eyes of every right-thinking parishioner or citizen of the town in which one lived, in my case, Banff, Macduff, or even the nearby village of Whitehills. Each and every transgression, from the trivial to the heinous, would be reported, we were led to believe, and dire consequences would follow as inevitably as night follows day.

All the characteristics that accrue to small boys so naturally – being untidy; sometimes being cheeky, or even swearing; farting; putting one's elbows on the dinner table; scuffing one's boots by playing football on tarmac or climbing walls, were to be firmly suppressed. First, a serious telling off, the second time, a smacking. There were few scruples in those days about corporal punishment. The more dangerous characteristics that accrue to larger and older boys, such as going with girls, smoking, or drinking anything more potent than Irn Bru, would be even more firmly put down. Yet more portentous homilies, perhaps a 'confined to barracks' for a not insignificant period and a variety of unpleasant penances, would follow.

'How often have I to tell you, David, that (Billy So-and-so or Jimmy What's-his-name) is not a nice boy. I don't want you to have anything to do with him,' my mother would shout after she or some of her spies had seen me making a catapult or kicking a tin can around with one of them. And the annoying thing was that these were all the interesting lads I met at or on my way home from school. The ones she deemed appropriate companions were always, it seemed to me, amongst the most boring or cissy of the lot of them. 'You must both be an example to others,' she would intone. 'Remember who you are!' Later on, in my teens, the same applied to girls. None were (in my mother's eyes, if not always in mine) good enough for 'sons of the manse', as my parents never tired of describing my brother and myself. Indeed, in one of my father's bookcases there lay for many years a sizeable volume with that very title. I confess to having glanced through it once in a while but was not inspired. It dealt largely, and in a rather self-congratulatory fashion, I thought, with the apparently successful lives and careers of my predecessors as 'Meenister's loons'. However, I couldn't help noticing that there seemed to be rather a lot of them recorded and wondered whether these laudatory chapters had served to found my father's aspirations for Tom and myself.

In terms of Freudian theory, there were in such an existence, the makings of a cripplingly severe superego, the unconscious conscience which outdoes in its severity all normal and rational ethical evaluations. Somehow, however, there must have been elements, less well observed, which militated against such a burden for later life, for it seems that neither I nor my friends have thought of myself as being unduly restricted by such a personality characteristic. Perhaps these very friends, very few of whom were 'approved' by my parents, supplied the necessary antidote. Perhaps too the fact that from an early age I have tended by habit and style to be an observer rather than a participant in the maelstrom of human interaction has played its part.

From my earliest years it must have been apparent to me that there were some features of day-to-day existence which were different from the experience of the many other children about me. Precisely when such a perception became clear to me is uncertain. Perhaps the first of several oddities to occur to me was how seldom I saw my parents. The second was how seldom we all sat down to an evening meal especially at the same time each day. Other kids seemed to be called in for their 'teas' at or about 5.00 or 5.30 p.m. In the case of my brother and me, however, high tea was very much 'a movable feast'. Sometimes it might be about 6.00, maybe 6.20 or 6.30, but quite often it could have been nearer 7.00. Then, it would have been really rushed and my parents would likely have shot out again by 7.25 p.m.

The tradition of the time was that both the minister and his wife, as far as a parish church in the Church of Scotland was concerned, were 'given' to the parish to serve in every way possible for much of their lives. My father never had a car but was committed to visiting his parishioners most days of the week when he was not officiating at some wedding, baptism or funeral. He might therefore disappear after lunch only to return, having walked many miles throughout town and country in the course of these duties. Occasionally, hospitable farmers and their wives might have given him an evening meal, but most times he would come in hungry for something – preferably not salad, which he, untutored in healthy eating, would scorn as 'rabbit food'. My mother's and his evenings also seemed to be taken up with other kinds of 'meetings' such as Guilds, working parties, and meetings of the Kirk Session about which I understood little and cared less. In consequence, my brother Tom (always addressed with full formality as 'Thomas') and I were largely brought up either by the maid current at the time or by a friend of the household, Miss Mann.

The latter had in fact been my father's landlady when he came first, unmarried, to Banff and lodged, in a way befitting the then assistant parish minister, in 'Broadcroft', a solid and respectable whinstone and slate detached villa on Bellevue Road, near the Glebe. She seemed, as do all older persons to the very young, to me to be a very old lady then. She may well have been, but perhaps less so than I thought. Her habit was to dress with the serious decorum she thought pertained to the manse and I doubt if I ever saw her in anything other than an ankle-length black dress, low heels, and, for outdoors, a long overcoat with a rather extravagant fox fur collar and a black felt hat, shaped like an inverted pudding bowl and with what looked like a dyed, and certainly dead, sparrow's wing pinned to the side of it. Occasionally, when she would give my small brother and me our evening bath and plate of Farola, or worse, castor oil or Californian Syrup of Figs, she might affect a cotton pinafore over her dress. My memories of her are, however, of uniform kindness and for many years until her death we visited her weekly, usually on a Sunday afternoon with my parents.

Plate 13: Myself, father and brother Tom, probably in the autumn of 1937

Curiously, I can remember almost nothing of anything she said, but a good deal about what she did. When we visited, her kitchen was the room in which she obviously spent much of her spinster life. She also gardened a lot – fairly expertly, because relatives had a seedsman and nursery business in Elgin – and my father was very pleased to take her advice on how to eradicate carrot fly or grow better tomatoes. In the kitchen I was fascinated by the incredible cleanliness of the 'range' (the fire grate and hobs) and associated oven. It was black-leaded and shining and trimmed on handles, hinges and some edges with brass which the most critical of regimental sergeant majors could not have faulted. The willow pattern plates, great, gleaming brass jam pans and tureens on the shelves around the opposite wall shone back at one from these other gleaming brasses and vied for my attention with the five or six beautifully made and maintained paraffin lamps with which the house was lit but which were removed to the kitchen each day for a ritual trimming of wicks, topping up with oil and polishing of the tall, tapering glasses.

For me, the best bit of any visit was an opportunity to study in detail a typically Victorian *objet d'art* which decorated her hallway. This was a glass case of some three feet tall by two feet wide and deep which contained an 'artistic' display of stuffed birds of the countryside, their nests and eggs. One feature of living in a small town surrounded by the sea and the open countryside was that as boys we were always aware of the natural history and wild life around us. We took a keen interest in animals and birds from the earliest of our school years. To see such a fine egg collection, and the greenfinches, a lark, a corncrake, a mistle thrush and some others mounted by the taxidermist amid natural grasses and on a branch of beech or such like was the cynosure of all small boys' eyes. Curiously, in the light of contemporary attitudes, my parents, though not overly enthusiastic, did not look askance at the collection of wild birds' eggs which I was later in my life to accumulate.

It is not unlikely that only in the post-war years did the problems of the depletion of our countryside by the combined effects of sprayed weedkillers, the clearing of hedges to form larger fields, increased urbanisation and thoughtless shooting for sport become apparent. When it did, then the collection by small boys, and others, of wild birds' eggs, the trapping of birds and animals for the taxidermist and uncontrolled shooting were reviewed with concern by the thinking public. In the late 1940s and earlier, many private houses as well as the local museums and libraries would have sported a number of glass cases like Miss Mann's and in many middle class homes at least one might have seen fine mounted and stuffed specimens of red squirrel, otter or wildcat. The gentry, of course, went one better and sported the odd stag's head and antlers in hall or dining room, or tiger skin rug on the floor.

To such trophies the worthy Banff shopkeepers had their equivalents. I well remember that even in the local butcher's shop when I went to collect the mince on a Saturday, a pair of (to me) huge Aberdeen Angus and Hereford bulls' heads, complete with rings in their no longer moist noses, glowered down from the tiled walls of the shop. Whether these were meant to intimidate customers tempted to beat down the butcher's prices or not, they certainly filled me with a certain trepidation, linked to uncertainty as to whether they really were stuffed or whether the rest of their powerful bodies were not simply hidden behind the wall.

The fishmonger too made his shop a place of interest beyond simply the fish on the slab by showing a huge mounted and stuffed salmon in one glass case and an even bigger cod in another, while an impeccably accurate and detailed model of a fishing drifter graced the side counter. Equally interesting and beautifully framed oil paintings of other fine ships, like the *Thermopylae*, a famous square rigged clipper, also graced the walls. More incongruously, there stood at the back of the shop two huge glass jars with brass lids and bases filled, I believe, with pears, skinned but whole, in brandy in one and more pears in gin in the other. The jars must have been about three feet high and what they had to do with fish was a constant puzzle to me, and possibly others. Perhaps their bizarre charm derived from that very fact. Tesco and Sainsbury's have never been able to match that! As it happens, I have recently confirmed that the two jars remain to this day in the possession of the fishmonger's family.

The manse itself was, like many Scottish manses of the day, an externally gracious villa of white-harled rear walls and sandstone masonry frontage, two storeys and an expansive loft, standing on the south edge of the town in a large garden with decorative trees and shrubbery at the front. The interior was, nevertheless, often cold and cavernous to a child's eyes. Having lived in it from a few weeks old, however, I did not really understand then that it differed so much from the ménage of other children around me.

Rooms, whether by habit or design, were allocated certain functions and a number of rules applied. For example, family life was carried on essentially in 'the parlour', what would now be called the lounge or living room. That was a large room with three high windows, two looking southeast and another at the side looking northeast. A sofa and two armchairs, one exclusively the property of my father; a large mahogany dining table and four upright chairs, a somewhat over-elaborate chiffonier and a more functional sideboard, and, in due course, the wireless, were the main furnishings of that room. A full-sized door at one side of the fireplace gave entry to 'the press' and under the window at the other side was a low cupboard, always bursting open, which contained some of our toys – a cigarette card collection in a large cardboard box, several Dinky toys, a wooden 'fort' with lead soldiers, some jigsaws, rubber balls and a catapult or two. Only family friends were entertained in there. The 'press' had nothing to do with the inquisitive, even inquisitorial, gentlemen from the *Banffshire Journal* or *The Scotsman*. It was simply the local name for a large cupboard with shelves and in this one, my mother had, in the year or so prior to the war of 1939, packed an accumulation of tea and tinned goods in anticipation of rationing. It served her well when, on hundreds of occasions in the following five years, she was to entertain and feed large numbers of servicemen and women from the various military establishments around the town.

Across the hall, the other main front room was the dining room. Only the famous and the powerful ever dined there, except perhaps if some of my relatives happened to be staying with us and my mother was 'showing off'.

We ourselves ate in the parlour (or the kitchen if we happened to be left to the tender mercies of the maid when our parents were away). Otherwise the main function of that room, which was rather 'posh', in late Victorian style, was to act as a 'consulting room' for parishioners and others who visited my father for advice or to arrange various 'hatches, matches or despatches'. From time to time, and often during the war, weddings, baptisms and communions would be celebrated in there. In its way, it was quite an imposing large room with expansive bay windows, a side glass door leading into the greenhouse, and another side window at the other side of the fireplace looking onto the garden. It contained a huge mahogany table (later gifted to the Health Board and recognised by me some twenty years later when, in Banff again, I took up post in the NHS) complemented by eight hide upholstered mahogany dining chairs and two matching carvers. There were two large sideboards, one of castle-like proportions, and a number of fine Farquharson and Raeburn prints along with an excellent Whistler, all of which mysteriously disappeared when my parents 'flitted' to Girvan after father's retirement. Another large 'press' also figured in a number of notable events in that room. Because of its usage, we were always obliged to knock before entering – although it was made quite clear that there was really very little reason for us to be in that room at all at any time. One might have thought that interviews with and counselling of parishioners might have taken place in my father's study, through the wall from the dining room. The study was, however. a *sanctum sanctorum* reserved for family or his very closest friends, when invited.

Plate 14: St Mary's Parish Church Manse, Banff, as it was in the 1930s

Dinner parties for the 'famous' were marked by my mother's usual preface. 'Now David, tonight we're having *people,* so I don't want you anywhere near the dining room.' She always talked of the main rooms of the manse as if they had capitals. *People* meant they were in some way posh or extraordinary and would not wish their evening to be spoilt by the sight or sound of urchins like myself or my brother.

We might have pricked the bubble of what passed for our good reputation by being either dirty, uncouth, unintelligent, or worse still, argumentative or overtly critical of the guests. It must be admitted that some of these guests, these *people,* were, when we occasionally ran up against them, sometimes literally, rather special, and usually quite charming. I remember in particular one evening, early in the war, when I was met halfway up the stair by a tall, immaculately uniformed and strikingly distinguished-looking soldier with a general's collar tabs and gold braided lanyard. Though his native tongue was Norwegian, he addressed me in English and then proceeded to test out my then, as now, fairly rudimentary knowledge of French. He was General Strugstad, Aide de Camp to King Haakon VII and his son the Crown Prince Olav of Norway, who had the decency to brush past us on the stair landing, thus forestalling my linguistic inadequacies being wholly revealed as he urged his man to continue to the drawing room for coffee.

Other distinguished guests in addition to those included various Moderators of the Church of Scotland, Lords such as Lord Rowallan, the Chief Scout, Lord Blades, one of the Scottish Law Lords who happened to have married one of my mother's cousins, and Sir Max Aitken, then the Group Captain in charge of Banff Strike Wing at Boyndie aerodrome. The royal Norwegians and several of the last named, though visitors at different times, were all very keen bridge players and would promptly repair, after the port, with whomsoever were their partners for the evening, to the drawing room upstairs for a prolonged session over the green baize, something which my father, less of a bridge afficionado than my mother, was none too keen on. How they survived my mother's penetrating post-mortems on their various hands I'll never know. Initially, when my parents played host to scores of 'other ranks' – as, in fairness, they did much more frequently than to officers – the whist and pontoon parties (which we boys joined in with after school) were held in the parlour rather than the drawing room. Soon, however, it became plain that the numbers of soldiers, airmen and WAAFs who turned up far exceeded the capacity of one room and often both the parlour and the drawing room would be fully occupied and an egalitarian democracy was restored, to my father's gratification.

The drawing room was upstairs above the dining room and of equal proportions. It too was not routinely open to 'the boys', Tom and me, except by special invitation. I have to admit that the drawing room, with a bright fire in the grate, its deep and comfortable easy chairs, flowers and pictures, was in its period style rather a gracious and welcoming room. As we grew older, the restriction on our using it was somewhat relaxed, since the drawing room, amid a general clutter of glass fronted display cabinets, bric-à-brac, card tables and easy chairs contained the piano. If we were to develop the social graces my parents wished for us, then piano lessons, at the hands of the church organist, were very much the order of the day and the drawing room perforce was required for practice.

It was also the centre for our 'Home' games in a peculiar little league formed within the parish. That was the 'PSE' or Pleasant Sunday Evening. The 'Away' games were in other people's houses. After church on Sunday evening it was the habit of several parishioners to convene at each other's homes, along with the rather irascible but effete church organist and his long suffering and long term fiancée, the local art teacher who was a reasonable singer and elocution mistress. We all knew intuitively, both because of the prevailing moral climate and for other unspoken reasons, that she could never deserve that title in any other sense. In some of the homes we were dragged to, like 'whining schoolboy, with his satchel, and shining morning face, creeping like snail, unwillingly to school', several of the group could play other instruments than the ever present piano. A local pharmacist was no mean performer on cello and/or clarinet and one or two of the butcher's family sang well. Others fiddled away manfully as the hostess for the evening prepared a frugal tea. When it was my mother's turn to play hostess, it was to the drawing room they all repaired. It was almost incredible how often I suddenly found out that I had some Latin version, an English essay or a geometry problem to solve at the last minute before Monday morning arrived. It was amazing too how such intellectual travail could beat a PSE hollow!

A curious phenomenon occurred in the drawing room every summer which much annoyed my parents but which occasioned more wonder on our part. On some warm days the whole room, and the windows especially seemed to come alive with bluebottle flies. One theory was that they were 'encouraged' by the flocks of sheep which grazed regularly in the wood and field across the wall on the other side of Sandyhill Road where we lived. The other was that they somehow managed to breed behind the rather elaborate though refined plasterwork cornices and central circle on the ceiling of the room. Whatever the true explanation, there immediately followed a vigorous campaign with the 'Flit' gun which was soon followed by a frenzied buzz on the floor all around us as the thousands of flies wriggled in their death throes. Our natural boyish aggression would have us vie for the spraygun but mother was adamant that we should not be let loose with it lest we inadvertently spray the noxious liquid on her precious aspidistras, potted flowers and fine china ornaments. In those days there were no such things as aerosols and the Flit-gun was a hand pumped spray a foot-and-a-half long, two inches in diameter and with a pint-sized container soldered to its underside for the insecticide. We were allowed to sweep up the carcasses.

If the parlour was the room for the family and, in general, open to all, then my father's study was, as already noted, the holy of holies. It lay behind the dining room and was protected by double doors some five or six feet apart. Both were generally closed. Through these forbidding barriers, the room was a pleasant square room with a single high window facing on to the back garden. In the centre of the room was my father's roll-top mahogany desk and matching swivel chair – a gift from his erstwhile parishioners at St Matthews Parish Church, Edinburgh, where he had been an assistant minister in 1913, and something of which I am now the proud possessor.

On each side of the cast iron and tile fireplace were two deep and large horsehair upholstered moquette armchairs both of which completely swallowed me as a small boy. Along the two walls which were uninterrupted by either window or fireplace were ceiling-high bookcases full of books. These were of course largely on philosophy, literary criticism and theology but there was a goodly smattering of others covering the classical fictional writers of English literature, geography, history and other languages. There was yet another huge 'press' adjacent to the fireplace which also contained mainly books on church history and local history as well as piles of manuscript, mainly sermons and other incidental writings. The room perpetually smelt of cigarette or pipe smoke and brass ashtrays littered the furniture. In some ways this only added to the room's special ambience. It reeked of scholarship.

In retrospect, I can now see that this haven of peace and privacy was a serious necessity for someone of my father's turn of mind and habit. The fact that even my mother would ask permission, if not to enter, certainly if she intended to spend any time in the room, meant that my brother Tom, the maid and I afforded it the status of something between a royal court and a secret spy HQ.

'David, where are you going?' my mother would challenge should I even hesitate opposite the study door half way along the corridor to the kitchen. 'You know your father's busy in there and doesn't want to be disturbed.' She defended him well, even if she half guessed that some of his claims to need a perfect academic solitude were founded, at least sometimes, on a baser need only to have some peace and quiet to himself when he could consume his *Scotsman* or an engaging book wholly untrammelled by the incursions of others. As I write this, I realise I too have used such stratagems in my time.

Only as we grew older and bolder would we venture into the study when he was out. The goals then were to get a 'shottie' of the fairly powerful airgun he kept in the 'press' to scare off the pigeons that had the effrontery to nibble at his early spring cabbages outside the window, or to pinch a fag or two from where he kept his supply in the third drawer down on the left of the desk. During the war his military friends kept him fairly well supplied with Capstan or Gold Flake apart from those he purchased himself. He was a fairly heavy smoker until he gave up precipitately when he was 72 on medical advice. It afforded him another thirteen years of reasonable life.

As for myself, smoking was manly, if a bit reckless, and very infrequent at age ten; little more than a quick and furtive draw in the gang hut at eleven; a bit more sophisticated in the 'scratchers' at the local Picture House at twelve or thirteen and eventually sporadic while we worked picking 'tatties' on nearby farms in the autumns of my fourteenth and fifteenth years. I gave it up just as I turned sixteen and it became legal for me to smoke.

The circumstances underlying such a dramatic and Pauline conversion were that I then happened to be fancying a certain girl who lived not on the road to Damascus but on the road to Portsoy. She and her (also quite attractive) pal came to watch us playing football for the school at interschool matches. We surreptitiously supported her at the hockey games. Having been beaten to the ball twice in a row by my opposing left back from Buckie High School in a certain game, I heard this fair maid comment to her pal that Sark (my nickname then) was getting slow and this was due to his smoking too much. That did it. Never did another fag grace my lips. Neither the rigours of university study nor the rather different ones of later life in the RAF impelled me to take up the weed again and for that chance overheard remark I have subsequently been very glad.

But to revert to the manse, if the study was forbidden ground most of the time for nearly everyone but my father, then the kitchen and adjacent scullery were 'an open city'. It is true that my father, during the years that we had a maid, would hesitate to infringe the boundaries of what he indubitably saw as women's territory. Later, however, towards the end of the war years when we no longer employed a servant girl because they had all joined the Services or The Land Army, he regularly took it upon himself to light the fire in the ancient 'Triplex' range and to make the porridge in the morning. He felt that nobody else could quite get the consistency just as right as he could himself.

In many ways he was out of tune with employing a servant. His own father had been a strong socialist and pamphleteer about the exploitation of the working class. Old Jimmy Clark, my grandfather, as a jobbing gardener to the landed gentry of Carrick, knew all about that. My father's political sympathies, though he felt it obligatory to 'the cloth' to disguise them, were well to the left of centre. It was therefore something of a relief to him when there was no longer a maid in the manse. My mother, also from working class origins, with her strong aspirations to the more obvious aspects of middle class status, regretted it more, though it must be said that she always worked in the house and in the parish as hard, if not harder, than any maid we ever had. It killed her in the end.

The kitchen, and adjacent scullery, were large rooms with stone floors and barred windows like a jail. Off the kitchen was a walk-in pantry, also with a very small barred window and off the scullery was what became a store room for bicycles and the like but it had a lavatory pan and the remains of a box bed. At the time of my father's predecessor in the manse it had been the maid's room – and pretty comfortless at that. My parents had had a bedroom built in fine fresh pine timber in the very large attic for our maid(s) and furnished it reasonably comfortably with bed, wardrobes, washing facilities, dressing table and so on. The windows were curtained and the door had a lock to afford the girls privacy against our insatiable curiosity.

The kitchen was mainly heated by the Triplex grate (not a patch on Miss Mann's gleaming *penates* up the Bellevue Road!) which also heated the water and oven. There was also a gas stove on which more and more of the cooking was done as time wore by. One of the fascinations of the Triplex was that it had a 'damper', a rod with a knob on it which, when it was pulled outwards, closed off the normal upward rush of the flue and opened a new vent somewhere in behind the back boiler. The effect of this was to produce a throbbing roar as the flames, compressed and offered more oxygen, heated the coals and dross to near white heat. As the water boiler warmed so did we. Our wooden kitchen chairs, rough with age and starkly brown painted, would be drawn in with the maid's round this homely glow. If the maid was in a good mood and her boyfriend was in, she would let us make toast. The crusty bread browned beautifully on the long wire fork and the butter melted in little gold waves as we savoured the heat and the companionship. Manses were in those days, unconscionably cold places but for such occasions.

The town had at that time its own coke-fired gas works down by the harbour and some of the manse rooms were gas lit as well. My father's predecessor in the manse was a Rev. Dr W. S. Bruce, a man of some distinction and literary bent but a man too who was more Harpagon-like in his domestic habits than many of his erstwhile parishioners might have known. My father, while still an assistant minister, would visit him in the study later to be my father's, to find Dr Bruce clad in greatcoat, scarf and woollen mittens sitting writing at his desk beneath a candle, with no fire in the grate and with all the gas pipes in the rooms hammered flat lest the gas bill became too high!

Even years later, I can remember that many of these pipes remained flattened and useless where they emerged from the wall, often over a mantlepiece, in bedrooms, on the stairway and in the hall. At least my parents when they moved into the manse had gas lights reinstated in the parlour, kitchen, dining room and study. We had only an oil lamp in the hall, however, until well into the war. Gas lighting required very fragile mantles and woe betide us if, in a boyish attempt to light up, we happened to put the taper through the mantle. It was a great day, quite late in the '40s, when we had electricians in to fix an arrangement whereby the gas in the main rooms could be lit by a battery and switch at the door. Later still came a full electricity service with all its convenience, lack of smells, good illumination and reduced fire risk. No wonder that even now I still delight in things like dimmer switches, low voltage circuits and halogen bulbs! All that in just over half a lifetime.

One of the features of the kitchen which fascinated me was a long row of bells, each about 2 or 3 inches in length and diameter which hung on foot-long curved springs at near ceiling height along one wall of the kitchen. These were all activated by a hidden arrangement of wires, levers and quadrants in behind the plasterwork of the walls which connected each bell to an S-shaped lever (of moulded brass with white ivory-like handles) in each public room and bedroom. These were rung to summon the maid who had to watch which one was still swinging on its spring in order to tell from where the summons originated.

Several of these had long since succumbed to rust and wear and tear but Tom and I would try them all just to hear the strange wheezy, creaky rattles and rubs the wires made in the walls. If, by chance, we'll say, we happened to pull a 'wrong' one, i.e. one which was still working, we could guarantee the combined wrath of the maid and our mother, at least one of whom would emerge from the kitchen to utter dire threats and sometimes a few well-aimed slaps for our experiments. The bell at the main front door was eventually replaced by a modern battery-powered electric bell in the hallway activated by a push-button. Because visitors (as everybody who came to the front door were called) were usually 'on business' to see my father, it was important that their advent should be noted effectively. Tradesmen, beggars, friends of the maid, message boys from the local shops, the fishwife with her wickerwork creel, Tom and I and often our friends were encouraged by my mother to use the back door. That had no bell at all but a remarkably effective large cast iron knocker. Unlike the others, Tom and I were not constrained to knock.

The kitchen and scullery were the scene of much that was interesting and colourful in my boyish life. Many of the maids who served us so well were lassies from the farming hinterland of Banff, mostly quite young but quite unsophisticated. They knew a lot of the lore of the countryside and could tell tales of the life in the bothies and 'chaumers' with a variety of embellishments which had been Bowdlerised from the versions of the bothy ballads which made it into print via the pen of Willie Kemp or G. S. Morris. The drama and various tribulations of country life which were thus related to us were closer to the world of Lewis Grassic Gibbon's *Sunset Song* first published in 1932, only five or six years before the period described here. The country girls we had as maids were unaffected, direct and deeply immersed in the toil and traditions of the farms and crofts of Buchan though inarticulate in expressing that. They felt, but could never openly declare, that their roots were in the land. Chris Guthrie might have.

And then a queer thought came to her there in the drooked fields, that nothing endured at all, nothing but the land she passed across, tossed and turned and perpetually changed below the hands of the crofter folk since the oldest of them had set the Standing Stones by the loch of Blawearie and climbed there on their holy days and saw their terraced crops ride brave in the wind and sun. Sea and sky and the folk who wrote and fought and were learnéd, teaching and saying and praying, they lasted but as a breath, a mist of fog in the hills, but the land was forever, it moved and changed below you, but was forever, you were close to it and it to you, not at a bleak remove it held you and hurted you. And she had thought to leave it all!' (*Sunset Song* p. 120)

Nearly all of our maids were kind to us and tolerated, even welcomed, us into their domain in the kitchen.

The ones from the town rather than from the rural hinterland were less fey and more worldly. One, rather more sexually precocious than most, would also invite us from time to time to visit her in her bedroom in the attic to watch her change uniforms. At that time we were hardly into our teens and perhaps less inclined or insufficiently knowledgeable to take advantage of such offers.

There was only one of these lassies of whom I have really unpleasant memories. She was the one, perhaps the first I can remember, who, while taking me for a walk one afternoon in a pushchair when I must have been no more than two or three years of age, began by berating me for some long forgotten misbehaviour and finished by tipping me, quite deliberately, out of the pushchair into a bed of stinging nettles. This torture took place near the end of the then unmade farm road now known as Colleonard Road. It is a measure of the impact it made on me that I can to this day remember not only the size and aspect of the nettle bed but also the adjacent iron bench which was then available there as a welcome seat for pensioners and other weary wayfarers. How the swellings on my face and limbs were explained to my mother I never knew. But I was never keen on being taken for a walk by that young lady again.

Another maid we had at about the beginning of the war was so withdrawn and shy that she would never come down from her eyrie in the attic when the Air Raid warning sounded. We would all repair to the 'black hole' under the stair (as it was called) which served as a bomb shelter but Margaret would dot about in the attic with a flickering candle while my father agitated about her safety but was too much a 'gentleman' to go up and fetch her down while she was in her nightgown. Mother, having called her once or twice, eventually gave up.

'Well, if she gets blown up, it's her own fault. We've told her often enough!'

Margaret was taciturn enough in a way which I now recognise was schizoid and she eventually left service of her own accord a year or so later. Annie, who succeeded her, after, I think, two others whose careers at the manse were for one reason or another, more short-lived, was with us for many years and to us boys was almost one of the family. She was from the town rather than the country. She was warm, accepting, direct and business-like about her duties and we all liked her. She was allowed some evenings to have her then boyfriend, and later husband, a gardener, to visit her in the kitchen and Tom and I would often find them sitting side by side at the Triplex grate when we, after a due interval, disregarded our parents' instructions to leave them alone since Annie was 'off duty'. They were amazingly tolerant of our intrusions and would have rather solemn and shy conversations with us until we were shoo'ed off to bed. We regularly went with her on her half-day (usually a Sunday) to visit her family in a wee house just off the Gallowhill.

'Come on, you loons', she'd say, 'an' I'll tak' ye tae see far I bide', as she reached out to take wee Tom's hand in her own red and work-calloused fist. These outings were, along with summer holidays in Lochgelly at my maternal grandfather's miner's cottage, my first real first-hand acquaintance with working-class life in the '30s.

One of the main features of such a life as we there saw on a Sunday was the cramped but socially close life that was enjoyed by Annie's family. We had so many rooms, most of which were large and decorated with all manner of artifacts, but so often empty of life. They had but one living room/kitchen where everything happened. All the stories of Edwin, the soldier, eventually away in the war, the squabbles after a boozy Saturday night, the dog being shooed away from the neighbour's baby who lolled happily in front of the grate, the clothes drying on a string draped over the fireplace like elaborate Christmas decorations never taken down and the dog-eared, sepia-toned photographs of ancient family members bespoke of a closeness and warmth that I never felt in the vaulted coolness and formality of the manse.

The irony of it all was that that family would never have guessed at my wistfulness about their simplicity and directness. They attributed to me, with all their diffident deference in the face of my childish hesitancy, a sophistication I singularly lacked. But these afternoons, together with my experiences in the miners' cottages in Lochgelly where, in the 1930s we spent our summer holidays with my youngest aunt and my maternal grandfather were potently formative of my political awareness of the interrelatedness between and the inherent value of all the citizens of our land. Socialism or liberalism in a formal sense was not then known to me, but these experiences, with others to follow at later stages in my life, ensured that the self-seeking capitalists of Torydom would never have my vote.

One previous maid at the manse, Ella, came from the farm of Luncarty on the road to Turriff and she too was wont to invite Tom and myself to visit her home on her day off, usually on a Saturday or Sunday afternoon. She was a 'Chris Guthrie' who could lead us out over one of her father's fields to admire a great bit of ploughing, point out to us the distant sea beyond the great sweep of the Buchan farmlands and return to watch as we were allowed to suckle a calf from the bottle of warm milk. In retrospect, I see these young lassies as remarkably forbearing and tolerant of two small boys who must often have been a pain in the neck to adults. Perhaps in a strange way these girls could see that we were deprived of the normal wide range of experiences and pals that were more easily available to boys from an ordinary home. While at Luncarty we would be taken to see the cattle in the byre, the hens running free, of course, and could even sit on the tractor seat and essay to turn the wheel, even if our little legs could not reach the pedals – which was maybe just as well! To get there we had to travel on the Bluebird bus which ran on to Aberdeen and then walk the mile or so along the country road to the farm. For some reason it always seemed to have been a fine day. It rather limited our style when we had to go there wearing our best kilt gear. Old trousers and a jersey would have better suited to jumping into the straw in the loft or fetching the eggs from the 'walk-in' chicken coops.

These country Sundays, and some when we sneaked off on our own to range along the seashore, make rafts, fish or throw 'skimmers' of flat stones over the river or calm sea, left me, and probably my wee brother too, a rich legacy of memories both sharper and more enriching than did many other aspects of our lives in school or in the manse. I have often been reminded of a poem called 'I Remember Sunday' by Ken Morrice. The late Ken was a warm, talented friend and professional colleague during the latter years of both our lives as clinicians in the NHS. It was always intriguing when I spoke with him as to whether I was engaged with the poet or the consultant psychiatrist. His readers and his patients all loved him.

> Yes, I remember Sunday as a boy.
> From Sunday-suited Sunday-school,
> From golden texts and dusty hymn-books,
> We fled to sunshine, young and free;
> And (while our elders contemplated tea)
> Became backsliders on the sandy slopes,
> Quick hours flowing with the tide.
>
> Salt water stained our polished Sunday shoes
> As pebbled barriers, contrived against the waves,
> Crumbled before the heedless sea
> Which swamped our cork-and-feathered argosy
> Till weary of playing Canute in the foam,
> suddenly guilty on a Protestant Sabbath day,
> We repented up the hill to home,
> Dishevelled sinners, too late for grace,
> And seeing God's thunder in our father's face
> Knew we were hungry sent to bed
> And cared not, me and Roy
>
> Yes, I remember Sunday as a boy.

Plate 15: Tom and myself (on right) with one of our manse maids, 1934

There are few occasions when I remember my parents both being at home and spending time with us boys during the early years of our lives. The fact that they were much older than most parents when we were born played a part in this as much as did the constant round of demands made on them both by the parish and congregation. By the time I myself was the age of my father then, my own children were in their thirties. In many ways he was more like a grandfather than a parent. He tried quite hard at times, doing his best to play at cowboys or to kick around a football, but these were no more than episodes.

By the time I was in my teens, near the end of my school career and later while I was at university, we had more sustained interactions. These, however, were essentially academic in content – discussions on philosophy, religion, literature or politics. My father was much more comfortable in such relationships. When I was just starting school he would occasionally 'hear my reading'. He would ensure that we possessed, and read, the *Childrens' Encyclopedia* and the *Childrens' Newspaper* – another rather prissy Arthur Mee production guaranteed not to corrupt the youth of the city.

'Ach, Dad', we would grumble, 'can we not get the *Dandy* and the *Hotspur* instead of that *Children's Newspaper.* None of our pals want to swap any of their comics with us if it's only a *Children's Newspaper*'.

'No, you certainly will not!', my mother would interject a good second or two before my father had worked out his arguments for or against our proposal.

'You know perfectly well that you learn nothing at all from that rubbish. It's a complete waste of money and time. If you both read all there is to learn in the *Children's Newspaper* every week you'd be doing a lot better at school than you seem to be.'

Father, drawing on his Gold Flake, retreated muttering, 'Good man, that

Arthur Mee. Look at how much you get from the *Encyclopedia*! Both of them were slaves to Calvinist doctrine and Victorian habits of thought. Moreover, they had, after much deliberation, paid a hefty sum of money for the ten volumes. Only by our ingesting their contents *in toto* would they feel they had got their money's worth.

It was ironic that about this time my curious (perhaps in both senses) little mind led me to ask 'awkward questions' about what ministers thought and did, and especially about God. Week in and week out, and often twice on Sundays, Tom and I were paraded down to the kirk where, to our huge embarrassment, we were then led by my mother, draped in a silver fox fur, to the very front 'manse seats'. We felt, probably rightly, that every parishioner's critical eye was boring into us to discern, by some sort of radar, the very slightest adverse feature of bearing, deed or thought. We were ourselves both secretly aware of several of these. Typically of my mother, she usually just made it into church in time, beating my father's ascent into the pulpit by split seconds.

The beadle would precede him, solemnly carrying in his outstretched hands the huge pulpit bible, climb the steps to the pulpit, deposit the 'good book' on the lectern, descend in his unhurried way and stand aside as he ushered my father into the pulpit. Once in, the beadle would clip a gold and purple braided rope across the pulpit entrance. As his gnarled hand snapped it in place I was reminded of the way a cattleman would clip the chain across the back of a stall once the cattle were in. Father's academic gown, purple, trimmed with ermine, was always impressive and he knew it. He would then raise both his arms aloft and intone in his sonorous voice, 'Let us worship God!'

My mind would quickly wander to wondering where the button eyes of the dead fox round my mother's shoulders came from or why should we have to worship God anyway. This Old Man in the sky seemed to have a lot of pull for somebody who was not real, never appeared and who seemed unable to get a wife for himself to have a son by. At home and in school I was encouraged to think for myself but here I was not encouraged to question. I would wryly remember once when I had, as a very small boy, been awakened by bad dreams of demons and ghosts.

'No, no, David. Go back to sleep. That's just your imagination. There are no such things as ghosts, or fairies or demons!' my mother reassured me. Now I was encouraged to believe not only in spirits and ghosts but in the Holy Spirit and the Holy Ghost. What made them so different?

Sometimes I would tackle my father about it. After all, he seemed to have a hot line to God and should know. His answers far from satisfied me. He would try to make distinctions between 'body', 'mind' and 'spirit' and say how God was the creator of all things but it all seemed to me that 'spirit' was a bit superfluous when I could get by with 'body' and 'mind' which I recognised – even in myself. It was said to be a good thing if the 'Holy Spirit' was with you, but I could never see any evidence that it was or wasn't, so, even then, I discarded it as an irrelevance. We seemed to be 'worshipping' in the interests of 'salvation' – a pretty dodgy sort of concept in itself – so that we might go to heaven rather than hell when we died. Being a child, I thought death too far removed in time to bother about it. In any case, as my mind roamed around these ideas while the sermon continued, I became preoccupied in wondering if Heaven would be such a great place, especially if it came to be peopled with most of the characters I met in church. When they got there, what age would they be – the age they died, or the age they liked best? Would they be naked or clad? Could they choose who they palled up with? Was football allowed? Would we be mixing there with Roman Catholics, Muslims, Episcopals or Hindus? Dad didn't seem to know so I thought it was all a bit fanciful, and Heaven probably hideously over crowded. At least in Hell they got burned up.

Christmas was also a time when belief was called in question. It was especially awkward when wee brother, Tom, was still young enough to believe in Santa Claus while I was not. Naturally, being a big brother, I would try to explode his world by telling him Santa was just his parents. But then, with the commercial acumen he was later to demonstrate so well in adult life, he sidestepped the belief bit by pointing out to me that if there were no Santa then instead of getting a present from Santa **and** one from Mum and Dad, we'd only get the one. At that, I decided to claim belief for personal and selfish reasons – as most believers seem to do.

The week leading up to Christmas was a busy one in the manse. A large Christmas tree would appear in the parlour and we would be encouraged to help dress it with glass baubles of incredible fragility, streaming tinsel and with no apparent thought about the huge fire risk, real coloured wax candles on tin clips which were fixed to the ends of the branches, and, on Christmas day, lit. Paper decorations were hung from the central gas lamp in the ceiling to the four corners and paper bells hung in the hallway. That seen to, our parents largely disappeared. Both were at various Guild functions, sometimes a wedding or funeral, visits to the hospital to see ailing parishioners and so on. Father had several church services including a midnight carol service on Christmas Eve and two on Christmas Day for which he prepared in his study. We were usually excused the evening service, having endured two within twelve hours prior to that.

At Christmas and birthdays we always got good presents like Meccano or, notably, in 1938, my first bicycle, but mostly we were seen, I think, as 'sons of the manse' to be trotted out for inspection as models of probity, diligence and good manners for other important adults to examine and, hopefully, admire. Every Christmas Day we had to put away the toys we'd received from Santa and otherwise in favour of accompanying our parents who diligently took gifts and visited parishioners who were sick at their homes or in the local

Chalmers Hospital. This was not country in which spirited small boys travel comfortably but we were told it was our Christian duty. As we grew older, we developed elaborate stratagems to avoid such activities – and not just the Christmas ones. Well into the war years I can remember how elaborate were my techniques of getting into the back door of the manse after school and out and off to football without being spotted by a parent when the Maintenance of the Ministry meetings were on.

These were occasions when all the ministers from the Presbytery, i.e. perhaps from twenty-five miles around, gathered at one of the larger manses putatively to discuss the management of the churches but actually to have a social chat over tea and cakes (plenty of both, as far as I could see) and to discuss the chances of a rise in salary. My mother was always very keen to introduce her boys to this black clad coven. Her boys, on the other hand, had nothing to say and could find nothing to interest them in this swarm of messengers of the Lord, but once entrapped in the parlour or dining room with them, appropriately polite responses had to be summoned up and by the time we got away, the football or catapult practice would be packing up. That was why the maid often nearly broke her neck on a schoolbag and/or blazer flung down in her way between kitchen and scullery.

But youngsters then, as now, were not brought up with only the influences of home to be wrought on them. Consequently, the *Childrens' Newspaper* was illicitly replaced by *The Dandy*, *The Wizard* or or *Hotspur*. While *The Childrens' Encyclopedia* was indeed devoured avidly by myself, there were other occasions when cheap little paperbacks about *Dixon Hawke and his boy assistant, Tommy Burke* took pride of place, especially for secret reading sessions under the blankets after lights out. We were fortunate to have school friends who took those comics regularly and who were prepared to let us have them when they were done with them, even without a swap. I think they were sorry for us.

Our early friendships were, as I have already indicated, not only tenuous but very rigorously monitored and although I think my younger brother came off better in this respect than I, it seemed to me that in the Primary school, nobody was good enough, in speech, social class or family background to become my chum and come back to the house with me, no matter how well I might have got on with him in the classroom or school playground. Naturally, I would compare my lot with my contemporaries and grumble to my parents that it would be fine to play with so-and-so but would always be met with some vague reason why this could not be. My mother would have heard him swearing somewhere or he couldn't come to the manse because his parents were not really married or he went about with other boys whose reputations were in some way, unbeknown to me, besmirched.

'It's very important that the manse sets an example to the whole community', I would be told. To me, these lads were just good company, interested in the things I was and it was far from obvious that either I myself or 'the manse' would suffer in any way if they came home with me after school or if I went to their place instead (as I did, secretly).

In retrospect, I see this rather censorious restriction imposed on me, however well-meaning it may have been, as having played a large part in my having grown up to be perhaps overly self-sufficient, interested in ideas, theory and relationships as phenomena observed in others rather than experienced at first hand or for their own sake. That aspect of my early experience may well have played a part in determining my ultimate profession. Not having been allowed to experience at first hand a great variety of relationships has perhaps determined my dealing with many at second hand and whetted my curiosity about examining the natural history of other people's relationships and motivational patterns.

By the time I was at secondary school (which I reached at the rather too tender age of ten) there were fewer restrictions, though habit established earlier took some time for me to slough off and I was nearly half way through the 3rd year before one or two pals could come up to get involved in exploits in our attic or garden. Girls, of course, were seriously frowned upon and I was never allowed to invite girls, even in the plural, into the manse. Trysts were therefore arranged in the shrubbery, outside the 'chipper' or in 'closies'. Later still, towards the end of the war, it was possible to possess a bicycle and that led to much more adventure. Tennis games at Portsoy, Macduff or Aberchirder allowed of even more contact with girls of our choice or football games with other lads.

Curiously, my parents had always arranged parties for Tom and myself when we were very small boys. Both small boys and some (very pretty) girls would be invited to these. Games and pastimes were arranged for us and jelly and ice cream dispensed in generous portions. The curious thing about these parties was that I always had the feeling, rightly or wrongly, that my parents were rather hoping that these early associations with 'the right girls' such as the doctor's daughter or the teacher's daughter, would later blossom into more adult, but approved, relationships. They never did, although I was quite fond of two of them up through the school.

But when sex reared its ugly head in adolescence my parents' policy changed radically. No parties then, and no hanging about round the chip shop or the Picture House with girls – especially girls from Macduff, Portsoy or Turriff that they didn't know! At least that was the official line. There were two great exceptions to our segregated existence.

The first was, in retrospect, quite bizarre. I must have been about fourteen, because the blackout was still in existence, when the telephone rang one evening and a girl's voice invited me to go to a 'Beetle Drive' with her in Aberchirder. Her father would call for me in his car on the evening in question and would guarantee to return me intact before the witching hour. I had no idea who the girl was and now can only remember her name as Elsie. My parents were rather taken aback (as I secretly was myself) but they must have decided that the use of the telephone, which was not at all common in people's houses in those days, and the fact that the father of this child had a car, which they had not, qualified this girl as a 'suitable person' for me to risk a game of cards with – provided the hall at Aberchirder was well lit and that we would be supervised by others. Came the night. The car duly drew up at the manse and I was whisked away to the throbbing nightlife of 'Foggieloan' as Aberchirder is universally known locally.

The lassie was a quiet but pleasant and quite good-looking girl who initiated me into the deeper mysteries of Beetle Drives, saw that I was plied with tea and sandwiches at 'halftime' and treated me to a somewhat tentative, almost virginal kiss and a cuddle as we walked to her home in one of the main streets of the village. There I was again treated to tea by her parents – I think her Dad was a long distance lorry driver with his own lorry – before the girl and I were again taxied back to Banff by him in near total silence.

Strangely enough, I remember that the girl had really sweet-smelling longish wavy hair, something that I first noted (and liked) in Janet, now my wife, when I first met her. Yet that girl and I never met again and I would not know her if I met her in the street. I have no idea how she came to telephone me in the first place and never thought to ask at the time. It may have been for a bet or a dare. I doubt she had worshipped me from afar. Nobody ever has! It was an episode which was a little time capsule, hanging in the space of experience, weightless but imbued with a delicate and truly innocent charm.

The second episode came about because our parents had to go off together to some series of meetings in Edinburgh for the best part of a week. For once, because we were older and the war was over, we were trusted to look after ourselves in the parentless manse. It was superb! We organised slap-up feeds from the 'chipper', illicit drinks by courtesy of compliant but older pals and ran parties for several nights with anybody we chose to ask. They were not all boys. The only trouble was that we were unable to persuade our parents to indulge themselves (and us) similarly on some other occasion.

If our contacts with girls were either covert or bizarre and limited to the near locality, some venues, with nothing to do with sex, were nevertheless such that, even in my more adventurous moods, I would perhaps not avoid them completely, but would at least feel more than a little guilt about a son of the manse entering them. These included the billiard room behind a baize curtain in the Carlton Café and another in the village of Cornhill. It was never entirely clear to me which particular sins were likely to be committed in these dens of iniquity, but even now, a smoky atmosphere, shadowy figures crouched along the walls and the click and rattle of cues and ivory balls still causes a frisson of guilt and apprehension. I was aware that 'old lags' from the gaol hung about there and that one could acquire 'French letters' but since at that time I was corresponding with a smart young French schoolboy at a lycée in Tours, I thought I could easily write my own.

Perhaps because of its propinquity to 'The Picture House', the Carlton's reputation, in my parents' eyes, had seemed to rub off onto the cinema. In many ways the 1930s and '40s were the heyday of the cinema, not only as a spectacle but also as a social phenomenon. There was little enough radio and of course no television at all then so a night out at the cinema became a major pastime and often, by means of Movietone News, an information source as well. It was not unduly expensive, 9d (old pence) or about 4p in contemporary money, would buy a two-and-a-half hour programme of news, a cartoon, a 'B' movie and 'the big picture', all in black and white of course. Even so, Tom and I were very seldom allowed to go to an evening show, only to the Saturday matinees until we were perhaps fourteen or fifteen. Then the zenith of our night life would be reached when we could go to 'the first house' (5.45 to 8.15 p.m.), follow that up with a bag of chips from the 'chipper' and a *Green Final* in which to read all the football scores. 'That's living!' we thought.

Earlier we had committed what my parents would have considered a heinous sin in our attempts to get to the cinema a bit oftener than they would countenance. Then, if you did not have the 9d for admission, you could get in for 3d plus a couple of used jam jars or lemonade bottles. (Presumably an earlier form of waste recycling!) Tom and I and, sometimes, another pal devised the stratagem of going round all the neighbours in the 'posh' end of the town, most of whom were known personally to us, with a barrow asking if they had any spare jars or bottles 'for the Boys' Brigade or the Scouts'. They did. We got them, hid them in our hut and saw several Hopalong Cassidy westerns and a few James Cagney gangster wars virtually for free. Our entrepreneurial flare was short lived, however, since we dared not push our luck by a second 'harvest'.

Partly, some of these exploits were occasioned by the fact that neither of our parents had ever had any money themselves, certainly not as children, and consequently they never had any consistent policy about giving us pocket money. Once in a while, and only after I had reached my teens, my father would slip me a half-crown or we could earn a few coppers by washing up a lot of dishes when my parents were 'entertaining' or by cutting the lawns (of which there were three!) but there was never any set sum allocated for pocket money. If we needed any cash, say, for a bus trip with the school football team then that would be forthcoming all right and of course, since much of my childhood was in wartime, even the weekly purchase of a quarter of sweets or a couple of Mars bars was attended by a parent because they held the Ration Books. There was little else available to buy other than perhaps a puncture repair kit for my bike or new laces for my football boots. Little wonder then that a few years later I was able to survive as a student in Aberdeen, paying all my books, note files, digs and transport out of an £88 bursary for the whole year.

Preparation for that studentship was something that was indeed well founded in the manse. When we did, from time to time, all sit down to a meal together, usually on Saturdays and Sundays, there was a good deal of talk. We boys were often bored by the more (literally) parochial chat our parents indulged in, but at least the contents of the *Aberdeen Press and Journal* and *The Scotsman* were consumed in detail by my parents. World affairs, whether in Aberchirder, Aberdeen or the Aberdare mountains of Kenya would all be commented on and anything 'educational' would be drawn to our attention. My father was always interested in cross-cultural comparisons or in the growth and development of ideas although he had terrible gaps in his knowledge of the sciences and tended to shy away from them. I would be expected to 'keep up with my reading' and to have an opinion (not always agreed with) on such matters.

One of the great positive aspects of life in the manse was that we did meet, sometimes for days at a time, a number of missionaries who were on leave or on lecture tours at home in Scotland after years abroad in quite exotic corners of the globe. They were, on the whole, less formal and less pompous than many of the home-grown variety of minister we were used to. At meal times and in the evenings they were often prepared to tell us about ways of life in undeveloped Africa, Polynesia, India or China.

Rev. Coulter, who had been a close friend of my father before either of them had married, was especially interesting for he had spent many years in Ceylon. Nearly forty years on, I was to remember some of his stories when I was out there, now Sri Lanka, as a consultant for WHO. As a boy, I was a keen vicarious traveller and these missionaries' tales and the *Children's Encyclopedia* section on Other Lands went a long way to satisfying that predilection.

A striking feature of those travellers' tales from abroad was that, almost without exception, those missionaries talked of the black, brown or yellow people they had lived amongst with both respect and warmth. It was abundantly clear that a cultural and economic gulf of enormous proportions existed between our, even then, war-torn country and theirs. It was equally noteworthy that most of these visitors to the manse, whether medical doctors or priests or both (as some were) could hardly wait to return to their bungalow on the veldt, hut in the jungle, or half-plumbed-in flat in some thronging metropolis such as Calcutta. On the whole, they were refreshing conversationalists, full of realistic insights into both their own contributions and what they expected of those with whom they worked. Religious dogma, trite aphorisms from the New Testament and too much preoccupation with 'principle' did not define the content of their talk as it often did when I overheard the talk from the boorachs of local 'dog collars'.

My father had a library of perhaps three thousand books, many of them

Plate 16: The public faces of the manse family c. 1941. The author is on the right

too specialised on theology or philosophy for my taste or interest, but he never grudged my borrowing these, usually of a more general literary kind, which appealed to me. Quite early in my life, perhaps when I was about five or six, I can remember the great debate as to whether the family could afford to buy, from a travelling salesman, the ten great volumes of Arthur Mee's *Children's Encyclopaedia* referred to several times already. My father's words were, 'Well, it's an awful lot of money, but can we afford not to buy it?'

These volumes are in my home even today, seriously outdated, even quaint in their style and values, but there is not the slightest doubt that I consumed them voraciously when young and I have no doubt that they contributed to a store of knowledge from which I continue to draw. Books in general were undoubtedly valued far beyond their monetary value in the manse. I doubt if there was ever a day when I would not find my father reading something of substance. Naturally I was encouraged to do likewise, though in the event, my persistence was not sustained. For all that, even now I find it hard to get rid of books, even after they have been read, and sometimes re-read. They have the elusive characteristic of encapsulating something of the world, something of the author's personality and vision and something too of the reader in that he selected the volume in the first place.

After more than fifty years, it is hard not to see that the modelling of behaviour I saw from my father in his study and from the nature of his conversations played a huge part in my life later. While I was at school it was perhaps not so obvious since I tended to get along in class on the strength of what some might have described as 'mither wit' together with incidental learning. The latter came simply from habits of discussion and a measure of pedantry from my father who could not bear inaccurate use of English. Spelling words like 'believe' and 'receive' was drummed into me. The distinction between 'casual' and 'causal', 'continuous' and 'continual' or 'solecism' and 'solipsism' was always to be made correctly.

'If you don't use language correctly, you'll never think accurately!' he would declaim, anticipating the cognitive psychologists of thirty years later.

One of the attractions which Latin held for him was that it was in his view 'a disciplined language', rule-dominated in its grammar and depending on accuracy in its constructions, declensions and conjugations. Perhaps that was why, as soon as I had passed 'the Qualy', as we knew it, or the Qualifying Examination as officialdom knew it, for it was the then equivalent of the '11+', he spent great chunks of the summer holiday thereafter sitting in the pine woods of Newtonmore where we were spending our first wartime holiday instructing me in the declension of *mensa* and the conjugation of *amare*. I had 'qualified' to go into the two language and two sciences stream in the Academy the following August and he was ensuring that I would not 'fall behind'. Whether he fostered fantasies that all the other boys and girls in the class would turn up on the day immediately as fluent Ciceros I never found out. Certainly it gave me a head start in Latin then which it seemed I was able to sustain throughout the five years I was at the Academy but the downside of it was that the actual class lessons became boring recapitulations compared to the others where everything was new.

It is difficult to know after all these years quite when the manse began to lose its influence on my development and habits of thought. Certainly, as my life at school progressed, both the content of my learning and the attitudes that went with it became more diverse and in some ways beyond the ken of my parents. Adolescent rebellion and an inherent independence of spirit began to assert themselves and I began to owe more allegiance to my pals at school and to wider ranging ideas in the many books from furth of my father's library that I then began to read. It has to be remembered that in those days the distractions of television and even of radio were non-existent. The radio depended on relatively expensive batteries and was consequently used frugally and mostly only with parental permission. Television was still more than a decade, for the few, and for the many, fifteen years distant. Reading therefore became a major activity and source of both knowledge and enjoyment. Curiously, I read relatively little fiction. In my parents' eyes (and to a lesser extent in my own) it had little to do with 'real life'. The prosaic and the humdrum were less dangerous and more true to the experience of most people than the high jinks of the drama and romance of novels. To this day I still prefer to read reference books, travel and biography rather than fiction.

Football and girls also took me out of the house a bit more than in the past and with the end of the war and blackout in 1945 it became possible to range more widely on my bicycle. Among other things I extended my affiliations from only the Boys' Brigade to the Scottish Youth Hostels Association (SYHA). The former had been virtually a compulsory part of my boyish life from early years in the Life Boys, who wore little sailor caps and rope lanyards, to the BBs proper who wore curious little pillbox hats in navy blue with white rings round them and white canvas haversacks tucked into brown leather belts. Founded by a certain William Smith, the BBs were hot on 'drill' and discipline. Marching to commands, PT, lessons on semaphore, morse and nature study prepared us for a healthy and supposedly God-fearing life. This was, in my parents' views, the perfect organisation for sons of the manse. The Puritan image was well sustained by this organisation and only slipped briefly during the yearly summer camps. These were usually held in some secluded valley up country or at a seaside town in Fife and 'senior boys' then were allowed some latitude to test themselves in less restricted situations.

Like most lads in such organisations, I was keen to earn all the badges available, the Physical Training, First Aid, Signallers, Campers and so on. There was even a Musician's badge which I qualified for on the strength (although I think, with hindsight, that was a fearsome misnomer) of my bugle playing in the marching band. The result was that in due course I was promoted to the rank of sergeant some time before I left, but not before we had savoured the high jinks which ensued when by some cataclysmic organisational mistake, the 1st company of the Banff BB camped in the adjacent field near Dufftown to a company of Girl Guides. Unfortunately, it didn't last because fearing what they must have considered our rampant sexuality, the Guide Leaders were in instant cahoots with the BB Captain to arrange for us to be moved several miles away forthwith.

By the time the war with all its attendant alarms and excursions had ended, I was beginning to feel a measure of anxiety about the impending 'Highers'. In those days the Scottish system was such that a candidate for this most senior of school qualifications (and the necessary hurdle to be leapt prior to university or college) had to opt to take, and to pass in all, of certain subjects. If you were to fail in one of those, then no certificate at all was awarded, no matter whether or not you had succeeded *summa cum laude* in everything else. It was a pernicious system which nearly every educationist and certainly every pupil was glad to see done away with a few years later.

Up to that point I suppose the privileges I had enjoyed at home whereby there was both a sufficiency of intelligent conversation of reasonably wide-ranging content and almost a surfeit of books had allowed me to survive at school on the basis of the exercise of 'mother wit'. But then the serious business of deciding which subjects I might be reasonably expected by my mentors at the Academy to succeed in had to be undertaken. Unfortunately, there arose a measure of conflict between my own views about this and those of the Rector. The latter, guided by the Principal teachers, took the view that English, History, Latin and French would offer me little difficulty. They were far from sanguine, however, about the prospects of my passing both German and Mathematics at Higher level. I reckoned that I had a better than 50:50 chance, and said so. Only later did I appreciate that part of their reluctance for me to embark on the reckless course of trying to get Highers in the whole lot derived from the fact that the number of passes or failures among those presented for the examination each year reflected on their reputation as teachers, and their narcissism demanded that 100% passes must be achieved, as it were, by them!

Having argued my stance with the redoubtable Rector to little effect, I was constrained to take the matter back home to my parents in the hope that they might back me. After all, I argued that failure would be my own loss and my own responsibility, not theirs, if I chanced my arm with all the subjects. Father, after much discussion, agreed and turned up in the Rector's room, along with myself and the other Principal teachers concerned next day after 4 p.m. To cut a long story short, it was eventually agreed that I would be put forward as a candidate for 'the lot'– and my blood be on my own head! There is no doubt in my mind that being the son of the manse was hugely to my advantage there and this was perhaps the last time that that aspect of my background was to be of any significant help to me in my life. First, my father was prepared, and able, to beard the lion – in his den. Second, he was articulate, knew the system well and was prepared to make a strong plea on my behalf, secure in the knowledge that I would then feel obliged to put in an extra bit of work once I was committed to the course decided. The result was that I then got cracking with some serious swotting to augment my casual but reasonably quick wits. Needless to say, when the results came out I had passed easily in every subject. But it was a relief – to all concerned!

One outcome of that small success was of course that I then entered and won a Bursary at the Aberdeen University Bursary Open Competition a month or two later. I had only completed the 5th year at the Academy but a bird in the hand was worth two in the bush so I elected to enter Aberdeen University later that year (1947) rather than go back to school for a sixth year. It was, with hindsight, probably a mistake for I was, and felt myself to be, at least for my first year at university, an immature student. But it meant that I was now living a large part of the year outside the physical and emotional shackles of the manse and for all the academic and ill-defined other benefits I had enjoyed in that former setting, I now began really to grow up – and to enjoy it. The manse suddenly became no more than an intermittent base for me during the university vacations and brief leaves when later I did National Service in the RAF. I was no longer quite so much its prisoner as I had been.

Postscript

The saga of the mysterious girl who invited me out to 'Foggieloan' some fifty-six or seven years ago developed and was amazingly resolved in 1999, some months after I had written the first draft of this piece.

Duff House Royal Golf Club, of which I have been a member for more years than I care to remember, has a Seniors' Section for the over 65s. It meets every Tuesday morning, fair or foul, throughout the year for regular Staplefords or the odd Medal round. We play in threes with whomsoever happens to turn up at the time. One morning I remarked to my mates on the presence in the group following us round of a chap I'd not seen before. 'Oh yes, that's Fred Stephen. He once had a small farm out Foggie way but now has retired in Aberdeen and comes out from there each Tuesday. He's a fine cheery chiel. I think his wife's name's Elsie.'

Some weeks later it so happened that I was drawn to play in a three with Fred. We chatted amicably and he referred to his wife, Elsie. 'I've only ever known one girl called Elsie', said I, 'and she was a schoolgirl from Foggie.' Well, my wife came fae Foggie an' a'', says Fred. 'I'll hae tae ask her aboot that story!'

A week or two later there was a party and presentation in the Club House for the retiring head greenkeeper which we all attended. My wife and I were seated at one side of the club room with some friends when Fred appeared at the other side of the hall from behind a pillar and gave me a wave. Somebody said, 'Aye, Fred's wife's here the nicht an' a'.' Ye'd better awa' an see this Elsie.' My story had got around!

I crossed the room to Fred's table and there was Elsie – THE Elsie! – but more than half a century on. She, bless her heart, recognised me immediately. I did too, now, though I doubt whether I would have, had I simply seen her pass me in the street and out of context. But there she was, the same features, the same hair, now streaked with silver, and just as cheerful and friendly as she must always have been. It was quite an emotive moment. We recapped the Beetle Drive, the drive in her Dad's car to and from Banff and a bit more as we shared a dram or two. Janet, my wife of over forty years, at last believed the tale I had told of my long lost teenage adventure which she had always thought to have been the stuff of fantasy. I wonder what else I can now get her to believe! Poor Fred has since died but I hear sometimes of Elsie from another of my golfing friends whose wife is Elsie's sister. It's a small world up here!

Chapter IV

THE ART OF COARSE EDUCATION: EXPERIMENTS AND EXPERIENCE

' ... then the whining schoolboy, with his satchel
And shining morning face, creeping like snail
Unwillingly to school ... '
(Shakespeare *As You Like It*)

'Learning makes a man fit company for himself.'
(Thomas Fuller MD *Gnomologia*, 1732)

Looking backwards, one of the first outstanding subjects which bulks largely in the recesses of a man's memory is the remembrance of his schools, his schoolmasters and his early associates when time was young with him, and he is surely a man devoid of sentiment and natural feelings if such recollections do not, as age creeps onward and the shadows begin to lengthen, appeal to him. Great changes have taken place in the matter of education since I made my first essay to understand 'the nature and power of letters, and the just method of spelling words.'

Thus, in his rather quaint and perhaps even archaic way did a certain Garden Milne Hossack, one-time Sheriff Clerk of Banffshire, open his speech, 'Reminiscences of a Sexagenarian', to a meeting of the Banff Field Club in the year 1900. A relatively old man for his time, he went on to detail aspects of his early 19th century education and of the personages both central and peripheral to it in a relatively entertaining way.

In the light of his comments, it is therefore some surprise to me that, holidays apart, my memories of the years of my own early life, prior to going to school, especially, are fragmentary. There was no way I could know it then, but the sporadic and short-lived contacts I had with my parents left me deprived of many of the natural closenesses and affectionate moments that other young children took for granted. Not having much opportunity to meet and play with other children of my own age meant that I did not then know what I was missing, but it surely played its part in making me the boy I was. By turns I was self-contained and a bit aloof, insecure and uncertain about how to relate to others, inclined to dominate my wee brother by dint of my superior knowledge of the world, but far from comfortable with other contemporaries. It was all too clear that my parents expected much of me but in what way I might be able to fulfil these expectations was never made terribly explicit. People would say things like, 'Now, David, you be a good example to others. Be a good boy, do what you're told and stick in to your reading and lessons!' And that was even before I ever went to school!

From Easter 1935, I spent some 4,615 days at Banff Primary School and later Banff Academy. With the exception of two, all were distinctly unmemorable. The two which jangle the bells of memory were tinged equally with foreboding; the first, with the uncertainty, anticipation and concern which are the proper emotions for a precocious four-and-a-half year old flung into the maelstrom of Primary 1; the second, much later, bearing all the accumulated urges to establish the unequivocal adulthood of the chip shop, the billiard saloon and perhaps even the tepid warmth of a premature sexual adventure characteristic of the sixteen-year-old. But perhaps that is a leap just too far ahead. The early days have their own story.

For a couple of days, trouble had been brewing in the manse. There had appeared an unpleasant amount of blue serge. My mother's youngest sister, my aunt Nell, a lady of unrelenting good humour and firm persuasiveness had come to spend a holiday in Banff, and bathing, paying attention and being in good odour had assumed a disproportionate importance compared with more usual activities. The latter might have included the exploration of the inner recesses of the coal cellar or re-glueing the slots and tabs of a cardboard model of the the *Queen Mary* – the ocean liner, not the Monarch!

Came the dawn, and there I was, resplendent in hairy blue jacket, hairy blue shorts (on the long side!) and hairless white knees (knocking), to be paraded for inspection and photography at the front door of the manse. There I was, stuck between my resolutely smiling aunt, a mystified but equally well-scrubbed little brother, and the

Plate 17: Ready to accompany my wee brother, Tom, on his first day at school, April, 1936

maid – whose softer contours were heavily disguised by a uniform starched into armour plate of white linen sharp enough to cut your finger on – if you were adventurous enough to explore it.

On the word of command – a command which rang hollow with falsity – 'You will really enjoy school!' the march to the gallows began. Flanked by the not inconsiderable figures of mother and aunt, I myself, resembling nothing more than a three-foot footballer/monk with a skull cap bearing the dread emblem BXA (the 'X' was meant to be a white St Andrew's cross, the B and A for Banff Academy) stumbled along the pavement for the half mile to school. The worset (woollen) blue socks with white bands on the turn-downs were at least mildly macho and would do for football later. The school cap, however functionally limited, aesthetically bizarre and socially carrying more than a whiff of the suggestion that its wearer was a cross between a thoroughgoing pansy or a Billy Bunter, was later to outdo the modern frisbee and teach lessons about love and hate.

The middle-class veneer so carefully lacquered over my personality by earlier influences stood me in good stead when faced with the initial peremptory questionings from the tight lips and blankly reflecting round spectacles behind which lurked the Primary Headmistress. The anonymous white faces of the other pupils were then of little interest to me, excepting those pallid ones on which a tracery of tears was etched, while I spent the first hours learning to learn slowly what I already knew. The bell announcing the mid-morning break caught Miss Peterkin's pointer half-way up the number ladder and transformed it into a magic wand which, at a stroke, announced playtime.

The jostling surge down the corridors and past the lavatories, rank with the urinary experimentations of small boys, ran out of steam as we debouched on to the tarmac playground. Immediate dispersal to a miscellany of football games, 'boolies', and the more secret cabals of the 'heavies' from Primary 6 and 7 left me gawping uncertainly at the foot of the steps. The reverie, if such it was, was suddenly disrupted by the simultaneous cry of 'You're a bap-faced wee bugger!' and the violent removal of my cap, together with just enough hair to make my eyes water, by a coarse and undisciplined member of a higher class – in one sense. He was also bigger, apparently more worldly-wise and in the mood for a challenge, whereas I, a virgin among harlots, snivelled fecklessly in my impotence to do anything about it. The cap meanwhile, like a frisbee, or a target at a clay pigeon shoot, curved gracefully up and away on the wind to land with a discernible 'plop' in a puddle on the flat roof of the lavatory.

Caught in that embarrassing hiatus between frustrated anger and arrant fear, I hesitated – and was lost. But not for long. A fresh-faced wee loon (as Banffshire lads were called) whom I was not conscious of having seen before in my life materialised from the whirling serge ectoplasm of the playground to pat my back and reaffirm my weakened faith in human nature with the immortal words, 'Nivver mind, Davie. I'll get yer bonnet an' gie 'im a bashin''. So saying, this seven year old Sir Galahad (real name 'Sanders' Rennie), shinned up the soil pipe, thus braving the double wrath of Miss Peterkin and the Janitor, flung down the sodden cap and, later that day, (and that bore the stamp of dedication to the good and the beautiful) found and thumped my tormentor. Never was there 'such a gentil, parfit knight' and many a day subsequently did we roam the Fir Widdie or guddle in the 'Bandies' at the mouth of the river Deveron, or otherwise in friendship, meet the sterner challenges of playground or classroom.

A few years later, in the early years of the war, an ominous thud and a pall of smoke over the Greenbanks marked the premature end of that same wee lad. He was blown to bits by a landmine intended to dissuade German invaders. He was probably trying to retrieve a ball from within the barbed wire surrounding the minefield for some smaller boy or girl. We all grieved for him, I especially, for many a long year.

Then followed twelve years of Primary and Secondary education which ended with some achievements but, above all, with a huge sense of relief. At intervals, when various people would enquire after my progress, they would mutter platitudes about these years being the best years of my life. I was never convinced. After the formal prize giving on my very last day as a pupil, I remember dashing down the flight of steps in front of the Academy, glad never to have to return and hoping against hope that further education would prove to be both a happier and a more rewarding experience.

It is true that I had jumped through all the necessary hoops, I had survived beltings, being shouted at in a relatively demeaning way and subjected to what might well now qualify as degrading and inhuman punishments. As far as my fellow pupils were concerned, I had enjoyed the sport and the company of a few and a sense of identity with many. Broadly, however, I regret to say that I took few really enriching memories, especially from my Secondary education. I respected my teachers and admired one or two but it was hard to get any impression that they actually liked you. In retrospect, I should perhaps conclude that I was not a likeable pupil but the plain fact was that most of my fellow students came away with similar impressions that they were not there to be liked. Perhaps the difficulty arose from the fact that the teachers would seldom reveal much about themselves as persons and hid perpetually behind the official façade of being our mentors and those we had to please if we were ever to make anything of our lives.

Such an early preoccupation with the Alpha and the Omega of my school life, sharp memories though they may be, does less than justice to a fair and complete history. There was no doubt that education in all its aspects was seen in our house as crucial to the effective and worthwhile living of life. My mother never lost an opportunity, in my early life especially, to remind me of how she had overcome the privations and exploitations of her nurse training at Dundee Royal Infirmary to become a Ward Sister – never quite saying, but often hinting, that that had in turn prepared her to become a worthy mate for a parish minister.

My father, the only one of my forebears to have benefited from a university education by dint of sheer stamina and self-help in the face of poverty and ignorance, was less direct in his endorsement of its value. But he demonstrated it by his love of books (of which there were 3,000 or more in his personal library) his wide knowledge of literature and philosophy, and his capacity to teach himself languages, including Ancient Greek, Hebrew, German and a smattering of Norwegian. It was equally clear that his inner life as well as his more obvious interactions with other people of all stations in life were imbued with a richness and depth that bespoke something the value of which was self evident. In retrospect – for it was lived through rather than observed at the time – it became apparent that my father was a cultured man with the common touch. My mother, by contrast, though she had many worthy qualities, was a common woman with only a touch of culture. She was, perhaps unconsciously, deeply aware of her working class origins, her lack of reading compared to my father and of her newer pretensions to the middle class and the bourgeoisie.

Father's roots were equally deep set among the workers and the exploited but I doubt if the notion of class ever entered his head. He was the equal of all who ever shared the time of day with him, Kings (literally) and Commoners alike. He would never tire of reminding me to value a man 'for who he is as a person and not for what he is in his job or station in life'. He possessed and had read most of the works of Mark Twain, Hazlitt and Emerson and had taken to heart many of their aphorisms about education. Where the former might have said 'Never let schooling interfere with your education!', the latter, in his first series of *Essays* would have said, 'What we do not call education is more precious than that which we call so!' Could he have been hinting at Daniel Goleman and others who are now writing about something called 'emotional intelligence'? Quite late in my school career I can remember my father trying to get me to write an essay on the famous quotation from Hazlitt's *Table Talk*: 'It is better to be able neither to read nor write than to be able to do nothing else.' Always happy to teach us the 'drills and skills', he made sure we never confused lessons with learning.

Remote though he could be from us all at times, I remember two particular occasions when my father played a very specific and direct part in my schooling. He never failed to play a part in my education. These occasions were, first, when I had just started Primary school and was being terrorised by a teacher, a certain Miss R. The shouting and slapping of desks with pointers and rulers was bad enough for most of us four-and-a-half or five-year-olds, but the crux came when one morning I succumbed to sickness on my way down to school and had to stop and vomit in the gutter. This delayed my entry to class by some five minutes, a heinous crime for which I was then strapped. Because I had to explain the red marks on my hand that evening, my parents took serious umbrage at the lady and hot-footed it down to the Primary Headmistress next morning with their complaints. Such unduly harsh behaviour toward very small children (even in these ancient days) apparently recurred several times in the course of this lady's career and she was to disappear from the school entirely the following year.

Schools, even Primary schools, could be the scene of considerable violence exercised upon the poor pupils. It was a tradition inherited from Puritan traditions and long established custom of 'Spare the rod and spoil the child!' Not many of us were, in our early years at least, as recalcitrant and inclined to innocent truancy as was Thomas Edward, the Banff naturalist, later to be honoured as an Associate of the Linnaean Society. He succeeded in being excluded from no less than three schools before he was aged six. Samuel Smiles, in his excellent and revealing biography of the man, *The Life of a Scotch Naturalist*, tells in gruesome detail (pp. 37–42) of a horrendous beating which Tam Edward was subjected to by a school master who strapped him repeatedly about the hands, back and legs until the boy was a mass of bloody weals which stuck his shirt to his back by the congealed blood. And it was all because some kind of creepy-crawlie beastie landed on the schoolmaster's jacket. Tam Edward had certainly the long-term habit of hunting for all kinds of natural history specimens, some of which might often be released in his classroom. On this occasion, however, Tam was innocent. The other children knew he was but were too terrified to declare in his favour and Tam himself was not to be browbeaten into admitting guilt when he had no reason to do so. The master then thrashed him repeatedly to extract a confession. None was forthcoming, so poor Tam was lashed till the master was totally exhausted.

I myself had not then read Samuel Smiles' book, but so frightening was this severe old spinster in my Primary 1 that I became almost incapable of listening during reading lessons. These were from little brownish-khaki books, the Radiant Way series, full of quaintly drawn black and white illustrations based on the letters of the alphabet but devoid of anything to grab the attention of a small child. Of an evening before bedtime, my father would sit me on the floor between his knees and guide me through sounding and pointing out the letters in this wretched book. He was patient and helpful and I began to get the hang of it

In the course of a wartime holiday some five years later in Newtonmore (thought to be an unlikely target even for the more assiduous of the German raiders) my father was at the core of a further signal initiation in learning. Having passed the 'Qualifying examination' rather precociously, I was due to go up to the Higher Grade, as we called the Senior Secondary part of Banff Academy just after the summer holidays and not long past my tenth birthday.

Among other things, I would be expected to learn French and Latin.

Father accepted that he could contribute little to my learning of French but he did reckon that he knew a bit about Latin. Every day during that holiday we would go walking or climbing in the hills and every day in the evening or late afternoon he would sit me down beside him, sometimes in the woods around our boarding house, and have me learn *mensa* – exemplifying the first declension of nouns, and to conjugate the verbs *esse* (to be) and *amare* (to love) as well as to start accumulating a rudimentary Latin vocabulary. It was well meant and I have to agree in retrospect that it gave me great confidence when I eventually sat in the class, but on the debit side, I became bored by knowing already what was going on in the classroom and such tutorials stopped soon after that.

My progress through Primary school was relatively uneventful though I could never feel that it was as interesting as some of the things that I could do at home. Reading round the class, as it was called, was something that bored the living daylights out of me. In this procedure every pupil would be asked to read a sentence or two of one of the set books, in sequence. Given that there was a huge range of reading competence within the thirty or more members of the class, this meant that all of us had to wait, with increasing irritation and boredom while the more modestly endowed struggled through a few words syllable by syllable. Some of us had read through the whole book days and days ago.

Many learning processes were heavily ritualised in these days. Every day we were lined up round the periphery of the classroom from the cleverest at one end of the tail to the dumbest at the other (based on the form shown in the previous day's exercise). Each was then given an arithmetical problem or other question to answer depending on what 'lesson' was being done at the time, such as Bible study, arithmetic or geography and so on. If you got the answer right you kept your position in the line, if not, you moved down below the next person in the 'snake' to get the right answer. It became quickly apparent to all the class that a group of the cleverer children were nearly always at the top of the line, whatever the subject tested, and that a number of poorer mortals would habitually end up at the bottom of the tail – and nearer the teacher, for getting the strap, if necessary. While this clearly boosted the confidence of the upper echelons, a steady erosion of self-esteem must have occurred in the case of the others. It was just taken as a fact of life amongst us pupils that some were cleverer than others and others were plain 'thick'. Whether this was because of nature or nurture was never a problem that we perceived – and to our credit, we never devalued the poorer pupils as people just because they could not succeed at mental arithmetic or whatever.

In the earlier Primary classes we quickly twigged that with minimal manipulation of right or wrong answers in these situations we could ensure that this process left one standing next to one's friend. By the time we were in the upper Primary classes, the first stirrings of precocious sexuality, found the same manipulation of right and wrong answers resulting in a position next to the current girl or boyfriend. Some of us, by that time, were just about beginning to learn about kissing – and a few 'practicals' were arranged at certain venues after school. The wartime 'blackout' was not an entirely bad thing.

Memories of the Primary school years include being dogged by my parents' preoccupation with which pupils should feature among my friends. Their obvious predilection that I should associate only with 'suitable' children tended to deter my revealing any details about with whom I was wont to spend my time in the playground or at weekends. Mother's choices for me tended to be amongst the relatively few rather 'wet' offspring of Banff's aspiring middle classes. They were all distressingly well-behaved, not very good at football and forbiddingly clean of voice and bearing. My best pals were, on the whole, admittedly among the brighter kids, but were generally keener on more adventurous pursuits and some occasional teacher – (and dare I say it), pupil-baiting. These were the lads who organised football after school, fishing at the harbour pier, or making rafts on the 'Bandies', a tidal limb of the river Deveron, just above the bridge.

Many of these activities followed a curiously seasonal pattern. There was a time in the year for 'boolies' (marbles) when iron shod heels would be used to rotate out a series of holes in the dirt surface of the playground and the relatively complex rules of fair play would be followed even by the dimmest of our number. Some of us, more committed to the game, would even play all the way home along the gutter of the streets. Mothers were persuaded to sew up boolie-bags from old shirt tails and the like. These accumulated the basic capital of the game in the form of a collection of 'glassies' half-inch diameter glass balls (we could not afford the few larger sizes in glass) with multi-coloured whorls of colour embedded in them, and 'cackers' in the case of which two or three variations in size were more affordable since they were made of baked clay. Personal collections were gradually accumulated by spending pocket money, occasional theft (from other boys or from the toyshop) and as a result of winnings on the pitch. Losses also occurred of course from reversals of the last two processes. The first throw of a 'boolie' could be a gentle pitch – as in the French boule – but thereafter the marble was propelled by the thumb being flicked over a curved first finger. There were, as might be expected, separate rules for 'one-holie', 'two-holie' or 'three holie' games. But then, with amazing suddenness, the season would close, as if by common consent, and our energies would be turned to other endeavours.

Amongst these would be bird nesting, for crows' or seagulls' eggs, and that was necessarily seasonal, starting with the former in March and the latter a month or two later. In the 19th century the whole matter of crows' nesting was formalised. Garden Milne Hossack, in the same 'Reminiscences' quoted from earlier tells how the boys were organised by the landed gentry in those days.

One red letter day which we boys looked forward to every spring was a holiday set apart for the 'Harrying of the craws' nests' in the Duff House grounds. When the eggs were supposed to be duly laid, and the crows' nests matured and in fit order for a foray, a polite message used to be transmitted to the Rector by the Earl of Fife (the fourth Earl James) by his lordship's head keeper that he would have pleasure in affording the boys a day's crow nesting. You may be sure the invitation thus extended was duly countersigned by the Rector and accepted by the school en masse. For the next few hours the unfortunate crows had a bad time of it. When I look back to these proceedings I often wonder how some of the more daring climbers did not break their necks or otherwise come to grief, but I suppose there is a special providence for loons under such circumstances.

Indeed there was one occasion toward the end of the Second World War when my young brother Tom and a couple of our pals went after crows' eggs in the selfsame Cra' Widdie on the Fife estates. Tom was an intrepid climber and, perched among the topmost branches of a very high Scots pine tree, isolated among its deciduous neighbours, he had just raided several nests scattered about the upper branches and was beginning his descent. Our habit was to gather the eggs and pop them into corduroy blouson tops we then favoured, thus to leave both hands free for the climb down. In the jargon of the day, he was in the process of 'warpin' ' in towards the trunk of the tree from the outer extent of a large branch, hanging under the branch by hands and feet as he edged closer and closer to the trunk where more secure hand and footholds were to be found.

We others had already reached the ground and watched with interest because we knew Tom had captured several more eggs than we. There was suddenly a loud crack and Tom with his blouson full of eggs plummeted down, scraping and bouncing through some lower branches until to our, and no doubt, his, huge relief, he came to a stop, much scratched and bruised, on a more substantial branch still many feet from the ground. His unexpectedly rapid descent was enough to leave us unsure whether our apprehension about his survival or our concern about what excuses we could make on our return home was the greater. Tom was simply left with egg on his face, and, at a quick glance, almost everywhere else. There on his new lower perch, he remained suspended, still high above the ground, while a slimy, sticky and fairly smelly yellow smear spread ever more widely about his body from the shattered eggs in his 'jerkin' (as we called it).

Only half aware of the fact that Tom had been incredibly lucky not to have fallen all the thirty or forty feet to the ground, we, callous to the end, laughed and joked about whether or not he liked scrambled eggs whilst he slowly and rather more deliberately than usual, made his careful way to the ground. He was not far from tears but pretended bravado. It was not the fact that he had been spared greater injury – or worse – but the fact that he would be on the end of a terrible thrashing for ruining his clothes (which were rationed at that time) that bothered him and also, of course, all his trophies, bar one or two which were miraculously still intact, were smashed. Somehow we succeeded in using such scraps of cloth and paper as we had about our persons, bunches of grass and damp sphagnum moss from the surrounding bogs to clean up his blouson sufficiently for us to persuade Annie, the maid, when we got home, to sneak it into a wash before our mother found out.

The sexagenarian 19th century historian never did explain what happened to the crows' eggs in his time. The uses to which our 20th century trophies were put varied dramatically. Crows' eggs, which often involved, as in Tom's case, quite hair-raising climbs of the tallest trees, were retained until they were rotten, simply as ammunition for throwing at rival gangs of boys.

Seagull eggs, and we climbed cliffs, not trees, for them, were, if not addled, or 'gorbled' as we called it, boiled or fried and eaten. They had a distinctly fishy taste but at that time the habits of the herring gull had not deteriorated to raking in rubbish tips from their more normal diet of fish offal from the boats or live sand eel from the sea. At the time we were clambering over the sea cliffs east of Macduff for these eggs, it was, of course wartime and the addition to our meagre diet of rationed foods was welcome.

For the same reasons, our after-school activities would move, as summer progressed, to the rocks and pools by the shore to catch shellfish such as lobsters and edible crabs and to the harbour pier where we would fish for saithe, rock cod and pollack (called 'lythe' by us). Smaller boys had to settle for catching the immature, six-inch versions of these, which fed the cats and were used for bait, but by the time one was able to cast a line from a ten-foot length of bamboo then the bigger fish were there for the catching. As in all fishy tales, there were stories of derring-do and mayhem to be told by some of us but the proportion of these which had a smidgeon of truth was tiny and the proportion which were wholly true was equally so. Two that I can personally vouch for may be worth recounting.

George was a couple of years younger than myself but was a frequent attender at the pier, occasionally with his elder brother. The presence of the latter was something of a relief to us since the story was that George could quietly become hypnotised by the patterned shimmer of sun on the water surface. He would gaze with increasing intensity at this, leaning more and more forward as he sat, legs over the edge of the pier, as did we all, until there would be a sudden splash and there was George, a non-swimmer, flailing about in the harbour eight or ten feet beneath us. Sometimes a swimmer would jump in and grab him before he sank and thrust him toward the iron ladder set into the pier wall, but on one occasion, no swimmer was present or prepared to jump in so I (a non-swimmer myself at that age) had to go down the ladder and try to grab him, by the hair, as it happened, and bring him yet again to land. Georgie would be 'greetin'' (crying) because his clothes were soaking and his mother would be on the warpath when he got home, but we all rallied round to lay out most of his outer garments in the sun while he shivered in his underpants and accepted, with a mixture of resentment and apprehension, our various adjurations to keep away from the edge in future and our descriptions of him as a 'daft wee bugger' or worse. The ironic aspect of these episodes was that George was subject to the condition of syndactyly whereby his fingers were partially joined together by a web of skin – perfect for swimming, we thought.

The second minor drama of a later summer at the pier took place when a boy I did not know at the time was fishing, like me, for saithe. He called out as his rod dipped alarmingly.

'Hey loons, look at this. Ah've got a big lythe!'

We crowded round to watch. The boy was having difficulty controlling his rod and line and two others went to grab his big bamboo rod and help to land the monster. Then it rolled over in its fight, some feet below the surface of the sea and we saw that it was no lythe, but a conger eel apparently about five or six feet long and very powerful. There was now a touch of apprehension in the air as we all wondered how we would cope if the beast was indeed landed on the pier. There were many tales of divers' airpipes being bitten through or fishermen's hands being bitten off by such aggressive denizens of the rocky deep. We need not have worried, however.

Two or three more minutes of struggling by the boys on the end of the rod made it entirely clear that they were either to be hauled bodily into the sea or the rod and tackle were to be forfeit to the conger. With a shout from its owner and a splash, the rod arced through the air, was tugged hither and thither while it still floated on the surface and eventually was seen to be heading for deep waters as it was drawn down by the sounding fish. A few days later, both rod and conger were landed by a fishing boat at Macduff, having been trawled up some miles offshore.

As spring wore into summer, football and fishing or making rafts, tree 'hoosies' or gang dens in the neighbouring woods took the place of boolies. Catapults were important weapons both for showing off and for warfare. The search for good Y-shaped twigs strong enough to resist the pull of strips of car or lorry inner tubes was on. Old shoes were robbed of their tongues to make the leather stone pouch at the end of the rubber elastic strips and collections of smooth rounded pebbles for ammunition became important. The defensive mining of our seashores early in the war severely restricted supplies of the latter so the gravel drive of the manse was a valuable source-reserved, of course, for the use of the 'Sandyhillers' gang – of which I was second in command. The Low Streeters and the Whinhillers could have no access to such riches.

The ideal catapult stick was about half an inch thick with the handle part (the leg of the 'Y') slightly thicker and longer than the arms and in the case of afficionados, whipped with string or leather bootlaces and occasionally weighted with lead to give a better balance when in tension as the elastic was drawn back. With practice, tin cans could be knocked off a dyke at 30 yards and pigeons or rabbits might be hunted if there were no rival gangs to harass instead. Parents of a later era (to say nothing of policemen and schoolmasters) would be appalled to know of the awful risks we constantly took with such weapons in these ancient gang fights. It has to be remembered that much of the action was when the blackout restricted evening visibility – indeed during much of the day during winter. Only Saturdays and the summer evenings were available for conflict. There were then only one or possibly two Bobbies roaming on the beat in town because most of the menfolk were away at the war and the models of macho behaviour before us were inevitably about winning or losing battles. After all, for most of our pre- and early adolescent years, we boys were effectively preparing to fight, in all seriousness, for our survival against the Germans or the Japanese.

In these circumstances, it was hardly surprising that we were very 'weapons oriented'. Catapults were prized because they were easily carried (and spirited away if need be). Bows and arrows were also constructed with varying degrees of skill and sophistication and one or two of us who had read of the cowboys of Argentina even tried our hands at making and using bolases. For these old solid sponge rubber balls about the size of a tennis ball were ideal. You could pierce them diametrically with a bodkin and thread heavy fishing line through, stopping it at one end of the ball with a large knot through a disc of plywood about the size of a sixpence. The cord coming out of the other end of the ball of about three or three-and-a-half feet length was then tied to the ends of the other two cords, also with their balls attached, to make, when laid out on the floor, a 'Y' shaped array with the balls at the end of the radii and the knotted ends of the cords at the centre.

In use, the balls were swung in horizontal rotation above our heads, held by the cords where they were joined together. At the crucial moment they were released so as to hit their target, preferably round the legs. The Argentinians brought down steers this way. We thought we could similarly fell a fleeing Macduffer – or even a German paratrooper – for later torture and inquisition. Unfortunately, the strings all too often either twisted round themselves or broke completely after wrapping themselves round trees or posts when we were practising. The gauchos may have had a knack that eluded us!

Curiously, and perhaps because of the watchfulness of our teachers, the gang warfare of evenings and weekends never seemed to percolate through to the school playground. There, football reigned supreme. Primary school football was clearly a group activity. The group formed itself around the ball like some sort of ectoplasmic accretion which pulsed, expanded and contracted with the ball-nucleus hidden somewhere in its midst. In common with its modified and more structured form of the secondary school, it was, however, no place for the faint-hearted. Whether the occasion was one of 5-a-side or of 25-a-side, its essence was total commitment to wielding one's feet, usually heavily booted, elbows, shoulders and even head in the cause of driving the ball between the cast down jackets which signified goal posts. Darwin would have delighted in the vision of big strong eight or nine-year-olds storming through the ranks of the puny by dint of sheer speed, aggression and well-aimed shin hacks. Only later would he have observed, a few years on, the more subtle skills of the 'wall pass', the 'through ball' and some notion of a game plan supplanting, at least in part, the mix of gaucherie and brutality so typical of the primary school exponents. On the boys' playground, as this battlefield was so naïvely described, voices could be raised, occasionally fists, when enthusiasm shaded into savagery.

The ball was mostly on old tennis ball or of similar size of solid sponge rubber. Real leather footballs were only available to the school teams on official occasions and were locked in cupboards during normal hours. The playground games were nonetheless fiercely contested and scores of 19–0 were less common than 4–4 or 1–1.

There were two main principles involved in team selection. The first operated when a game was already in progress. It simply meant that if your pals were on one side, especially if the best players were also on that side, then you simply added yourself on to the mob playing in that general direction. These were the occasions of the 19–0 wins. The second principle operated when a game was set up *de novo*. The two best players, usually Primary 6 or 7 types, would call up alternately from the assembled mob their chosen teams, starting first with the next best player to themselves, then the next (in their eyes) and so on until, as the crowd of anxious selectees dwindled, the few to be picked last were torn between swallowing back their deeply eroded self-esteem and electing to try to play better this time, and skulking off with some muttered excuse that they had their good shoes on anyway and their mothers would shoot them if they got them scuffed. These peer evaluations about things which 'really mattered' always seemed to be much more important than the rank order lines of the classroom which reflected prowess in trivia like arithmetic or geography.

It can hardly be without significance that most of the sharper memories I have of Primary school life are about peripheral activities, play and personalities rather than about the kind of things I was supposed to be learning and the content of lessons. In those days, the latter seemed to comprise lots and lots of 'drills and skills', the former more than the latter. Modern ideas of the linking of knowledge to everyday life or even of the linking of one subject with another were unknown. If they were known, they were not practised.

Only one teacher enlivened my days at primary school. She was a certain

Mrs Kelly, teacher of Primary 6. For one thing, she was a 'Mrs'. In those days, the vast majority of primary school teachers were spinsters. In the case of some of them, they had decided to forego the 'pleasures' of marriage and family in the interests of pedagogy; and in the case of the others, pedagogy was the only resort of the plain or the embittered who had not been offered the alternative of marriage or a sexual partnership.

Mrs Kelly was, however, a youngish widow with a gentle manner and a ready smile for all her pupils, not just for the smart or the middle class. We later discovered that she was friendly with a Miss Grant who, in Primary 4, had shown some of the qualities and attitudes which we found later in Mrs Kelly. She eschewed wielding the 'tag' or tawse, except for very occasional social rather than academic misdemeanours. Although she did stick to some of the 'drills' we were used to, there were many occasions when she simply talked intelligently to us about various aspects of a puzzling world. She did try to lead us to see how a knowledge of reading and grammar ('English' as it was called – though we all spoke the Doric Scots dialect out of the classroom) related to communicating effectively with others, how 'History' and 'Geography' were related subjects about people and our world and how 'Arithmetic' was not just chanting the 'Tables' but could help us to become better carpenters, bankers, farmers, painters and so on.

I had been fortunate to discover the trick of reading (and spelling) very quickly by the end of Primary 2 or 3 and though I found the books supplied for schoolwork very boring indeed, I was lucky to have at home a large library of magazines, newspapers and books to dip into. Of these the most important by far were the ten large, morocco-bound volumes of Arthur Mee's *Children's Encyclopaedia*. He also edited the *Children's Newspaper* a rather priggish and proper weekly for good Christian boys and girls. My parents naturally favoured this above the *Beano* the *Dandy* or the *Wizard* which my pals were wont to collect from the newsagents and pass around at school. I read it without enthusiasm but did gobble up with some avidity the contents of the *Encyclopaedia*. True, the Chapters headed 'Bible Stories', 'Poetry', 'Art' were all skipped in favour of 'How things Work', 'Geography', 'Natural History', 'Transport' and so on. But by the end of the next year or two I had, with pleasure, consumed, and largely remembered most of these elements of the volumes' contents.

Partly this was because I was a rather sickly lad on frequent occasions during my early boyhood with such ailments as measles, fevers, tonsilitis and something then described as 'acidosis' but which I can find no reference to in contemporary medical textbooks. Off school, often for more than a week at a time, I spent my time reading in bed, making cardboard cut-out models and doing jigsaw puzzles. All of these activities were more educative, positive and interesting than what went on in the classroom. Looking back, I can see that I might have been influenced toward hypochondriasis and using illness as a way of problem solving by dint of the fact that my parents were often more solicitous about me and actually seemed to care more for me when I was ill than when I was well.

Perhaps what really cured me of any such tendencies (for they never did emerge at any time in my later life) was the experience of being despatched to Kepplestone Nursing Home in Aberdeen for surgery when my tonsils and adenoids finally became too troublesome. There had been several visits from our family GP culminating in a long bus trip to Aberdeen to see a Consultant ENT surgeon, a Mr Otty. It was decided that I should have my tonsils and adenoids taken out soon and there then followed, a week or two later, a further expedition to Aberdeen, to the nursing home where I remember some distress when my mother, who had accompanied me from home in the bus, departed saying she'd see me after the operation. I am sure I must have had alarmist fantasies about what the latter entailed though they remain repressed to this day.

The nurses were kind enough but when the rubber mask for the anaesthetic was placed over my nose and mouth I am sure I must have been bawling with apprehension. An hour or so later, I was being painfully sick into a steel dish back in the ward. My throat was burning and bleeding and I was told I could only have ice cream to eat – and that not for an hour or two. Eventually my mother reappeared with even more ice cream and after some more unpleasant days of a sore throat and little food, I was sent home to recuperate. I decided that hospitals and ill health were not fine and should be avoided at all costs.

Back at school, the old routines had continued as usual but with the added distractions introduced by the war. Gas mask fitting and practice, air-raid warning drills were added to the scholastic ones and visits to the brick and concrete air raid shelters behind the school interrupted the even tenor of our ways. (Readers interested in reading more about this will find it in this author's *One Boy's War*, 1997).

Apart from that, the same old classroom distractions continued, only, because we were growing older and wiser, more discrete. The girls sitting in class behind us would surreptitiously offer to show us their knickers etc. etc. if we would show them ... ! The actual arrangements as to time and place for these momentous revelations were mostly omitted because some other less sneaky class person would spoil it all by pinging bits of ink sodden blotting paper at the back of the boys' heads with rulers. Sooner or later of course they were caught and reprimanded – or worse. For all that, my memories of Primary 6 under Mrs Kelly were far preferable to those of preceding classes and I did take much more interest in acquiring some knowledge under her benign tutelage. For once, I went to school each day, if not with enthusiasm, at least with some freedom from the raw taste of fear in my mouth. For a whole year I had never been strapped. Because of how my parents had indoctrinated me it was much more heinous for the minister's son to be strapped (for whatever reason) than for 'ordinary boys' to be similarly punished, so most of my days at school became simply 'escape and evasion' exercises to avoid such ignominy.

After that year of bliss, we moved into the Qualifying Class – the 'Qualie' – under the stern aegis of Miss Mitchell. I did not know it then but she was to become the nearest thing in the life of a schoolboy to a Drill Instructor corporal in the RAF I was ever likely to meet. She did everything 'by numbers'. We marched up and down the stairs in strict tempo to her rhythmic clapping and stentorian 'One..two..one..two..!' Victor Sylvester was sloppy in his so-called 'strict tempo' dance music compared to this bunned martinet in tweeds and brogues. We placed our books, jotters and pencils exactly on the desk surfaces as instructed. We picked up our pencils or pens simultaneously and wrote on the command. There was only one correct way to hold a pen or pencil and a ruler smack (sometimes using the edge) over the knuckles ensured not only that that method was used but also that the actual penmanship (as it was called) was ruined by pain and swelling. Our only purpose in life was to do 'exactly as I am telling you' and to pass – or, in some cases, inevitably, to fail 'the Qualie'.

The latter was the dread equivalent in the late 1930s of the '11+' examination which elsewhere determined for ever and ever what calibre of secondary education you were to endure. The Scottish educational system at that time was, at Secondary level, entirely and unashamedly streamed. The 'elite', with the highest marks in the 'Qualie', a series of tests including a standardised reasoning (IQ) test as well as tests of English and Arithmetic attainment, would move into the 'A' stream and take the usual subjects such as Maths, English, History, Geography, Art and Science, plus two languages, French and Latin – and perhaps German as a third language in the third Secondary year. The next 'layer' of ability would go into the 'B' stream and take the usual subjects plus one language. Into the 'C' stream went the next batch to take the basic subjects, no languages other than English, but Domestic Science in the case of girls and Woodwork, Metalwork and Technical Drawing. The 'tail-enders' went into the inglorious 'D', 'E' or even 'F' streams where they were given a gentler time in the basic subjects, mostly recapping what they had not learned in the Primary school, plus Gardening and First Aid, both subjects which might have benefited all of us. Little were we to know that at the end of six years of all this, the last term at school, after the Highers, would be a short time when we were afforded the luxury of taking, even in abbreviated form, these very subjects!

Parents were perhaps less well aware of the implications of this once and for all sorting process than they were to become of the later 11+. There was therefore much less fuss about it in the homes of pupils or in the press. It was an inevitability. People knew their place – or ought to – and, perhaps because most of the men were away at war, the results were faced with acceptance or resignation. Perhaps there were few 'false positives', i.e. those who gained higher grading than they were worth, but it is very likely that there were several 'false negatives', i.e. those who did less well on the test day than they might have been expected to and who were thus consigned to a school career which, for example, might have ruled them out of a university education later.

Maybe I had passed 'the Qualie', but at that stage I was a pale, skinny and none too prepossessing wee lad not yet old enough to join the Boys' Brigade or the Boy Scouts. The prospect of moving to Banff Academy where we had to go to different classes for different subjects with different teachers, many of them men, filled me with foreboding. No longer would we use the familiar wooden framed slates on which we had scraped with our slate pencils and spat and rubbed with the end of our jacket sleeves for years. No longer would the ephemera of the knowledge explosion be so easily eliminated by a hasty rubber when we had to submit exercises written in ink! No longer would we see the same familiar faces at the desk next day, exchange the same schoolboyish cheeky remarks, occasional smut and other pleasantries.

Mungo Park or David Livingstone venturing into the wilds of central Africa could not have felt any more trepidation for their future than did those of us who were to move to the 'big school'. The solid whinstone and dressed sandstone of the latter stood no more than several hundred yards from the building we were leaving. It was not unfamiliar – but it was threatening now. We felt then that we knew nothing, that all the gloomiest prognostications of our ineptitude from Miss Mitchell and Mrs Kelly were now about to be fulfilled. The 'Reccie' (Rector) at the Academy not only had the 'All-seeing Eye' but was also a known torturer and sadist, and that unspeakable initiations would be wrought on us fledglings by the toughs of 4F. I was even too young for my voice to have broken or my face to have come out in spots. It did not bode well.

One of the more daunting experiences of that summer of 1940 was that I had to accompany one or other of my parents to the bookshop in Low Street where school books, and brown paper to cover them, could be bought. Books on Latin, books on French, Science books, books on Geography, History and even Arithmetic all had to be purchased and prepared for the new life in the Academy. No more would I search for the better slate pencils with half their length covered in prosaically patterned coloured paper. No more would I have to ask my mother to save her empty Eau de Cologne bottles for the water supply necessary for 'wiping the slate clean'. That had now been done in several senses and I was starting from scratch in an entirely new fashion.

Chapter V

MORE COARSE EDUCATION

'If you think you have a problem you should see the headmaster.'
(School Notice Board)

There is little doubt that I was too young to be thrust into the 'catch as catch can' of a Scottish Academy secondary education having just turned eleven a few weeks before. But that is awareness born of hindsight. Nor was 1941 an easy time for most children. Britain's fortunes were at a low ebb in the war and the random mix of evacuees and locals now stumping up the double flight of concrete steps in front of the school were all aware that the fathers and elder brothers of many might never be seen again.

Several of the male teachers, including Mr A. S. McHardy, the Rector (Headmaster), had not been called up but were considered to be in Reserved Occupations. Although some volunteered for the Services over the coming months, most, with the lady teachers (all unmarried), remained in the Academy till the end of the war.

The disciplined seriousness of the classroom was, however, relieved greatly by the weekly sight of several of these same male teachers, enhanced by a leavening of postmen, butchers, bankers, undertakers, plumbers, grocers and the like in an entirely different role. Their various bodily frames became the supports for all the khaki uniforms too ill-made to suit any self-respecting private soldier in the regular army. They were the local detachment of the LDV (Local Defence Volunteers) or 'Look, Duck and Vanish!' boys, as they were better known. The acronym was later changed to the Home Guard – better known subsequently as 'Dad's Army'. If memory serves aright, the 'Reccie' was an officer. He tried to ensure that those of his staff who, by standing and waiting, also served, responded with the quivering promptitude he normally expected from his juvenile charges. He was noted by us, delightedly sniggering behind our hands, to fail quite regularly in this endeavour.

He did not, however, fail from Monday to Friday when he monitored the behaviour and learning of his several hundred town- and country-raised pupils. From the moment when we lined up in class files to march into school, all boys at one main entrance and all girls at theirs at the other end of the school, we were under scrutiny for the slightest sign of misbehaviour, lateness, untidiness or talking to each other. The latter was not encouraged. We were living through an era when pupils were talked at, not with. The critical scrutiny of our masters was unremitting each day until the nearby church clock struck four and we debouched as a shouting, scampering mob – free, for at least another seventeen hours! I still remember the sense of relief from fear, contaminated only a little by the thought of how I might cope with the mountain of homework to be tackled that evening.

For five years, homework dominated every day. A natural procrastinator, I would sneak in the back door of the manse, dump my schoolbag in the lobby by the scullery and quietly sneak out again to play football or go down to the harbour. There was some hazard as I went round the side of the house, toward Sandyhill Road and freedom, because the large casement window of my father's study had to be passed. Mostly, I could bank on his being out on his pastoral duties. If not, a peremptory banging on the window would result in my prompt return to homework. Occasionally, the window would be open a few inches at the bottom and the muzzle of a .22 heavy calibre air rifle would emerge. This happened mostly in the Spring when father was waging war against the enterprising wood pigeons bent on decimating his young cabbage plants. Even then, I could not but lift a whimsical eyebrow as I set this image of the crouching, slit-eyed sniper against that of the black, purple and ermine gowned figure who led his congregation from the pulpit in ' ... all things bright and beautiful ... ' of a Sunday morning.

I have been impressed by how much other autobiographers seem able to elaborate upon the emotional content of their lives and to express it in 'purple passages' of immense personal insight and subtlety. At various points in this story I have stopped to think why it is that similar memories and analyses are so sparse in my own recollections. Joan Bakewell, in her autobiography, *The Centre of the Bed*, referring to her early relationship with her mother writes,

> I, too, want to write rapturously, of candlelight and cushions, of creamy days and the stroking of soft skin. And I would like the feeling of that early happiness to linger, to be all-pervasive, to hover down the years and illuminate my growing self. And, of course, some of it does. If I hold my ear close to the past I can hear the echoes of laughter, of warmth and colour and kindness. The child's earliest comforts. (p. 13)

Wistfulness, and a tincture of regret, creep surreptitiously into my consciousness as I read that, but, apart from the fact that my own experience of early relationships was so unlike hers, I have concluded that my parents, both in their relationships to each other and to my brother and me, were seriously constrained. Their mutual expressions of emotion became increasingly eroded further by their relatively stereotyped perceptions of how they should behave and present themselves to us and the world. Aware of their own new-found social position in the manse and of their lowly beginnings, they were quick to punish but slow to praise; quick to anger in themselves but deeply resentful of any shown by us, hesitant about and wary of the warmer emotions in general. We boys were meant to work hard and 'be good'. Demonstrations of emotion showed weakness so we suppressed them. School tended to teach the same lesson.

So it was that Tom and I simply failed to express any emotion at all – at least until we were out of the school and the home environment. By that time an habitual phlegmatic and relatively unemotional acceptance of what life might fling at me had become a self-protective habit and 'feelings' became progressively harder to assay, or even experience. I had concluded that I should reason things out for myself, learn to be self-sufficient in as many ways as possible and be chary of the unsettling effect of any undue emotion, pleasant or otherwise. Growing up in the midst of the most extensive and intensive war the world had ever seen also had its effects. We could not allow ourselves to show whether we felt fear or not when the throb of German bombers, the crump of bombs or the rattle of machine gun fire filled the quiet night air. Our friends at school all just had to assume that their Dads and big brothers would return at the end of the war. They dared think no other thoughts – and certainly not aloud. As boys, we empathised so much more with the aircrews who flew out over the school around midday each day in their Mosquitos from the airfield a couple of miles away on attack missions over the fjords of Norway that we hardly grasped the significance of the lines etched into the faces of the young wives on High Street. They gazed at the sky as the returning warriors crossed the coast again at teatime. They knew how many aircraft went out at midday and counted with ferocious intensity to see whether they were wives or widows.

We learned to be phlegmatic about never quite having enough to eat and making do with one set of clothes for school and one 'for good' (like church, funerals and prize days) and nothing else. Our mothers darned and patched, patched and darned, turned shirt collars or cuffs and spirited football shorts from spare blackout material. These varying facets, even parallel universes, of our school and home lives left effects on our adult lives which a subsequent half century of wildly different experiences has not erased. Again, Joan Bakewell, three years my junior, and from a rather different setting, describes in her autobiography some of these effects.

> From our early years we learned to make a little go a long way. Many of us have remained thrifty throughout our lives. The impulse to save leftovers, hoard elastic bands and save paperclips amuses our children. The habits learned as matter of survival have stuck with us anachronistically in a world glutted with goods. Where now the economic imperative is to sustain consumer spending, we grew up believing that spending was wasteful and wrong. We learned as a generation to be

satisfied with our share so that others did not go without. It shaped our left-leaning politics. We came to believe that ambitions for ourselves, the acquiring of wealth beyond that of others, the lure of fame and success were glamorous and exciting, but somehow reprehensible. The children of the war took its influence forward into their lives'. (p. 53)

The remarkable thing was that our parents and teachers were able to infuse our lives with as much normality as they did. Come what may in the world at large, our task was to pass our Highers and move on to jobs or university. Scottish Academies of the 1930s and 40s had standards to sustain set in the previous century – and often with values more appropriate to that. The 'lad o' pairts' was part and parcel of Scottish history, even mythology, and it was always assumed that, among us, there would be new examples of that splendid breed. The term was used to describe a clever child of very humble origins who, in the ordinary way of the time, might not be expected to achieve, nevertheless struggles against various adversities to gain a significant position in the governmental, economic or academic world. There are those now in educational circles who would maintain that the lad o' pairts was no more than a myth, but taking examples since the Enlightenment only from the north of Scotland, it is hard to argue that such men did not exist.

By our first week in the Academy the Rector would have reminded us all that former pupil, Sir Patrick Duncan, Governor General of South Africa, had been a 'fairm loon' from a few miles out the road. That Lord Mountstephen had been a local boy who finished up building and owning the Canadian Pacific Railway. Thomas Edward, who was expelled from three schools by the time he was six and spent his working life in Banff as a cobbler, became the discoverer of several dozen previously unknown species of crustaceae and a naturalist of European fame. He was elected as an Associate of the Linnaean Society and awarded a pension by Queen Victoria on the recommendation of none other than Charles Darwin. In Cromarty, Hugh Millar, also from humble circumstances, became a national figure both in literature and geology while James Ferguson became an FRS on the strength of having, among other achievements in physics and mathematics, invented the planetarium. They all emerged from humble, even poverty stricken, homes with no advantages, but set examples which every pupil in the school was expected to emulate.

The general point made to us in almost every Morning Assembly in five was that, lurking in our snuffling and shuffling midst were several clones of these eminences who would in due course and with proper application of effort emerge as world figures in something or other. The spur to fame would be regular thrashings with the strap (called the 'tag' or 'tawse') for inadequate effort, stupid mistakes or insolence.

Every teacher possessed a 'Lochgelly'. Little did I know when we went on holiday to that smoky gem of West Fife that coal was but the least of its exports. It also supplied most of the armament for Scottish teachers in the form of two- or three-tailed leather belts with carefully embossed and tooled handles which were wielded with enthusiasm and accuracy by most who possessed them. Some were so hardened by soaking in brine (the belts, not the teachers) that they could be used as pointers in class.

I was to learn that few days would pass at the Academy when the swish and crack of the 'tag' would not echo round the classrooms and hall. Only two of the teachers who taught me were known never to use the strap. The classes of Mr George A. Scott (English and History) and Miss Lydia Taylor (Art) were oases of learning and peace in which we drank deep of the ideas and information they imparted and in which there was never any problem of discipline or anything else. In all other classes we lived under the constant threat of violence. So uncomfortable could it become that it was quite common for some of the girls in the class to fall in a faint to the floor as we waited in the corridor to enter some classes between periods. They were, as a matter of principle, never strapped but they felt keenly the miseries of their male fellow pupils who were. After a year or two of this, the Rector's wife, for one reason or another, prevailed on him to send his only daughter (in my class) to Morrison's Academy in Crieff. We all knew how embarrassed she could become watching her father in one of his rages. I succeeded in being strapped only a few times. Two or three times for disciplinary infringements and twice that I remember for inadequate performance in Latin in the 5th year.

In the late 19th and early 20th centuries teachers and ministers of religion were held in high respect in Scottish communities. It was to them, along with the doctors and solicitors, to whom people first turned for advice, information

Plate 18: Part of Banff Academy in the 1940s

and other psychological support. They were the most fully educated persons in the towns and villages. Only the finest graduates of Scotland's four (then) ancient universities might aspire to these professions. It was a matter of mutual respect for each of these professions amongst themselves and also between the townsfolk and them. This was a climate which was entirely consistent with the rule that all of us schoolboys and girls would, respectively, salute and bow to a teacher were we to meet one in the street either during a school day or at the weekend. It was not a rule which my friends and I were inclined to observe, especially in the case of those teachers whom for one reason or another we did not respect.

So it was that, one lunchtime, two of my friends and I were idly conversing in the street when we spied the approach of one 'Hairyhips' Munro, an angular and arid maiden lady of uncertain age. She was known to be liberal in the use of her tag, but it was not the hardest in the school. On impulse, we decided that our hands would touch no forelocks but would remain in the deepest recesses of our trouser pockets as she passed. Her gimlet eyes recorded every detail of our identities as she sniffily tossed her head as she passed. An hour later we were called to her room to be punished for our insolence. We held out our hands and took four lashes apiece like men. We had, of course, previously advised our fellow pupils of this exploit and were thus enthroned as heroes as we blew on the red weals on our hands and wrists.

Another similar occasion occurred when we marked a fellow pupil's gasmask case with 'the Mark of Zorro' (after seeing the film) and were similarly dealt with. I was probably aged about twelve then. Four years later, however, I was twice dealt with as an individual in the Higher Latin class by Mr McHardy, the Rector, who taught Classics. These episodes I have bitterly resented ever since. Whereas the two former might well have represented my psychopathology and immaturity, the two latter represented his.

As it happens, I was reasonably good at Latin but we all hated our sessions when Mr McHardy would intone 'North and Hillard' while we blanched and reached for the dreaded book. These two erudite gentlemen were the authors of a book of translation exercises from English to Latin entitled *Latin Prose Composition.* One day I erred in giving the word *rus* the wrong gender. For someone about to sit Higher Latin this turned out to be unforgivable. He fussed and shouted at me before the whole quivering class, very few of whom could by this time remember what the gender of the wretched noun was. Finally, 'Go for my strap!' he shouted. It was not his habit to carry this into the classroom. Were it to be used, the recipient would be further tortured by having to walk all the way to his study and ask his secretary for the strap which the victim then had to carry back, stewing in his own apprehension. The Rector was a violent wielder of the tawse. So, almost big and sturdy enough to have given him a bloody nose, I had to stand and take two or three lashes.

As that school year was ending we were to sit the Highers at the end of

March 1947. In February we were given Preliminary tests in preparation for the real thing. I did well with something like 85% in marks. In fact I was top of the year in Latin in the Prelim. at least. However, that was not good enough for Mr McHardy. He went through the papers and marks of all the others in the class, praising some and chastising others verbally. However, I was shattered when he turned to me at the end and said, 'Clark, go for my strap!' There was a gasp from the rest and 'What for, sir?' from me. He picked up my paper again, his hand shaking with ire. He was a bit exophthalmic anyway, but this time I thought his eyes would really pop out. 'I had great expectations of you, Clark – and what do I get? – several silly errors with the subjunctive and future perfect tense which I thought you'd learned in class IV – and for you not to know the verb *fremere*, that was disgraceful!' I suppressed a smirk. *Fremere* is the verb 'to snarl' which perfectly described his tone. He continued, 'There was no need for you to make ANY errors in that paper. Hold out your hand!' And so I took two on each hand and loathed him for evermore. Of course I did get my Higher Latin, but I'd have got it without his assault.

The same man insisted, quite unilaterally, that during my final year at school I would report to his study every day after normal classes to study ancient Greek (the only pupil in the whole school to be subjected to it) since he was convinced that I would follow my father into the ministry. By then, nothing was further from my mind, but he would listen to no reason. One good bit of spin-off from that was, however, that I learned what, much later, a well-known Banff Town Councillor called 'the Acrylic alphabet'! The other was that the ancient language bears some relationship to modern Greek. That let me get to grips with that language many years later while sailing in the Ionian and, following several fine holidays in the various Greek islands, becoming a Hellenophile for entirely other reasons.

Education was a rigorous business throughout Scotland in those days. The war had just ended before I left school and everybody was aware that there were great new expectations of social progress. Attlee had replaced Churchill (to my mother's great disgust) and 'opportunity for all' was the watchword. Thousands of servicemen were wandering back from all corners of the globe, surprised and delighted to be alive and determined to pick up their education from where it had been so rudely interrupted by Adolf Hitler, or move into new jobs as they struggled to get to know families which had grown in their absence.

Opportunity for all probably did obtain during the thirties and forties, in primary schools, where one teacher taught her own class for a year at a time, all the way up to the Qualifying Examination. But in the Academies, High Schools and Grammar Schools there reigned a strong streak of elitism with ruthless streaming throughout the six secondary years. The better teachers did try to give more time to pupils who were finding some subjects or topics within a subject difficult but generally, clever kids were pushed to excel, as we have seen, to produce the perfect performance. The teachers never quite appreciated that the 'lads o' pairts' excelled in their own time through their own motivation and in subjects they chose!

My six years in the Academy were a strange mix of what I saw as pressures upon me. They are difficult to write about because I regret my passivity in the face of my parents and some of my teachers – a passivity which saw my being propelled into a language based course rather than a science based course. My mother's ignorance of both and my father's own predisposition to language skills, together with what I later discovered was the hope on the part of both of them, and of the Rector, that I might follow in my father's occupational footsteps, all led to my being advised to leave behind, after two years of each, both physics and chemistry. The former, even in its elementary form, intrigued me, although I was much less comfortable with the latter. Chemical formulae were generally puzzling to me because of the negative transfer from algebraic and trigonometric formulae. Nevertheless, one of the mnemonics which still lurk somewhere in my cerebrum is

> Johnny, finding life a bore, drank some H_2SO_4
> Johnny's father, an MD, gave him $CaCo_3$
> Now he's neutralised, it's true
> But Johnny's full of Co_2

In the third year we were introduced to German, having already had two years of Latin and French. There was also English, Mathematics, History and in my final year, Greek – into which, as I have declared, I was press-ganged by the Rector. Geography, which I had liked and done well at, and Art only lasted for two Secondary years except for those who were to specialise in it. Then, at the end of the third year, it was discovered that if I progressed as I was doing, I would be just turned sixteen when I would have completed my Highers and the university would not then accept a student below a minimum age of seventeen.

So it was that I was advised to spend another year in Secondary 3 on the basis that it had been the first year in which I was taking three languages and some consolidation could take place if I repeated it. I was very concerned about this because it would look to my fellow pupils as if I was being 'held back' in a way usually reserved for the dunderheads, in spite of the fact that they all knew that my class marks were perfectly all right. Had I foreseen that, I would have much preferred to have spent the extra year in Secondary 2 when I was trying to master the science subjects. As it turned out, the extra year in Secondary 3 was a total waste of time. I had already done all the work and became lazy and disenchanted, more concerned with the football field and trashy novels. The teachers noticed it too and gave me what was perhaps a deserved hard time.

If some of our teachers were hard-driving traditionalists with first-class degrees, rigorous in their demands for perfection, at least on the part of the 'A' stream pupils, there were a few who were idiosyncratic caricatures of Scottish Academy teachers. My double time in the third year allowed me more time to observe these rather more than the others. One such taught, or nearly taught, us French and German. Curiously, she was much liked, if not loved, by her pupils, perhaps because she was the only teacher who would from time to time use in the classroom the Doric dialect we all spoke out of school. Her family and Christian names were always reversed in order so she became known as Mackie Jean. I never found out why.

Unlike almost all my fellow pupils, I did not experience the Doric as the common currency of everyday speech at home. King's English was the order of the day in the manse. Neither of my parents had their origins in the North East and my father, though understanding the Doric, used it only when he thought it appropriate with certain parishioners. My brother and I were never allowed to use it at home but of course we had, all our lives, spoken in the dialect outside of the manse. My parents considered the Doric to be a careless, bucolic form of speech unsuited to the elaboration of more complex concepts and debate. Nevertheless, it was the speech of all our friends and of nearly all their parents. We switched it on and off at will with no trouble at all without even considering ourselves to be bi-lingual. In the playground, and on Saturdays and Sundays, the Doric was spoken. In school, except in Mackie Jean's class or by the janitor, 'proper English' was the rule.

I still recall Mackie Jean calling to the last boy in to the class room, 'Carter, ee're the last een in. Ca' tee the door! The last class I hid wis that sweir tae learn that I'm connached.' In French, she would produce the most amazing mnemonics when we were struggling with vocabulary. 'David Clark, fit's the word for 'to spit'? Struggling to remember, I would then be told it was *'cracher'*. She went on, *'Cracher, cracher*, because it **crashes** doon on the pavement!' Some other pupil, failing to remember the word for a seagull, would be told *'mouette'* – because it **ates** wi' its **mou**!' Such unorthodoxy seems to have worked. I have never forgotten these words – ever. Jean Mackie had been brought up in the rural hinterland of Banff and I doubt if she ever considered the Doric to be other than the true language of her land.

Some other teachers were idiosyncratic in a less benevolent way. Mr Sutherland, who taught Higher Mathematics, had the beguiling habit of keeping his strap soaked in a jar of brine to harden it. As his wrath expanded to match our fear and ignorance he would straighten out the stiffened leather and use it as a pointer on the blackboard. Sitting, quailing in the room through the wall, and knowing that the next period was to be Maths, we would listen in dread anticipation to the tap, tap of 'Suds's' strap echoing through the wall. None of our teachers, with the exception of the great Mr Scott, was ever given to praising any of our efforts no matter how successful these had been. Even in the fifth year, 'Suds' would berate the three of us Higher pupils as we sat behind each other in the right hand row of desks. He was tall, ramrod straight backed and immaculately dressed, dark suit and collar and tie. I now recognise him to have been a control freak, obsessional, and even slightly sadistic in his ways. He was even the Captain of the local Boys' Brigade and brought the same personal style to that.

Rattling the upright cane chair behind his desk he would intone in a rising crescendo, 'There's Carter, there's Kramer and there's Clark – and they're all fools!' A long pause followed as he glared at us. 'Carter, you've a tongue the length of Bridge Street and a brain the size of a split pea. Kramer, you're a fool, have always been a fool and will always be a fool! And Clark', as he rolled his eyes heavenward in mock incredulity, 'You...are...getting... WORSE!' Yet we all got Higher Maths later in the year. The split pea brain became a headmaster, the fool became a lecturer in civil and mechanical engineering at an English university and wrote a textbook in his subject and the one who was getting worse – well, history records ...

For those of us in the 'A' stream, it was clear that the one preoccupation of all our teachers was that we, or at least most of us, should end our school careers with as many Highers as possible, and win some Open Bursaries at the competitions run by most of the Scottish universities at the end of our 5th or 6th years. The local, and even some of the national press, was always fully geared to reporting on such things, to the greater glory, always, of the teachers, and occasionally, to that of the pupils. Of that, more later.

During the most critical years of my time at Banff Academy all of us, pupils and teachers could not but be aware that the war raged on in the wider world. Some of my impressions of a boy's life in general during these years between 1939 and 1945 I have already recounted in my book *One Boy's War.* It was to the great credit of our teachers that they succeeded in having us concentrate at all on our lessons in the face of the counter-attractions of going out on our bicycles the two miles to the RAF Banff Strike Wing airfield to watch the daily drama of several squadrons of Mosquitos and Beaufighters take off, formate over the town and subsequently dive to just above sea level and head for Norway. School had usually finished by the time they, or some of them, returned, shot up and sometimes on fire, about tea time. We would watch the young wives of the pilots in the High Street as we pedalled by, anxiously counting the planes back in as they looked up, worry etched on their faces.

Often our history lesson at midday would be interrupted by history in the making. The heavy, powerful and insistent roar of over a hundred Rolls Royce Merlin engines would start as no more than a slight quiver of the window glass. In a few minutes, however, the whole school was throbbing and all other sounds were masked as we glanced out of the tall windows to catch sight of some of these famous aircraft. Rockets, bombs and cannon, clearly visible to us as they orbited the town in flights of three or four at little more than a thousand feet, declared that they were 'loitering with intent' while the rest of the squadrons were in position to join them for their attacks later in the afternoon in the dangerous canyons of the Norwegian fjords. In 1944 and 1945 that was a daily occurrence. The details of their exploits, victories and losses, are fully documented in Andrew Bird's book *A Separate Little War*.

We were disturbed not only by such activity but also by nights disrupted by air raids when the wailing siren would rouse us from broken sleep to head for the shelter. Many times we might hear the distinctive throb of German aero engines in the distance. Then we slept on. But if the threat sounded a bit too close parents would usher us from our bedrooms and we would shiver away an hour or two in our dressing gowns under the stair. Bleary-eyed, we struggled back from sleep just in time to get our porridge and toast and run down to the school at 8.45. There were no concessions and our total attention was still sought in class. Many of the teachers were themselves either Air Raid Wardens or Fire Watchers so they too had had disturbed nights – as they were not averse to reminding us should our heads drop a bit by afternoon.

Plate 19: Banff Academy soccer 1st team 1946/7. Author is extreme left, middle row; his younger brother Tom is kneeling, right

In many ways the pressures imposed on us in school distracted us from the more terrible aspects of the war. Entering the classrooms and going about our scholastic business was like living in a parallel universe when compared to the time we spent at home or on our own peculiar boyish ploys. Only once do I remember these parallel universes merging – if just for an hour. That was the early morning of 6 June 1944. Those of us with radios had been glued to them in the hour before school as had our teachers. It was sensed that something big was afoot. In the school there seemed to be a reluctance even among the teachers to start the day's work and I can remember us all racketing around the cloakrooms for a long half-hour before Mr Scott, our English and History teacher, came down the stair from the staff room and herded us into his class. Other teachers suddenly appeared and did likewise with their pupils. All were agog with the news. They had just heard the BBC's John Snagge announce that Operation 'Overlord', the assault on Northern Europe, had commenced a few hours ago and tens of thousands of troops were, even then, landing by parachute, ship, landing craft and gliders on and beyond the shores of Normandy. Many of the kids guessed, often correctly, that their dads or big brothers would be amongst those thousands. Many were buoyant and even gung-ho about their prospects but others, often girls, were more reserved and thoughtful. We all, with our teachers, were desperate for more news and the normal class topics were discarded that morning for an analysis of what this momentous event might mean for all of us.

We were lucky to have Mr Scott during that hour. He had always been a teacher who could engage his class in the learning process, almost without our being aware that we were really having a lesson. What was listed as an English period could become an exploration of the nature of creative writing and an hour of history might very well deal with the nature of our parliamentary system as compared with the Communism of our allies of the Soviet Union. In retrospect, I can confidently declare that he personally accounted for any capacity I might have developed for systematic thought, not only about language and literature, but about almost anything else. The other teachers dealt with lessons. He dealt with learning – and did so with flair, good humour and considerable wit. Only much later did we all discover that he had volunteered for military service very early in the war only to be turned down because he had earlier suffered badly from pulmonary tuberculosis and was considered unfit for service.

All other classes seemed to me to have become a perpetual exercise in stress management and harm avoidance. The notion of reward, even by word of mouth, for good performance seemed to have eluded almost all the other teachers. The only motivational plan they seemed to have engaged with was that of endless punishments for what, in their eyes anyway, were inadequate classroom and homework performances. Strapping, punishment exercises and essays and, most potent of all for nearly all of the boys, was withdrawal from the sports period (football) on Wednesday afternoons. The Rector was no sportsman and had little or no interest in athletics or games so he was all too ready to cancel sports periods for one reason or another. He succeeded in teaching me and many others to hate him. My father could never understand that. As far as he was concerned, the man was a fine classical scholar with a first class degree and that was that!

Many of our teachers then were of that academic calibre and I can well remember hearing my father discuss with my mother potential new incumbents to teaching posts around Banffshire. Father was for many years on the Education Committee of the Banffshire County Council and he, as one of the selection committee, would receive application papers from all the aspirants. There was no shortage of these then in spite of the war and he would mutter something about 'needn't bother with all those who don't have 'firsts'. I'll just consider the other qualities and experience from within that bunch'. He was aware that those with the best brains might not make the best teachers, but, other things being equal, those who had high intelligence and wide ranging knowledge and culture at least had something to teach! In his view, that would easily compensate for minor defects in their understanding of the child mind or the pressures of the classroom.

Growing up in an atmosphere in which such incidents were part and parcel of daily life was, of course, quite unlike any other household. There were always 'official' sorts of things going on, morning, noon and night and both our parents seemed to have little time for simply sitting around and being with us for anything more than five or ten minutes at a time. They really did seem to work something like an eighteen hour day. As our education progressed they played a smaller and smaller part in it – apart from monitoring that our homework was being done. As I moved into my later teens greater distance grew up not only between them and me but also between my brother Tom and me. He was following a less academic course than I and being two academic years behind me and with a totally different set of friends we began to live almost separate lives. We did meet in the football team, however, and there was some pressure on me to keep my place in the first XI in the face of his soccer prowess. Fortunately, we did not play in the same position so were not in direct competition, but I was aware of some anxiety each Friday as the names of the team for inter-school matches went up on the notice board at three o'clock.

One of the strangest features of growing up in the manse was that neither my brother nor myself thought very much about what we would do with ourselves after school. All through the war most of us had half expected that the conflict would continue and that we would in due course become soldiers, or in my own case, a Spitfire or Mosquito pilot. Our whole secondary education had taken place in wartime and we only knew of schoolteachers, some doctors, postmen and ministers and some shopkeepers who were not away fighting. What I was clear about, however, was that I would never follow in my father's footsteps, no matter what pressures might be put upon me. Tom felt the same.

Working with my hands was something that I found quite rewarding. For some years Tom and I had both worked at the 'tatties' (i.e. potato harvesting) on various local farms – a back-breaking job if ever there was one, and I did enjoy making things like simple woodwork or small two-valve radios. I had become a bit of a fitness fanatic from my middle teens onward and cycled, ran, played football, badminton and tennis at every opportunity. It had become one of the ways of breaking out from the shackles of the manse regime. But what actual job I might get was another matter entirely.

Neither of my parents, fortunately for them, were at all driven to earn money. They did not strive for worldly goods. They had the rent-free manse and just enough to get by on by way of food, clothes and the occasional holiday with relatives. The occasional half-crown a week doled out to Tom and me was irregular and soon spent by us. Father did, from time to time, suggest I should look for a job in the Civil Service although I do not really think he had much of an idea about what that might entail. To him, it simply signified security and tenure. To me it signified boredom and rigidity – and certainly not the kind of work to which I would sally forth each morning for the rest of my life with a light step and whistling some merry melody. I suppose I had thought, in my loose and inaccurate way, of journalism. But then I'd also thought of civil engineering, architecture, interpreting, and, after a dose of Somerset Maugham, of being a swashbuckling young District Officer in the Colonial Service. My Highers would only allow of some of these.

It came as something of a surprise when George A. Scott challenged the English class one afternoon to tell him what we all would do after school. 'Clark!', he pronounced, 'You'll be going to university, won't you?' I had never given it much thought, though I'm quite sure my parents had assumed that I would. It felt like a decision-making moment. I heard myself saying, 'Yes, sir!' and immediately thought, 'What am I letting myself in for?' Perhaps the folk-lore of stories of licence and debauchery that went on at the Bursary Competition in Aberdeen University had been enough to lure me to the Groves of Academe.

The recognised first step toward entering university – or even any form of tertiary education in those days was to get one's Highers, more properly, the Scottish Higher Leaving Certificate. There were 'Lowers' for the less academically inclined but anyone with aspirations to university was required then to have at least three subjects at Higher level. I was to sit mine in the spring of 1947 and with the predicted influx of ex-servicemen after 1945, it was confidently expected that only those with four or five Highers would be accepted at university. Messrs McHardy (Latin) and Sutherland

(Mathematics) were not confident of my prospective success in their subjects and hesitated to put me forward for five Highers. My father and myself, if truth be told, were both confident that I could achieve the necessary level in both these subjects so there followed a rather acrimonious debate between, in the Blue corner, Dad and myself and, in the Red corner, the two Principal Teachers in question. The ring was the Headmaster's study. This, I think, is where my middle class origins stood me in good stead since it would have been unheard of for a working class parent to challenge such a powerful pair of dominies. We punched our weight and won on points.

Much of the heat in the arguments stemmed from the fact that Head and Principal teachers of that day saw the Higher results of their pupils as a commentary on their own prowess rather than that of the pupils. Failures would count against them in some way and they could not countenance that! Failure also loomed large before all pupils at this time too since they were themselves all too aware that failing was easy. There was a totally iniquitous rule in these days that if a pupil were, for example, put forward to sit five Highers and failed only one of them then all the others would also be deemed failures regardless of what marks had been achieved in them.

In retrospect, the manifest unfairness of that system seems almost unbelievable but it placed huge stresses on every pupil sitting these wretched exams.

In 1947 there was another unexpected stress which took the form of a terrible snowstorm which began some weeks before the Highers and lasted well into them. It was, in fact, one of the worst winters and spring ever experienced in Scotland. For myself, living within a mile of the school, it mattered little, provided I rose early enough to dig a way out of the house through the eight foot drifts which blocked the doors. Many of my classmates were, however, from outlying homes and farms which became totally isolated for weeks at a time. The plan was, therefore to have them billeted with friendly families in the town of Banff for the weeks preceding the examinations until after the exams.

An excellent administrative solution, it was thought. However, for us as pupils it was an unprecedented opportunity to make closer friendships especially with the more attractive country girls than we could ever have achieved in normal circumstances. In no time we had discovered their billets and spent the dark nights pestering them to come out sledging, or whatever, not always unsuccessfully, and thus seriously disrupting all of our revision and study schedules. I usually tried to slip quietly out of the house when any meeting of minds with the girls from the country was likely. Consulting with a male school friend about an alternative construction in a geometry theorem was fine. A light-hearted chat with a girl in the lobby of her 'digs' was quite another. Any suspicion on my parents' part that such might be impending would, at the least, trigger yet again the sonorous admonition to 'Remember who you are! Boys from the manse must be a model of propriety and a good example to all others!' An example of what? I would wonder with adolescent sophistry.

For myself, the contretemps with the Rector about my proposed five Highers had to be justified by ultimate success so I did work quite hard into the night. My father's study was still a *sanctum sanctorum* so I had to work at a little card table by the bed in the freezing cold of my bedroom. The linoleum was often slippery with frost because my parents were fresh air fiends and would not allow me to close the window ever. There was no heating of any kind. We had at least got electricity into the manse by the year before so I was allowed a 40 watt bulb to write by. It seems that Parish ministers of that era were all parsimonious in the extreme with regard to burning any sort of fuel. Perhaps because the war had just ended and we had habits of frugality in all things, my father was always going around the house switching off lights in empty rooms. Worse still, when we first lived in the manse, my parents found that my father's predecessor, Rev. Dr W. S. Bruce, had had all the gas pipes other than the centre ceiling ones in the large rooms, hammered flat so that they could not be used. They remained as long as I lived in that house.

Anxiety reached a crescendo as the days of the examinations approached. Parents were worried because we all looked so wan and peaky. We felt it. However, the various papers and orals came and went and we awaited the results with feelings of total powerlessness. Curiously, the teachers themselves seemed in the end to take pity on us and became fleetingly human for the next few weeks. During the short period before the summer holidays we had the option to give up some academic classes in favour of such as classes in woodwork, first aid and cooking! I laboured for weeks on producing a dovetail joint in two pieces of incredibly hard beech. Little did I appreciate it at the time, but seven or eight years later I would be turning those skills to better use making some furniture for our little house just after I was married and had no money. As my beech wood dovetail joint gradually came to look more respectable and 'Speedy' Cochrane, the teacher, had stopped repeating his injunctions to us not to waste good timber, ('Watch what you're doing with that wood, boys, it doesn't grow on trees y'know!') our anxieties had switched from sitting the exams to awaiting the results. In due course, the buff envelope came in the post and inside it the magic card to turn the skies brighter, wipe the pallor from our faces and spell relief for me and my parents. I had my five Highers after all! I was relieved that it now seemed likely that I might go to university. My parents were relieved that they would not suffer the indignity of several of my friends achieving better passes than I had.

Between the end of term and the publication of the results my father had actually taken me in the bus to Aberdeen with the specific aim of letting me see what a university looked like. I had of course seen pictures of the dreaming spires of Oxbridge but these were remote – and English! Our boyish subculture automatically sustained the notion that such places were for the snooty and the effete, so much so that when my father suggested one day that if my exam results were good I might apply to go to Cambridge, I immediately rejected the idea. Some months later when at last I could visit Cambridge did I deeply regret my brash rejection.

Nevertheless, the visit that summer of 1947 to Aberdeen, the Gothic granite extravaganza of Marischal College, my father's wistful walk past the sober granite front of Mounthooly Church where he had preached so successfully twenty years before, and then the stroll together down the Spital towards King's College was exciting and impressive. It was a lovely summer day and even if it was during the vacation and very few students or staff were about, the warm sandstone of the Crown Tower emerging from the yellow-green embrace of the surrounding trees immediately engaged me. A walk into the Quadrangle and through the cloister-like front of the Elphinstone Hall as well as a glimpse of the Library and the Chapel suddenly stirred feelings that were as unexpected as they were intense. This was a place I could enjoy and be enriched by. I began to dread that my application to become a student there might be unsuccessful.

Some of us, having studied quite hard, were of a mind to try the Aberdeen University Bursary Competition a little later in the year. Once the Higher results were known, our teachers were also keen that we should try to leap through this final hoop. There were several reasons for this. First, we had had the achievements of our schoolboy and girl predecessors thrust down our throats in assembly after assembly in school. Second, we had accumulated such a store of knowledge for the Highers that it seemed a pity to waste it. Third, and most important of all, it was a chance to get away from school into the city on our own for a week, discover what living in 'digs' would be like and spend riotous evenings with the prettiest and cleverest girls from all the surrounding Academies. What fantasies we harboured about the debauchery and lubricity in which we would indulge come evening time. Most of us sixteen and seventeen-year-olds had hardly been away from home all through the war, so a week in the city was the stuff of our dreams. The reality turned out to be much tamer.

My parents had contacted a neighbouring minister whose son was already in Aberdeen in his first year of medical studies. He had digs in Holburn Street and it was there that I was to spend the week of the exams under the surveillance of Mrs Stuart, the landlady. Two hours in the Bluebird bus from Banff and a smart mile walk to No. 339 on the Sunday evening preceding the exams led to our introduction. To my discomfiture, my parents had insisted on accompanying me in the bus to Aberdeen and all the way to Holburn Street. They were to return home later that evening. Mrs Stuart was genteel and welcoming, even effusive, in the presence of a 'dog collar'. But a mere hour after their departure she reverted to type and then subjected me to a litany of rules and regulations governing our stay there. Some food was still rationed so we were told that butter etc. for all of us 'stewdies' would be mixed together in dishes on the table but that each of us would have our own half-pound jam jars of sugar in the press. Stealing from one of these would lead to instant dismissal from the lodging. Slightly abashed, I spent the evening chatting to Kenneth, my room-mate, about his experiences of the Bursary Competition the year before. I had a whole free day before my first exam on the Tuesday so I could revise on Monday.

Perhaps the least of our motivations to sit the exams was the possibility of winning sufficient money to keep us at university either in part or in full. Living through and being alive at the end of the war had made us relatively unworldly in such matters. My parents had always cared little about money – and had little, so I suppose I had assumed that a grant from the County Council might see me by.

There was a body of tradition too in sitting the Bursary Comp. (as it was always abbreviated). In 1906, Neil Maclean's book *Life at a Northern University* was edited by a certain W. Keith Leask as a Quatercentenary edition of the 1874 original publication. Since the book was published by the Rosemount Press, Aberdeen, under the auspices of the Students' Representative Council of Aberdeen University, it is not hard to deduce that it tells of life at Aberdeen University.

Leask, in his Introduction, writes: 'During the last week in October in 1853, when the days were visibly shortening and the leaves in the Chanonry were falling with a browner shade, the following notice from the Aberdeen papers would be on the tables of the teachers all along the North, conveying the important information about the number of vacant bursaries to be competed for at the ensuing Competition:

> The Annual Competition for Bursaries will be held in King's College, as usual, on the last Monday of October, at Nine o'clock A.M. Of the Twenty Bursaries to be disposed of on this occasion, there will be one of the annual value of £30, one of £20, one of £18, one of £17, one of £16, two of £15, two of £14, two of £13, three of £12 and six of inferior value.
>
> Candidates for these Bursaries are required to bring with them Certificates of their age, signed by the Ministers and Session-Clerks of their respective Parishes, as four of the above Bursaries ... can only be given to Young Men, natives of the British Empire, who have attained fourteen years of age.

While it was the case that in 1853 it might be that one could be too young to sit the Bursary Competition, there was no upper limit. Maclean goes on to tell of working ploughmen, tradesmen and others who tried it several times before winning a bursary which might free them from the soil or the workbench and lead to a more academic life. Indeed, in those days, the first requirement was to learn Latin. The whole examination was written in the ancient language so such candidates would pester the life out of the local schoolmasters or ministers to coach them in the mysteries of *cum* taking the subjunctive, the difference between noun endings in the second and fourth declensions and so on. No wonder that the North of Scotland regularly threw up more than its fair share of 'lads o' pairts'!

Our own schoolmasters left us in no doubt, even in 1946, about the traditions we should maintain in our own efforts to win a bursary. We shrewdly suspected that they were really anxious, not so much that we poor pupils would prosper, but that the good name of the Academy and of themselves as teachers would be enhanced should we win – especially a top bursary. However, by then we were at least spared writing all our answers in Latin – although, as it happens, I did that myself in one of the papers – the one in Latin. Moreover, the examination week itself had by now moved from October to the Spring of the year in which the Bursaries would be taken up. First came the Highers, then the Bursary Comp.

At the end of the war, the competition to enter university was, for school leavers, intense. The government had instituted a Further Education and Training (FET) scheme for all those who had been fighting for us for the past six years with the result that only about 10% of the university student population would comprise gangling and spotty teenagers like myself.

It was really quite important therefore to win a bursary since that would significantly enhance one's chances of being accepted as a student. Such was the insouciance of youth, however, that that issue seemed to influence me and the few pals from Banff Academy relatively little.

The actual examinations were held in the Mitchell Hall at Marischal College. This too impressed, even overawed me, with its high vaulted roof, stained glass windows and, to a country lad, immense size. Within the year, familiarity would bring contempt and we would laugh disrespectfully at the stories of how some of the engineering and medical students had filled a couple of dozen contraceptives with helium and left them to hover in the highest neuks of the self-same vaulted roof until they were shot down with airguns. The spaced desks, overweening silence and suppressed tension of the examination room was tangible on my first morning with an exam paper in front of me. Without exception, every other student in the room appeared to be infinitely more learned and intelligent than I. They were teenage men and women of the urban world, some from private schools in Aberdeen and the south. They all seemed to write so much that they were up asking for another examination book before I had written even a page. At the time it did not occur to me that that was due more to their expansive penmanship than to the quickness of their minds. My micrographic and crabbed little hand simply crammed more words into every page. It still does!

After three hours of intense effort we debouched into the Marischal quadrangle to compare notes with any other students we recognised – and some we didn't. I can remember talking to one large and erudite looking chap with a Gordon's College blazer – one of the ones who had headed the trudge to the front to acquire a fresh examination book – only to find that what he thought were good answers to one of the questions were, to my mind, total rubbish. It left me in a state of conflict as to whether to depend on my own store of knowledge and analysis or to doubt it so much that I would hardly trust myself to write another paper. Further brief chats with other hopefuls, however, reassured me greatly.

One event and one event only stands out about the next day's exams. I caught a glimpse of a girl emerging from the examination hall and heading for the nearest bus stop. She was animatedly chatting to some friends, was neat and slim and had lovely bobbed hair which bounced as she walked. I immediately knew I had to see her again and wondered there and then how I could possibly find out who she was. The whole episode did not bear rational scrutiny. I, and probably she, was but seventeen. In fact, I think I had a couple of weeks to go to reach that age. I had not even spoken to her and manse life had not allowed me a great previous experience of either extended or intense relationships with girls. In Banff and neighbouring towns. I did know several whom I could take to the pictures, go walks with, play tennis and so on – often enough with the usual kiss and cuddle tempered by teenage innocence. Some even declared that they 'fancied me' but I never quite believed them so my response to this fleeting glimpse of a girl I'd never met surprised me considerably. I consoled myself with the thought that if she was doing the Bursary Comp. then she would eventually finish up at Aberdeen University too.

As for evening high jinks, dissolution and depravity, it came to no more than a sneaky, underage half pint in the Students' Union, a few brief and unproductive chats with some of the girls who were also anticipating the student life to come in four months' time. None wanted to come to the pictures where it was dark, warm and there were 'chummy seats' that their mothers had warned them about. All seemed to move in self-protective groups of three or four and even most of the boys as well seemed anxious to curtail the festivities in favour of another hour or two's swotting for the morrow. The best I could manage was a chatty mile walk to Holburn Street with two pretty Huntly girls where my turning in to No. 339 saw my Brief Encounter end on a high note of emotional intensity with the unforgettable words, 'See you in the morning then!' No doubt they enjoyed a quiet snigger to themselves about the callow youth from Banff as they continued to their digs further down the hill.

And yet, that week in the city, for all the mental effort of the exams, for all the minor social successes and major sexual disappointments, was acclaimed by nearly all the participants as a huge success. We were, as they say in more modern times, at the bottom of a big learning curve. And I had a 'big project' – to find out more about the attractive, chatty lassie with the bouncing brown hair! At the time it suddenly seemed more important than the results of the examinations.

Twelve years had passed in which this human putty was moulded, sometimes with leather, into a form recognisable by a few of the more percipient pedagogues as a school leaver. A Utility-bound copy of a Conrad novel with an economically illuminated book plate inside the front cover proved that I had come top in mediocrity in English, and, driven on by the unremitting apathy of the average seventeen-year-old, had allowed myself to be persuaded that University offered me tastes of a freedom, even licence, unknown to the 5th year – except for those would-be dissolute and crafty mortals like us who had succeeded in getting themselves involved in the Open Bursary Competition.

Little wonder, then, that the final day prospect of a church service, a Prize-giving, (with dreary speeches heavily overconcerned with the Puritan virtues of aspiration, toil and persistence) and, as in the beginning, more 'good suits' and clean shoes failed to exercise its magnetic charm. 'Freddie's' or the Carlton Café both seemed infinitely preferable in spite of the dire threats of the Rector that absentees from the formal proceedings would not only incur the wrath of God, and besmirch the name of civilisation in the Northern hemisphere, but would also make him VERY ANGRY, call for his strap and withdraw his recommendation that we should enjoy the sinful pleasures of a higher education.

The call of the wild was nevertheless too strong, especially since a preliminary 'recce' of the Carlton the day before had confirmed that some of the queans from the upper classes (of the school, at least) would be there, nostrils twitching with the scent of maturity and freedom as they crouched over large strawberry ices. The Carlton had in the earlier days of the 'thirties and 'forties always borne a certain air of mild disreputability.

There were, it is true, no batwing doors to be brutishly shouldered aside as you stubbed out your fag on the downy cheek of a Primary 6, but there did at least hang a green baize curtain separating the inner sanctum from the bland civility of the outer café. Faint wreaths of blue-grey tobacco smoke and less faint and much bluer language issued from round its edges as lithe bodies beyond the mystic barrier danced warily around the coloured ivory balls on the tables. They hefted their cues ominously as they, slit-eyed, weighed up suckers for the hustle – at least until the bell for the end of 'playtime' rang. That place had atmosphere – if you could but find it in the surfeit of CO_2. Old lags from the gaol in Reidhaven Street told of bread and water, birchings ('D'ye ken this – they rubbed saut intae the scars!') and sages of immense worldly experience enlivened our fantasies with stories of a richness and lubricity to make Eskimo Nell seem like one of the Virgins who buried her talents. My mother was not keen on the Carlton.

Thus it was that, with a couple of my pals, school ties tucked away in pockets and jackets casual over our swaggering shoulders, we self-consciously swung down the Back Path, scorning the half-anxious, half-admiring glances of less audacious mortals from Secondary 4 and 5 going in the opposite direction. Having stopped smoking as soon as I was sixteen, a chew of gum was as much as I could manage in the face of my pals' Capstans or Woodbines. Ere long the familiar table tops of the Carlton were reflecting our bravado into the eyes of some of our friends, male and female, either lucky enough to have left school the year before or simple enough to see the huge irrelevance of a Prizegiving to 90% of the pupils.

Plans for a game of golf in the afternoon were well under way when a white and plooky face, wide-eyed with the first glimpse of the ultimate horror, appeared at the door to announce that 'Scottie' was actually on his way down to cleanse the temple of its usurers, Pharisees and other reprobates. The Carlton could hardly survive that! Its Seal of Disapproval would be gone for evermore. Had it only been the Rector, all would have been well. That would simply have awarded the place its Gold Seal – but 'Scottie'! It was no place for him, the one human being who, during my Secondary school years sustained in me any ambition to be educated, who enlivened the days and many otherwise dull books with his kindly irony and critical comment, not only on mine but also on the author's work. Our faces, blanched with apprehension, demonstrated that this was a call for retrenchment and reform that had to be heeded. With one accord we stashed the chewing gum under the edge of the table, stubbed out the fags and were to be seen, neat, scrubbed and, of course, innocent, taking our homily like men in the main hall of the Academy half an hour later. I still think the story about Scottie was a malicious rumour spread about by some jealous slob from Secondary 4. But it worked.

A week or two later, the *Press and Journal* published the Bursary Competition results in all their tantalising detail. That morning, scores of anxious eyes from Shetland to the Mearns, from Dufftown to Peterhead and beyond scanned the small print to see who had performed *summa cum laude* and who would slink away, quietly ruminative about the injustices of this academic world. But there was my name, not at the top of the list but at a reasonable level which surprised me and pleased my parents. It would surely assure me of a place at university – where I might see that girl – and I'd better consider what sort of a degree I should undertake. All these years in school had left me desperately short of worldly knowledge about the range of occupations and professions available to me and equally short of awareness about what subjects I should study to enable me to explore them. I was suddenly very sensitive about my innocence and my ignorance and it took some time to reduce both.

Five Highers and a Bursary might have seemed at the time to be the mark of a successful and liberal school education. My teachers and parents evidently thought so, even if my mother, with her usual flair for deflating me, nagged me relentlessly, and uselessly, about not winning the First Bursary as So-and-so from the Academy had done a couple of years before. It was just as well I never mentioned the girl I had seen and taken to at the Bursary Comp. – that would have raised a storm since mother had no doubt that only Princess Margaret would do for her son of the manse! I have subsequently rejoiced in my escape from that!

And yet, looking back, my first seventeen years had left me far from being a rounded personality and I still struggled for self-confidence and a clear sense of my own identity. The manse had thrust an identity of sorts upon me, but it was paper-thin and lacked the robustness that life away from home would demand of it. To some extent that was due to the immaturity common to most seventeen year olds, but more so to the impositions and constraints thrust upon me by manse life and parental expectation. Tom, my wee brother, did not feel this so acutely, partly because he was the second child and partly because he was less 'Bolshie' or combative in thought and style than I. Perhaps for that reason, he was also my parents' favourite son.

Having watched in later years my children and grandchildren grow up around me, one huge difference between them and me as a child is that in my own childhood I never had a close friend. They are surrounded by them. In those early years, those I felt attracted to, of whatever sex, were never 'good' enough, for my mother especially. Bonds could only be established on the football pitch, the playground, or even the classroom – but never at home. Some did their best by inviting me into their homes after school but that inevitably led to Gestapo-like questioning as to where I had been when I got home.

I learned, in the case of both adults and children, to be an observer of others rather than a participant with others but was never able to luxuriate in the warmth of a close friendship of my own. The debit side of that was a sort of isolation, but the credit side was that I developed unusual self-sufficiency very early. My father had shown a similar developmental pattern in his own life though I am less sure of the dynamics in his case. He was inclined to say things like, 'Don't depend too much on others and then you'll be spared any disappointment when they let you down.' Some must have let him down more than I knew.

It only occurred to me, long after, that my parents had never seemed to have cultivated close friends either. There seemed to be two main reasons for that. First, they were simply so committed to the work of a parish minister and his wife that they simply had no time. What are now called windows of opportunity in which they could sit down and share a meal or even a cup of tea or glass of sherry with neighbours or friends simply did not occur. All those who did appear for meals in the manse were 'official' guests, a variety of church or civil dignitaries during peacetime and myriad soldiers, airmen, officers and gentlemen during the war. These occasions allowed of a wide range of acquaintances but few real friends as their lay neighbours knew the word. There were few occasions when I saw my parents sit down together for a cup of tea and a chat and even fewer which also included Tom and me. Even our own family mealtimes which might have been expected to bring us together were often disrupted by my father having to leave for a marriage, funeral or other sort of meeting and my mother's having to go to the Guild or such-like. Tom and I had very little time with them together except during the month's holiday each year and even then it was mostly our father who would spend time with us. There was therefore very little modelling of ways to handle close friendly relationships.

The second influence to limit our opportunities and capacity to form friendships of any depth derived from a climate of social attitudes prevalent during the first part of the 20th century among 'the professional classes'. This was a widely held view that it was not appropriate for the local sheriff, doctors, lawyers, ministers and so on to mix too freely with the generality of the local population lest their professional role be prejudiced by over-familiarity. Happily that is now seen as an erroneous view but it nevertheless underwrote many of the constraints I felt so keenly as a boy. 'Remember you're the minister's son!' rang too often like a knell in my ears.

It is often said that many family patterns tend to recapitulate quite without conscious effort on the part of those concerned, but, beyond that, I have tended to the view that the very fact of growing up in a Scottish Presbyterian manse in the early 20th century conduced to some restriction and distortion of one's social world. There is no doubt in my own mind that that sort of background, manse inspired or not, played a large part in my eventual choice of career.

Chapter VI

A BID FOR FREEDOM

'If you cannot be free, be as free as you can.' (Emerson *Journals*, 1836)

Nearly three months of freedom followed my joyous departure from school and my Higher subjects had already largely determined that I would enrol in the Faculty of Arts at Aberdeen University early in October 1947. Following on from my short stay with Mrs Stuart at 339 Holburn Street, Aberdeen, during the Bursary Competition, it was agreed that I would move into 'digs' there in due course. But – there was the small matter of finding two pounds two shillings and sixpence every week of term to pay for bed, breakfast and an evening meal at her wholesome establishment. I would share a room with Kenny Cameron, the Gamrie minister's boy. There would be books and notebooks to be bought, fees to be paid and the time had come for me to begin to assert myself by wearing something other than a school uniform. I would save up for a new tweed sports jacket and flannels.

My parents did express some pleasure in my academic successes so far, but were already beginning to oppress me with homilies about working hard at university, keeping away from distractions like 'bad company', girls and drink – everything that I dreamed of! I even began to get paranoid about their having already primed Mrs Stuart to spy on me and report to the manse at regular intervals. They had not, of course, but because of what we might nowadays call their 'management style' up to the present, I could not help allowing such unworthy thoughts to enter my mind. I decided therefore, in a sudden drive for autonomy, to take a rest from all the mental endeavour of the past year and to engage in some physically challenging activities during the summer holidays before university in October. These were so planned as to get me out of the manse for long periods.

On previous autumn holidays during and after the war my brother and I had both worked on farms 'at the tatties' – potato lifting – and during the previous summer holidays I had worked for a week or two as a labourer harvesting at the farm of Paddocklaw, a few miles from home. Mr Milne, the farmer, or 'The Mannie', as he was known to his workers, was quite happy to take on a strong 'young loon' during future holiday periods. I was therefore ensured of work (and earnings) for several weeks during the second part of my holidays.

During the few weeks before that, I decided to cycle round the British Isles – a project that I had harboured for more than a year and had supported by a fairly strict training schedule on my old wartime 'black bike'. During the previous summer holidays, Sandy Kramer, a classmate, and I had undertaken a fairly lengthy tour of Scotland on our old wartime bikes. We stayed at Youth Hostels, made our own food when we arrived at each hostel, and pedalled about 50 or 60 miles per day. Even on our old machines, single geared and rusting, the bikes, that is, we could average about 12 mph.

Plate 20: Sandy Kramer and the author (right) setting out to cycle round Scotland in July 1946. It's interesting to compare the clothing and bikes with 21st century gear!

After school in the spring of 1946, we trained in the evenings by cycling from Banff to Huntly and return by a 42-mile circular route, Banff to Cornhill and Rothiemay to Huntly and home by Aberchirder. Occasionally we would reverse that route but that was less appealing. What we lived for on the first circuit was the long 10-mile run downhill from Aberchirder to Banff to end our trip. That was exhilarating.

For the big tour of 1947 I decided that the old 'Utility' black bike of the war years had to be sold and all my meagre savings (with some paternal help) would go toward a four gear, drop handlebar, blue and silver Rudge Pathfinder touring bike. It was still a long way from the lightweight miracles of engineering sported by present day lads, but I still remember the wonder and delight of buying it from Cheyne's of Aberdeen – also in Holburn Street. I took

Plate 21: The author setting out from Banff on a 2000 mile single handed tour of the UK, July 1947

the bus in to the city, collected the bike and cycled home, rejoicing in the luxury of using the four gears – with unnecessary frequency. My average speed shot up to 15 mph or more and I was home in Banff for a slightly late high tea. Sandy Kramer, brother Tom and my parents were there to 'Ooh' and 'Ah' with the rest. The round-Britain trip now seemed like a piece of cake!

Sandy and I planned our tour in detail and pre-booked all the Youth Hostels, north to south and back again. In the case of one or two like Edinburgh, Cambridge and London we allowed ourselves a day or two's rest to enjoy the local sights. Carrying no tent, we could not afford to chance getting in to some of the busier hostels at the height of summer – and, by pre-paying, we did not need to carry so much money with us. One night at each of eighteen hostels, provided we cooked all our own meals, cost a total of £1.7s (one shilling and sixpence a night) Even so, I bought myself a canvas money belt to carry the money I'd need on the way. I'd never before carried so much- all of £5! I began to wonder whether I was taking my quest for autonomy too far.

Then came a blow. We had never had any problems on previous cycling trips or otherwise and had seemed to find each other congenial company but a couple of nights before we were due to set off, Sandy announced that he was not going to come! He never gave me a reason. I wondered if he had just become a bit overawed at what we were undertaking or whether it was just laziness. It occurred to me also that his parents might have treated our proposals for the trip a bit light-heartedly, thinking we would never see them through. Then when it looked as if we were serious all along, they had chickened out of allowing his participation and he had been unwilling to tell me that.

In retrospect, I have often found it remarkable that my own parents were so tolerant and open in permitting me, only just seventeen, to take on such a venture, especially once they knew that I was to go alone. It is true that the roads were in those days much less busy than they are now. There were no motorways at all; some allegedly main roads were often little more than tortuous country lanes, and in Scotland, single track and with severe gradients. My equipment was primitive, largely Government surplus remaining from the war and I had to limit what I could reasonably carry if I were to keep up the daily mileages I had planned. Perhaps they were beginning to sense my drive for independence and self determination and I had underestimated their capacity to do so.

For myself, however, I had so built up my own expectations and had been so personally confident of success in my discussions with my parents and wee brother that I could not possibly withdraw from the project just because one of my pals had done so. The loss of face would have been altogether too much. So off I went, on my own, right on schedule.

The first day of that journey was indubitably the worst. The route was from Banff to Feughside Youth Hostel, near Banchory – not an unduly long or hard first stint. The first dozen miles were spent burning up the early adrenalin of initial excitement. Then came the rain, and the wind. It was right on my nose and in no time rivulets were running down the front of my yellow oilskin cape from the edge of which they assaulted my legs and feet with unremitting accuracy. The rain was not meant to penetrate the high collar of the cape but it still ran down from my hair under the collar and was gradually soaking my shirt. The cape too was offering so much wind resistance that fatigue soon began to conspire with ill temper and unmanly thoughts like 'Why the hell am I doing this, anyway?' and 'I've only done about twenty of the two thousand miles and I'm knackered,' began to chip away at my resolve.

But there was no way I could face returning to the manse and feebly declaring that I had given up at the first sign of adversity. That would have completely undermined the big plan to break away and assert my own identity which was what the trip was all about, at least in my own mind. Sandy's absence had simply emphasised the importance of my going it alone –

although I had no doubt that had he been pedalling and cursing alongside me in the rain and gale the travail would have been less. So my sodden feet were pressed even more firmly on the pedals and after an hour or two the wind and rain relented, the cape came off and my mood lightened. The reward for my dogged persistence on that first day was that I very seldom required to wear the rain cape at any other time on the whole trip.

The rolling wooded farmlands of Buchan gave way to more conifers and heather as I approached Deeside. Traffic was light and I was soon descending through Banchory from the north and down toward the Falls of Feugh, roaring over the rocks, brown and cream after the rain. As I pre-heated my little brass Primus stove in the Youth Hostel prior to preparing a simple meal I had time to assess the other hostellers and compare what seemed to be their attitudes with how I was feeling at the time.

Three Glaswegians were presiding over a billycan of unidentifiable 'stew' with multiple profane incantations but general good humour. They were chaffing a pleasant looking young girl with a familiarity that led me to believe that they were one party but she soon tired of their banter and went off to chat with a couple of young cyclists who had arrived just as wet as I was and were draping clothes over a line near the stoves which we had all got going by now.

Another pair of cyclists from the Scottish Midland belt, including a heavily built and foul-mouthed thug, leered at all the young girls with ill-disguised lasciviousness. He may have sensed my concern – and innocence – for he opened his horny hand to show me a contraceptive. 'I'll be intae the wids wi' her efter ma supper!' he intoned to all and sundry. It was probably the first time that I'd actually seen a 'Frenchie' as we were wont to call them. The scene and setting were all quite unlike the manse.

Several of the hostellers went for a walk after their meal, including the girl and the thug, but the outcome of the drama was never known – to me anyway! Two or three of us went to watch the falls, and any salmon that might be jumping. We exchanged notes in a rather desultory fashion about our day and the plans for tomorrow but little of those interchanges could be said to contain any sort of self-revelation on the part of any of us. Back in the hostel I checked my gear for the morrow and rested my weary bones. The day had been physically and emotionally quite taxing. 'This must be the independence I'm after,' I thought. But it was at a price.

The planning of the trip had set about 60 miles a day for the first few days and slightly longer stints thereafter as fitness improved. Day two dawned fair and the next challenge was the climb up the Cairn o' Mount, scenically beautiful but lonely and a hard climb in the course of which I was, even with my four gears, reduced to walking the bike up some of the steepest bits. On one of these, in thickening hill fog pierced only by the keening cries of buzzards and curlew and other strange animal noises, I watched as two unusually large hill rams engaged in some very fierce mutual butting. The victor stared me out as the vanquished fled downhill into the heather and made as if to assault me as his next competitor. I expected him to run off but he stood his ground as I approached and I looked around for some hefty stone to deter him with should he charge. I felt at a distinct disadvantage as I pushed the heavily loaded bike up the long hill. If I re-mounted and tried to pedal in my lowest gear I'd have made little more progress, and almost no faster. I was certainly not going to retreat downhill. Surrounded by some of the oldest hills in the world, I could see many boulders which were beyond my powers to lift and myriad stones which were too small to be effective but nothing fist-sized that might have constituted minor armament. The big black-face stood facing me in the middle of the single-track road as the distance shortened to several feet. I shouted some ill-defined imprecation inviting him to depart in peace – 'Bugger off, you black faced bastard!' was what it sounded like, and lo and behold, he did!

The descent from the summit of the Cairn was, though it tested both brakes and nerve, exhilarating and the sun again broke through as I wove my way through the red earth of the Mearns toward Brechin. I was to see much more of that locale in due course, but that is another story. My target for the day was the charming cliff-girt village of Auchmithie, near Arbroath, where I took the opportunity to telephone my parents (at Banff 107 – there were few telephones in those days) and to wander over the beach below the cliffs in search of the agates which abound in that area. The run to Edinburgh the next day was uneventful, but for the novelty of waiting for the ferry to transport bike and self across the Forth at North Queensferry. The railway bridge was as russet and imposing as ever but the road bridge was then no more than a dream.

My self-confidence was increasing by the day and I remember catching up with two other cyclists on the outskirts of the city and riding alongside them as we exchanged notes about our trips. They had hostelled in Edinburgh before and were able to accompany me directly to the hostel at Hailes House where, for the first time, it was possible to purchase a cheap evening meal rather than crouch over the Primus once more. Sheer luxury! – and 177 miles completed.

The following three days saw me climb over Soutra Hill and down through Lauder and Carfraemill as I headed for Jedburgh and the hostel at Ferniehirst Castle – very grand but a bit bare and functional – and then on over the border at Carter Bar, another long uphill slog, and down again into England. I was in alien territory now and half expected to be harried by the ghosts of 'Proud Edward's Army' or even more literally oppressed by these 'foreigners' with their funny posh accents. It turned out that I was much more oppressed by the Romans and their propensity for making long straight roads up and down hill and dale with no thought to contouring more gently for young cycling hopefuls like me. The switchbacks from Otterburn to

Edmundbyers where I was to spend one night were wearisome in the extreme. Every time I drive over them nowadays I am reminded of that long hard afternoon the first time I traversed them. On I went next day to Barnard Castle, a very busy and popular hostel with cyclists in particular, where I was now able to enter into the spirit of the cycling confraternity and swap tales of derring-do with the hard men of the National Clarion and other major cycle racing clubs. The simple fact that I'd pedalled over 300 miles to get there accorded me suitable accreditation.

I had never previously been aware that there were clubs of cyclists on pared-down lightweight machines who road-raced every weekend in time and distance trials in the course of which they covered nearly 25 miles in an hour! These young bloods could be recognised by their massive calves and thighs, bikes that you could lift up with a finger, and no heavy panniers or stove. They sported only a soft cloth bag over their shoulders and one or perhaps two drinking bottles clipped to the chassis bar which went from just below the handlebars to the crank. Some even had goggles and baseball caps on back to front. This was 'the big time'! They were inclined to scorn the cycling hostellers who had pedalled up for the weekend from Darlington or York as effete picnickers. Unexpectedly, they became quite pally with me when they discovered I had come all the way from Banff (which they had never heard of) and that I was in the course of a virtually non-stop circuit of the UK. In the morning they invited me to join them as they departed and I did my best to keep up with them, on through Darlington, for 20 miles or so before I gave up and settled for the rest of the day to my more normal pace.

My target for the day was York and the hot pace of the early morning had made what was the longer than usual run seem less forbidding. Happily, the weather had by now become hot and sunny and the long, flat Vale of York shimmered under a pale blue heat haze. I pedalled on, revelling in the luxury of flat country after the ups and downs of the Borders and Northumberland. In Northallerton, the old town quiet in the sun, I visited a small grocery to replenish my food supply and buy some stamps. My genial summer mood was then shattered by the sudden revelation that I was an alien in this country. On being offered a Scottish pound note in payment of my purchases, the rather cool and sniffy lady behind the counter stubbornly refused to accept it. 'We don't take 'em foreign notes 'ere. They ain't legal currency.' I remonstrated, saying that I'd had no difficulty in the last shop, also English, that I'd visited. She was, however, adamant and pointed to a Post Office where I could change the note for a 'proper English one'. Had I seen another suitable shop nearby, I would most certainly have done my business there, but time was short and I needed to be on my way. So I gave in and sheepishly returned to pay for my milk, sausages, eggs, biscuits and a tin of steam pudding with an English pound note.

This acid rejection of my honest Scottish cash was so unlike the open acceptance that I had received from my English Clarion Club racers of the morning that I began to wonder whether my reception by this southern race would gradually become more hostile as I wended my way south. One of the disadvantages of cycling long distances is that there is plenty of time to turn over such thoughts in the absence of any other soul with whom to discuss matters. Cars, lorries and buses could whizz past, but only very occasionally would one meet up with a fellow cyclist or two. When that did happen, one had then to consider, not whether there might be a clash of personalities, but whether keeping in company with him, her or, more commonly, them, would either hamper by forcing a slower pace or exhaust by having to press on unduly speedily as I had done earlier that day. As it happened, that exigency did not arrive that day, so my transit of the pleasant country towns of Thirsk and Easingwold was one of unalloyed pleasure, enhanced by my very first experience of a purpose built cycle track running alongside the main road. For ten miles or so I rejoiced in that six-foot-wide strip of reddish tarmac free from the buffeting of vehicles which gave me too little clearance and with no need to refer to my map.

In late afternoon, the Gothic towers of York Minster appeared on the horizon just in time to counter my deepening fatigue. The heat had taken its toll. I was headachy and I needed to drink more. By the time I had reached the Youth Hostel I was ready to slump on my bed but decided to slake my thirst, get on with making a meal, and head out again in the evening to explore the ancient and historic old city. In the end, all I could manage was a visit to the Shambles, the Minster and the Walls. Over my meal that evening, however, I had met in with a small group of hostellers who had been in each other's company that day and were due to continue south like me. Three of them were girls from France. It turned out that my schoolboy French (remember I was fresh from my Highers which included that language!) was slightly better than their English so they gravitated to me as a welcome change from the monoglot English they had been travelling with. As a consequence, much of my evening in York was spent with Marie-Thérèse.

She turned out to be nearly two years older than I but we got along well. She was good looking, relaxed and vivacious and was spending some months travelling prior to going to university in France. Both of us were deeply impressed by our half-hour in the Minster. A Roman Catholic, Marie-Thérèse knelt in prayer. She told me as we wandered back to the Hostel that her parents had farmed near Caen for many years but she was praying that they would recover both personally, financially and emotionally from the terrible loss of their farm during the war. The battle for Normandy had raged furiously over their land, flattening the farmhouse and most of the farm buildings. They were living temporarily in Caen until the ravages of war could be restored but she feared that her father's heart was broken by the loss of his land and his animals. It was then that she told me, with a wry smile, that her family name was Le Râsle. It meant 'death rattle!'

In contrast with the cosy parochialism of a Scottish country kirk, the Minster, with its soaring vaulted roof, memorials and solemn atmosphere enhanced by quiet organ music moved me to a mood, if not of devotion, but rather quiet meditation. Its history weighed on my shoulders but its function still left me sceptical.

Returning to the hostel through the Shambles there was a funny little episode which hinted at the simple bonding process that can occur, quite unplanned, between fellow travellers. At one of these shops which specialises in all the worst, taste-free examples of tourist tat, we all six of us went in and each of us bought a bicycle-shaped brooch bearing the York coat of arms. Not too long ago I caught sight of mine in a tin box in the house. It had probably lain there for the near sixty years since it came off the red polo-neck sweater where it had been pinned under the red and white SYHA (Scottish Youth Hostels Association) badge. I wondered about the fate of the others.

In spite of the fatigue I had felt earlier, Marie-Thérèse and I talked quite late into the night, each of us doing our best with the other's language. As the others left for their bunks, it emerged that the French girls had decided, in the interests of having more time in Cambridge, to take the train there, bikes and all, in the morning. We planned to continue our conversation when I reached Cambridge in two days' time. There were now two girls in my life, the girl from the Bursary Comp. and the girl from Caen. And yet I perceived them differently. The first, whose name I did not even know, had stirred me in a way which Marie-Thérèse had not and yet there was a spontaneous rapport between us which we both seemed to recognise and value.

Before I slept, it dawned on me that in little more than a week and three hundred miles away from home, my project was working. I had grown in physical strength, independence, personal assurance and a clearer notion of who I really was. I was not 'remembering who I was', I was discovering who I was.

The name of my next destination was not one that inspired me with confidence. It had the entomologically threatening name of Tickhill, near Doncaster and was to take me through some of the more heavily industrial parts of south Yorkshire. I crossed the river Ouse in Selby in the first rain I'd seen since those miserable, sodden first hours of my trip. It wept for the Yorkshire workers waiting in the dole queue and the silent dockside cranes. Yet I was happily directed toward Doncaster by a cheery housewife whose gestures were unequivocal but whose lilting south Yorkshire accent left me grasping for meaning. 'Eh, lad, ye'll easy find Tickle on't rod to Worksop!' So off I pedalled again toward the slag heaps, shunting yards and stark, frowning factories of Doncaster. 'Tickle', for that is what it sounded like to me, crept up on me through the nondescript mix of industry, field and hedgerow. This grey land shyly hid itself from me in a mix of smoke and drizzle as if it were aware of the inner contrasts I was drawing between what I now traversed and the clean, brisk air and open land of the north. Its reticence was entirely understandable.

Tickhill was no more than a handy staging post. The hostel was less than half full but the relatively shorter run I'd had that day allowed of a better than usual evening meal. A day-old *Daily Mirror* left in the kitchen by a previous hosteller offered a chance to catch up on what was happening in the wider world. Clearly, the world was wholly sustained by squabbling politicians – 'He was called to resign!' – nearly naked dancing girls, – 'How'd ye like a pair like this in your back yard?' and footballers with strangely long shorts – 'The Rovers need supporters too!'

I wished I'd brought a book but settled for close scrutiny of the map for tomorrow's leg to near Grantham. It promised more rural surroundings and an end to the rain. It kept its promise. I opted for a more easterly route by East Retford, Newark and the A1 since it seemed flatter. Later I wished I had headed for Worksop and on through Sherwood Forest simply to establish for myself whether this was a place where Robin Hood might have created all the myths. Instead, I did make fast progress, though at the cost of breathing diesel exhaust and suffering constant buffeting from the busy traffic on the A1. Nowadays, Tickhill is just off the ceaseless throb of the M1 but then, even the A1 had only a few stretches of dual carriageway and I was never again to find the luxury of a dedicated cycle track as I had near Easingwold.

An hour's brisk pedalling did, however, take me again into the rural scene, through East Retford, about which I remember little, and on to a fairly boring stretch of road to Newark. After the usual stop there to re-provision there was just the business of surviving the increasingly heavy traffic and burning off the miles. It would be pleasant to report that these solitary hours gave an opportunity to consider the great verities and think great thoughts. I cannot – and have never met a cyclist who could make such a claim. What one does find is that the rhythm of the physical effort takes over and one finds oneself matching some silly melody to the steady whirr of the wheels and the tempo of one's breathing and the pressure on the pedals. One that I remember as fitting the situation quite well was a tune from the Laurel and Hardy films called the Donkey Serenade. It seemed to match my rhythm in top gear at about fifteen miles per hour. It was all pretty thalamic stuff and my prefrontal lobes did not have much to do with it.

I remember little about the Grantham hostel except that it seemed enormously grand in a passé kind of way. Those I shared it with that night seemed strangely aloof and kept to their tight little in-groups. I was beginning to see something of the southern attitude to northerners – of whatever country and the conviviality of York or Barnard Castle or Edinburgh. Yes, Edinburgh even, was missing. But I slept well in the knowledge that the next night would see me in Cambridge and, I hoped, the company of my young French friend.

The morning was brilliant. It was the rule that every hosteller had to carry out a task specified by the Warden before he got his membership card back and could go on his way. Mine was to clean two of the windows, inside and out. My damp rag and squeegee were plied to the soaring melody of a couple of skylarks, unabashed by a relatively uninspiring environment so long as they had five or six acres of grassland to nest in. My mood lifted accordingly to match that of Shelley's 'Blithe Spirit':

> Higher still and higher
> > From the earth thou springest
> Like a cloud of fire;
> > The blue deep thou wingest,
> And singing still dost soar, and soaring ever singest ...
>
> What objects are the fountains
> > Of thy happy strain?
> What fields, or waves, or mountains?
> > What shapes of sky or plain?
> What love of thine own kind? What ignorance of pain?
> > With thy keen joyance
> Languor cannot be:
> > Shadow of annoyance
> Never came near thee:
> > Thou lovest; but ne'er knew love's sad satiety.

What romanticism was this that had so subtly infiltrated my consciousness that such verses could spring to mind? The Highers were finished. I didn't need the quotations: but the sun shone, the window panes shone, the larks still trilled in the blue, and I expected to see Marie-Thérèse that evening. There was just the small matter of another seventy-five miles or so. The faster I did it, the sooner I'd see her. 'The Donkey Serenade' turned into 'The Dashing White Sergeant'.

Over the first twenty-four miles to Stamford I made good time, good enough for me to spend a half-hour enjoying the fine Georgian houses in mellow, golden stone and watching the small boats on the River Welland which flowed right through the town. Because I'd run out of paraffin for my Primus stove, I spent a little of my cash on a scone and a cup of tea. Disreputable though I must have seemed to the casual observer, a well-spoken old chap lingering over his cup opposite me was apparently glad to dispense a little of his town's history. Apparently the religious orders in Norman times had built many houses and schools and the town also prospered in the 12th century through the wool trade and later through the passing trade afforded by the stagecoaches. He twinkled, 'Just like this teashop's doing from you!' I wryly credited my presence and limited expenditure with negligible effect on the Stamford economy. But I had enjoyed our conversation, even if he'd never heard of Banff, and I began to think that not all the English were bad.

It was in the café that I noticed a spot on my right arm which was a bit sore and seemed very inflamed. I remembered having seen what looked like a cleg or horse-fly settle there soon after leaving Grantham but I had brushed it off – not soon enough, it seemed. Two hours later, as I laboured up the long Alconbury Hill five or six miles out of Huntingdon, every irregularity of the road surface was translating itself into a throbbing equivalent halfway between my wrist and my elbow. I felt hotter than I should have done even in the misty summer sun and more tired than I should have done now that my general fitness was not in doubt. There had appeared a nasty boil-like lump but the best I could do was to find a chemist in Huntingdon who could sell me some analgesic/antiseptic cream. Normally, I'd have been taking a keen interest in the nearby aircraft activity round RAF Alconbury and the leisurely river scene in Huntingdon. Another fine town with a goodly share of Georgian buildings, it had been the birthplace of such different souls as Samuel Pepys and the Protector, Cromwell. As it was, I was feeling too miserable to explore it for anything other than pain relief.

The last flat, straight sixteen miles to Cambridge took just over an hour but it had seemed an age. I tried cycling with only my left arm on the handlebars but the right seemed to throb just as much hanging limp as it had done while in its normal position. Even the sight of Ely Cathedral, clear, though sixteen miles off to my left, whose great tower had guided travellers since the Middle Ages over the flat fenland for twenty miles around, failed to excite me as it should have. In due course I found my way to the Youth Hostel where I decided that cooking my own meal was not something that attracted me. I would spend all of 1/6 (about 15p in modern cash) on a cooked meal in the dining room. The tough self-sufficiency that made me consider this English habit effete and unmanly had crumbled in the face of my temporary weakness.

Nevertheless, I went thereafter to the washroom to change my shirt and wash the one I'd been wearing. Lo and behold! There was one of Marie-Thérèse's friends busily engaged in her own laundry. "Allo, Daveed! Ça va? I go tell M-T!' My arm felt better, but still looked nasty.

Almost immediately, it seemed, Marie-Thérèse appeared, smiling a warm welcome which suddenly disappeared when she saw what looked like a huge boil on my arm. 'Ooh là là! I 'ave been talking viz an Americain here who is 'alf a doctor. Je vais le chercher de ta part.' I was not too befuddled to miss the 'ta' rather than 'votre' but was unsure whether the usage was that as to a child or to an intimate. I just hoped.

In a few minutes she returned with her pals and a handsome young American who explained that he was half-way through a medical degree in USA. He took a look and opined that I needed surgery – within the next five minutes! A stove was got going and he asked if my pocket knife was sharp. I was proud of the fact that both blades were well honed at all times. The smaller of the two (it had a better point) was then held in the flame and the surgeon advanced on me with intent. Unlike most of the Westerns I'd seen, there was no preliminary half-bottle of whisky to swig down, no gag to bite on and a singular lack of drama – all quite disappointing. There was, however, a growing and interested audience in the laundry room, including Marie-Thérèse. I would take it like a man!

My saviour ran the cold tap in one of the sinks, rubbed around the area of the boil with some meths from someone's Primus supply and cotton wool from the warden, asked me to hold the arm under the tap and promptly lanced the arm efficiently and effectively. It would be wrong to suggest that it did not hurt but there was a satisfying eruption of pus and gunge which he cleaned up further with a cotton bud. There was also a sudden relief of pressure and pain, apart from the sting of the cut. He filled the significant hole which remained in my arm with the antiseptic I had bought in Huntingdon, bound up the arm with a bandage also supplied by the warden and we all went out for a drink. I felt better already!

Cambridge in the warmth of that sunny summer evening was totally engaging. It more than lived up to my fantasies of what an ancient university town should be. We gazed into the quadrangles of some of the historic old colleges, wondered at the sight of the occasional young Don in his black gown flapping by like a low-flying bat on a bicycle and hung over the bridges to watch the last of the day's punters.

It may have been sympathy for my fragile post-operative condition, but Marie-Thérèse was solicitous that I should not be bumped by the others. She took my other arm and by accident or design we lagged behind as we wandered along The Backs, talking in our funny mix of English and French. She wanted to hear about farming in Scotland, the sort of school I had gone to – and about why I was travelling alone so far from home. It was heady stuff, for I had never previously talked at length to any girl about anything very much – and certainly not to an attractive girl who seemed interested not only in what I had to say but in me as a person. How could I be the son of *un prêtre* and not be religious, she wanted to know. She had some doubts but she thought she would find it hard not to be a Catholic. She did not plan to read philosophy at university but thought that it might still be interesting.

I was quite bowled over by this charming *gamine* who unaffectedly took my hand as we walked back to the hostel. When she suggested that it might be better for me to stay another night in Cambridge to make sure that my arm was not going to give further trouble – and reminded me that she would not be moving off to London for another couple of days, I was an easy conversion.

As it happened, my next planned leg of the journey was to London to stay for a long weekend with my aunt Mary (my mother's eldest sister) in Sydenham. I was sure she would not be too worried if I turned up a day late.

Not so many people had a telephone in these days and as she was one such, there was no way I could communicate directly with her. She was a resilient sort of person, as was my married cousin, Millie, who lived with her. Having been bombed out three times during the war, losing all her possessions each time, to say nothing of her husband and son, the process prepared her well for any later vicissitudes that life might fling at her.

We all made cocoa when we returned to the hostel and the group chatter dissipated somewhat the excitement and emotional warmth I had felt in this girl's company. It was hardly believable that we had met only a few days ago and yet now knew so much about each other. I certainly liked her very much and she seemed to enjoy my company. My naïvety showed up, however, when the Warden, who had allowed us all extra time already, finally called 'Lights Out' and we had to head for our separate dormitories. Marie-Thérèse hung back in the corridor with me, put her hand on my arm, and looked up at me, very close. 'Bonne nuit, David. Dors bien.' I took her other hand and reciprocated the wish. It was only when I got to bed that I realised she had wanted me to kiss her. That would now have to await the morrow. I hoped she would feel the same then. But there had never been moments, or hours, like this in the manse!

In the morning, the young American insisted on changing the bandage on my arm but reassured me by saying it looked OK. He thought it was a good idea for me to spend a lazy day and go on to London later and shot off on his own venture. I was very grateful to him, even if the arm was still a bit sore.

That day passed in a blur of new impressions, not only of the city but also of myself. Marie-Thérèse's friends went off to try their hands at punting on the river while we bought a few things for a picnic and decided to explore some of the back lanes and villages on our bikes. She was keen to have a look at Girton, the ladies' college, and later we wandered south toward Fulbourn. Virtually part of the city now, the centre of Fulbourn then was a typical English village green surrounded by pinkish houses and an old church, quaint with its flinty walls and pantiles.We found it was dedicated to one, St Vigor, a sixth century Bishop of Bayeux, whose name seemed to have been brought to England by the Normans. Not unnaturally, Marie-Thérèse was thrilled about this and was sure she would investigate the matter on her return to Normandy. She could cycle to Bayeux quite easily. 'Trente-deux kilometres de chez moi, seulement!' she declared, with such an air of finality that I was convinced she would.

We brewed up with my Primus in a sheltered shrubby patch near a tributary of the Cam, ate our sandwiches and apples and talked at length about ourselves. Several times I was acutely aware that she was eighteen and I a year younger, chronologically, and perhaps even more emotionally. But I was sure that I would have tried to continue this relationship, no matter how tenuous, had she lived an awful lot nearer Banff than she did. We exchanged addresses and promised to write to each other as soon as we got home again. Yes, we kissed – several times – and I think she was better at it than I was!

Unfortunately, like so many teenage romances, ours, in spite of many letters in both directions, petered out after a couple of years. During vacations, some of these arrived at the manse and I, to my huge irritation, was subjected to vigorous interrogation especially by my mother about 'that French girl you seem to have taken up with'. 'You can't know much about her background or her parents or anything!' She was still afraid that I'd miss out on Princess Margaret. However, the worm was turning and I reasserted my capacity to judge what was good for me in no uncertain manner. I'd probably have been less firm a year or two ago. My parents retreated, bristling.

Marie-Thérèse and I went off to our respective universities, were too poor to arrange any sort of meeting either in France or Scotland, and eventually she was the first to declare that she had found a young Frenchman as a new soul mate. Up till then I had been too chicken-hearted to tell her that for some months I had become obsessed by my Brechin (for that was where I had found out she lived) lass with the bouncy hair. I must admit that I have often wondered what became of Marie-Thérèse, because even the few days I had known her were for both of us an enjoyable and wholly good experience, in every sense.

We had a sad parting the following morning but since we had promised early letters to each other and the hope of meeting perhaps the following year, I pedalled my way brightly, a four-speed Dick Whittington, to see whether the streets of London were paved with gold. It was another long haul but the weather remained fabulous and my arm seemed to be healing quickly. I made fast time through Royston and Buntingford to Ware, thirty-three miles in just over two hours, but the progressively built-up areas of outer London slowed me simply because I needed to check my navigation more frequently and because there was so much more traffic to negotiate. As a result, the next thirty miles needed half as much time again and was more tiring.

I found the scale of things had changed dramatically. Till now I had enjoyed more or less the freedom of the road and bowled along under wide skies and with the woods, fields and hedgerows offering a constant kaleidoscope of changing patterns all of which seemed almost a complement to my physical effort. Now, the oppressive press of dull architecture, the frequent halts for traffic lights, the near-misses from red buses, all seemed hostile and threatening – and, although I found half a crown in the gutter at one point – there was no gold in the streets at all. London was entirely new to me. This was, after all, the first time in my life I'd been in England and the sheer size of the conurbation was something I could only wonder at.

Wearied though I was by the long haul down through Enfield, Tottenham and Shoreditch, no sooner had I reached the Thames Embankment than I felt reinvigorated by the famous sights of London then laid before me. In fact, I probably added a mile or two to my route by following the Embankment west all the way to Westminster, doubling back up Whitehall to round the Nelson Monument in Trafalgar Square and then head south again past Westminster Abbey and the Houses of Parliament. This was the London of the *Children's Encyclopedia* and the geography books, of myth and of history. It may have been England – but I was impressed and intended to return the next day for a fuller exploration. But time was short if I was to reach Auntie Mary's at Crystal Palace Park Road, SE26, before tea time. So I cracked on past the Elephant and Castle, Camberwell and Dulwich toward Sydenham and Penge.

By then the excitement of Whitehall and the rest had faded and the busy anonymity of the city crowded in on me. Only as I passed through the poorer areas did I actually see many people stop to talk to each other and I found myself fantasising about what all the others in the taxis, great trucks and bustling about in the streets were thinking. Many looked as if they were not thinking very much at all, just worrying. Not many were on bicycles.

It would be good to see aunt Mary again. I had seen her only once when she visited Lochgelly some years ago while we were there. She was a bulky lady and that visit caused some consternation about the bedding arrangements there. I remembered her as being quite jolly though she was inclined to disparage people she did not like, unlike my mother who could disparage anybody. My married cousin Millie, ten years my senior, and her husband, Bill, lived with her in a second floor flat in Crystal Palace Park Road. The prospect of a proper bed, a bath and a meal began to encourage a faster pace. I even found out that Crystal Palace Park Road was actually named on my map of greater London and therefore relatively easy to find.

The house in question was approached through a small drive. It was obvious that it had once been a rather grand private house of some distinction, now reconstructed as several flats and apparently untouched by the ravages of war compared to some of the quite large areas of destroyed and bomb-damaged shops and homes I'd seen on the way. On these, rosebay willow herb now smothered the memories of laughing children, doors banging, till bells tinkling and the rows and the badinage of working women. Here there was a strange silence as I climbed the stairs to the second floor flat and rang the bell. I rang it again and heard it ring inside. There was no other sound. Certainly not that of approaching footsteps. Mildly frustrated, for I had written some weeks ago to say when I'd reach London, I banged the door quite heavily.

At that, there was a movement from the flat below and a middle-aged woman emerged to scrutinise my bike and panniers leaning against the wall near her door and then cast a bilious eye over myself. She was apparently not much taken with what she saw.

'You lookin' for Mrs Wickens, then?' she asked with a slightly hostile air. 'She ain't 'ere. Some Scotch friends of hers came 'ere a couple of days ago and they've all gone off for an 'oliday. The 'ole lot of 'em.'

Deflated, I shuffled downstairs and explained who I was and my circumstances. That seemed to mollify her a bit and she said she'd have given me a bed for the night if she'd had room – but she hadn't.

'I tell you wot! I'll get the phone number they left me of where they are an' you can give 'em a ring.' 'Use my phone!' she added generously.

She might not have been so generous if she had known how long it took me to get through to aunt Mary. The phone number was for the holiday camp at which they were staying, at a place near Chale, along with three or four hundred others. Then the staff there had to check in which chalet Mrs Wickens was berthed before putting through the call. Eventually a rather shocked Mrs Wickens told me how she'd written me a letter a fortnight ago to say they would be away and I would need to find a hostel for the night. Of course that letter had only reached Banff one or more days after I had left and would be waiting, unopened, my return.

Explaining that there was no way I could find a place for the night in a Youth Hostel in or around London at such short notice, I suggested I might find a cheap B&B. She then proposed that I ride down to the Isle of Wight and stay for a day or two with them in the holiday camp. She clearly credited me with more physical and mental resilience than I thought I had. It was nearly 4.30 p.m., I had just cycled 75 miles already that day and was not really in the mood to double that. 'We'll wait up for you', she intoned. 'Just come in the gates and head for the third last chalet on the left on the row nearest the sea.' So off I set again, heading for the Portsmouth Road.

Again, greater London brushed against me all the way through Epsom and only when I reached the Leatherhead area and got beyond Guildford did I begin again to admire what was, in the late sunshine, rather a pleasant piece of countryside. Many a wistful glance did I cast at the folk now gathering round tables outside the country pubs, their working day ended and feeling none of the concern I was now experiencing about perhaps not reaching Portsmouth in time for the last ferry to the Isle of Wight. By the time I had reached Petersfield I had lost interest in the countryside and could see nothing but the miles to Portsmouth on the signposts – and it was not just because, even in midsummer, the light was beginning to go. A quick spurt for the last eighteen miles took me right into Portsmouth and no more map reading for navigation. I forgot my pride and simply stopped and asked people the quickest route to the ferry. There was only one more that night and it was almost ready to leave for the short crossing to Ryde. I carried my bike up the gangway and slumped on a bench in the cabin where, happily I could enjoy a sumptuous meal of a cup of tea and (no expense spared!) two slices of fruit cake.

The street lights were coming on in Ryde when it dawned on me that I would need to remember to swing the little dynamo against the side of my rear tyre to power my lights. I had not bargained for pedalling into the night, but my most direct route to Chale, at the very southernmost part of the Island, was by several secondary roads and lanes where I would need to be seen by any other traffic. It came as something of a surprise to me that the island was so hilly, or maybe four or five hundred feet eminences just seemed so much more tiring to an exhausted young man. I remember signpost names like Downend and Rockley but had no wish to linger. It was now quite dark and I was ready to look for a barn or haystack where I could simply lie down and stop pedalling. But I knew that if I did, I would sleep immediately, and for many hours.

Then, suddenly, a signpost proclaimed Chale and I was briefly stronger again. There was even, reassuringly, a separate sign for the holiday camp, still over a mile away. In due course I cycled right past the gatehouse unchallenged, turned left, found the right chalet with a light in the window and virtually collapsed at cousin Millie's feet as she opened the door. She and her husband, Bill, were the occupants of that hut. Aunt Mary's was next door, but they had two beds and would double up in one single while I was afforded the other. My final bravado of that very long day was to pretend that I was fresh and that 145 miles on a bike in a day was easy. In fact, my legs were like lead and my whole body was screaming for sleep. I swore to myself never to try 145 miles a day again – and I never did!

Bill gave me a can of beer and a packet of crisps as I climbed into bed. I had protested that I could sleep on the floor but they insisted I take his bed. They probably thought I was as tired as I must have looked. My polite protests were weak and when he shook me awake at breakfast time I found that I had finished neither.

It was considered that I needed two days to recover from my marathon before heading back to the mainland and the road north. There was certainly no way I could cycle further south and remain in the UK. How it was wangled by my relatives I never knew, but I simply accompanied them to the canteen for every meal they took, ate heartily, played table tennis and football, took a dip in the pool or the sea (in my cousin Charlie's swimming pants) enjoyed the odd half pint in the evening. They all went dancing later but, in my khaki ex-Desert Rats shorts and sweaty shirts I would have been less than *persona grata*.

Cousin Millie, who I was seeing for the first time, seemed to spend, for a woman ten years my senior, rather more time with me than I found entirely comfortable and could even become flirtatious, even in her husband's presence. Maybe I was in the process of substantiating my psychological independence compared to how I had been in the manse, but this was beginning to rock the boat a bit and I was glad to leave and settle down to the more monk-like daily habits of a north-bound long range cyclist. Thus were my anticipated days in the Metropolis replaced by the disinhibited, noisy, jolly and largely proletarian drunken fiesta of a holiday camp with an accounting and security system so lax that my additional presence in its midst was never noticed from the time I entered till I cycled out on the third day there. I could never have paid for it since I was by now down to not much more than £2 to see me home to Banff. I had set out with a fiver in my money belt and the cousins had all generously chipped in for beer money and even the price of the longer ferry from Cowes to Southampton. That allowed me to see more of the Island as well as to shorten my route to Streatley in Oxfordshire where I had a place booked in the hostel.

It would be tedious to detail much of the rest of my trip. In Winchester I put off a little time to look at the Guildhall and to shop for my evening meal. Newbury I bypassed, turning off on to the B4009 for the final hour. The rolling, wooded countryside, interspersed with what I thought were very attractive villages, even with greens and cricketers, was doing its best to stereotype what I had always thought it would be like in England. Somehow it went with the posh accents and the slightly stuffy attitudes I had come up against from the few casual conversations I had on my way. To get back to talking with other cyclists, walkers, and, as I remember, at Streatley, canoeists, was friendly and relaxing.

The next day took me through Oxford where I was able to compare the 'dreaming spires' with those of Cambridge. Perhaps my memories of the latter were enhanced by emotional overtones which had little or nothing to do with Academia – but I did prefer it. It was also, of course, a busy commercial city for which the motor trade sustained a large proportion of its non-academic population. As I progressed later that day through Woodstock, past Chipping Norton – a strange name to a northerner's ears – and Shipston on Stour, the weather, which had been remarkable throughout my trip, was very hot and I was perspiring freely on many of the long slow climbs over the wolds. Twice I succumbed to thirst and, not remembering who I was, pulled off the road into country pubs with Falstaffian names on their signboards like 'The Woolsack and Crown' or 'The Golden Wheatsheaf' to order a shandy – strong drink, and me not even eighteen! But I fought back the guilt, just as my brother Tom and I had when we sampled the Communion wine back in the manse and topped up the bottles with water, on the basis that if He could do it to water at a wedding in Cana, He could do it anytime. Yes, I suppose I was gaining in confidence without quite becoming a hopeless psychopath.

My target was the grand looking but very busy Youth Hostel at Alveston Manor, near Stratford on Avon. I had reserved a place there for two nights in the expectation that I might explore the town, the stamping ground of one of the most remarkable men of all history, and also give me a better chance of being able to book a seat in the then new Shakespeare Memorial Theatre. Its setting, amidst weeping willows on the river bank where swans and other river fowl paraded seemed to me suitably romantic. The box office told me that I could get a stalls' ticket for *Troilus and Cressida* on my second night so I was able, before then, to visit the usual sites, the birthplace, Anne Hathaway's cottage and so on, soaking up as much of the atmosphere as the constantly bustling crowds of tourists would allow. They were, in 1947, just getting into their swing following the widespread restrictions of wartime and in the absence of much foreign travel then, places like Stratford were heavily overloaded.

When, eager to see a stunning cast perform a play I was not then familiar with, I turned up in my cycling shorts and shirt, only to be told that I was not properly dressed to enter the body of the theatre. I remonstrated, recalling Petruchio's comment in *The Taming of the Shrew*, which seemed to be exactly what I was doing with the box office lady,

> Our purses shall be proud, our garments poor;
> For 'tis the mind that makes the body rich;
> And as the sun breaks through the darkest clouds
> So honour peereth in the meanest habit.

She relented a little and was finally persuaded that I, in my meanest habit, might stand unobtrusively at the back of the stalls, provided that I slipped in after nearly everybody had taken their seats and that I slipped out again before the final grand exodus. Agreement was also reached that, as I was not getting a seat, I be refunded half of the cost of the ticket I had bought the previous day.

Back in the hostel that night, I found myself impatient with the prattle of the cyclists and hikers after the resonances and complexity of speech and thought I had come from.

> As in a theatre the eyes of men
> After a well grac'd actor leaves the stage
> Are idly bent on him that enters next,
> Thinking his prattle to be tedious.
> (York, in *Richard II*, 5. 2. 23)

I reflected that my first experience of Shakespeare being acted had been at one of Donald Wolfit's 'over the top' performances of *Macbeth* in His Majesty's Theatre in Aberdeen. He had, with his gross overacting and personalised tricks of speech come close to converting the Scottish play from a tragedy to a comedy. Now I had been captivated by the way in which the cast in Stratford had brought the play alive. Their trick of making elaborate Shakespearean speeches sound just like normal conversation, changing slightly the tempo and inflections yet keeping the scansion where necessary, between people who knew each other in all their moods somehow gave a new life to the read or written word. As soon as I got home I read the play.

My next day's ride allowed me further glimpses of the best of English rural scenery through Worcester, where I spent an hour looking around, and on up into deepest Shropshire where I was due at a hostel called Wilderhope Hall and reputed to be haunted. It was in Worcester that I met in with cyclists who were travelling at least for part of the way with me toward Church Stretton. Initially they thought I must have taken my bike on the train from Scotland. They had come from the Bristol area and found it hard to grasp that I had cycled alone all the way from north Scotland. In the course of the morning I discovered just how fit I had become and was constantly having to wait for them to catch up.

We talked much more about Scotland than about their lives – which was what I wanted to know about. They were a bit taken aback when I told them that nearly all the Youth Hostels in Scotland were 'self cookers' where there was no canteen supplying cheap food over the counter but on the other hand were pleased when I reassured them that the hills in the Highlands tended to be long rather than steep and that I had found the Northumberland hills and even some of the wolds of the south harder work because of their sudden steepnesses. That was the last group I joined up with until I cycled in to Settle in Ribbledale a few days later. Because I had taken on to go much further than they, I duly parted their company and my introverted whistling to a Scottish tune as I matched its rhythms to the pedals reasserted itself. Past Long Mynd and the Wenlock Edge the country became less wooded and seemed very empty. When the Gothic castellations of Wilderhope showed up, there was even more ominous cloud in the sky than I'd seen for more than a week. It was a bit spooky. In the dayroom after our meal that evening we stuck together rather longer than usual before turning in. Unaccounted creakings and chain rattling, however, failed to accompany the odd footfall on the squeaky boards of the corridor outside the dormitories. That was simply someone whose bladder was smaller than his imagination.

Chester, the next day was a lovely old city – from *castrum*, a fortress, as our Latin teacher had constantly reminded us. As I crossed the bridge over the Dee, it was a proper river. Away to the west was where Charles Kingsley had watched the sands when ' ... the western wind was wild and dank with foam' and where

> The western tide crept up along the sand,
> and o'er and o'er the sand,
> And round and round the sand,
> As far as eye could see.
> The rolling mist came down and hid the land;
> and never home came she ...

Looking west from the high points of the town it was in fact a misty sunset but in spite of the sad story of poor Mary sent to call the cattle home, I felt none of the menace of the sands of Dee. Instead, centurions pacing along a vallum perhaps, the odd pole with SPQR (*Senatus Populusque Romanus*) emblazoned at its head leaning against a wall, helmeted soldiery cleaning up a chariot, and other images of that ilk populated my imagination. I was summarily brought to my senses by a brush with a bus as I rounded the next corner. It was just a reminder not to get either too abstracted or too cocky just because I was well into the return half of my journey.

There were other things to compel me to a more sober mood next day. The first hour was pleasant going and quite flat. That took me to Knutsford's leafy suburbs, but as I approached nearer and nearer to Greater Manchester, green turned to brown and grey and the next couple of hours required careful negotiation of city streets with frequent recourse to the map. Wilmslow, Cheadle and Stockport seemed to run into each other and to cap it all there began to fall a steady drizzle, the first to wet the roads since my first day. As the industrial grime and 'dark, satanic mills' encompassed me, only the grubby cream and wine-red buses offered any spark of colour.

My mood began to deteriorate from the pleasure I had in knowing that the necessary mileage today was a mere 54 miles to the depression I felt about the environment so many people seemed to have to see out their lives in, day after drizzling day. The final hour from Hyde through Stalybridge to Mossley, near which I hoped to find the hostel of that name, was no more than six or seven miles. That was because I had so many stops to check my navigation through endless dingy streets of faded brick houses and miles of poor shops and smaller factories of one kind or another. The rain had driven all but a few Lowry-like people from the streets and the few I asked had no idea whether there was a Youth Hostel in Mossley or not. 'Eh, lad, thar might be. Ee'll 'ave t'ask again when tha gets there!' This was not entirely encouraging, but I pressed on until the rust brown of the houses and the deep black of the coal pits began to be separated from each other here and there by swathes of dirty, heathery moorland on the low hills to my right. Low cloud grabbed at me from their tops.

When I planned my trip, I had hoped to take a more direct and northwesterly line from Chester, perhaps via Preston, but no hostels along that line had vacancies. When I finally arrived, it was quickly apparent to me how I had been able to secure one at Mossley. This hostel was a worn-out looking house, perhaps in happier days, the home of a prosperous mill owner. It felt damp from the outset and I was, at the time of my arrival in late afternoon, the only resident. An hour or two later I was joined by a couple of walkers, a middle-aged man and his wife, who had been driven off the moors to the east by the poor visibility. I had already used my little Primus stove to prepare my meal but was struggling to get a small fire going in the grate in the dayroom when my companions arrived. They lightened the atmosphere considerably and quickly held a newspaper over the fireplace to increase the draught over the few pieces of dry stick I had been able to find. We laughed about the prospect of setting the chimney on fire but concluded that a bit more soot and smoke would not be noticed outside.

The couple had been walking, east to west, over Saddleworth Moor but had found it damp and difficult in the poor visibility. They knew that this hostel was not busy for they had used it before. The rest of the evening went really well. It was the first time that I had met any older people in a Youth Hostel. The man had fought with the Army in Europe from D-day till the end of the war and his schoolteacher wife was knowledgeable about the industrial North of England. Both had a knack for story telling and could have talked all night. Moreover, they seemed to be happy to do so with an ingenu like myself. This encouraged me in the belief that I was not so much remembering who I was as discovering who I was – the aim of the whole exercise. They heard a bit about my origins, and, as my confidence with them grew, my attitudes and expectations as well. We parted in the morning with mutual good wishes.

It was still a bleak journey north, skirting Rochdale toward Todmorden and on past cotton mills perched on quite steep little hillsides. Little noise or activity could be discerned from the road but, in my head, I could still hear the rattle of Hargreaves' spinning jenny and Arkwright's 'mule' rattling down from the 18th century. But now there was 'trouble at mill' and stiff competition from other lands.

There was some high moorland to be crossed and then I skirted Burnley toward Nelson before these products of the Industrial Revolution of more than a century past had diminished and more open country prevailed again. This was a land which did not attract tourists other than industrial historians – and they were not on bikes. From Nelson I climbed up over the high moor toward Gisburn. A leaden sky had frowned on all these miles of moribund manufacturing. I wondered what many of the young men and women, promised a brave new world when they returned from the war, would have given for steady jobs and a chance of a holiday, even on a bike like me, breathing deep, most days, of crystalline fresh air and surrounded by the hills, streams, woods and pastures of our glorious Kingdom.

No sooner had I harboured such thoughts than I came up on four cyclists just remounting after a short break. They were local, from the heart of Manchester and were heading, like me, for the hostel just north of Settle. For once I was lucky and had found similarly paced compatriots. We then shared sporadic chats as we switched companions en route and the last hour of our cycling day simply flew past. There had been relatively few occasions throughout my journey when I had enjoyed this sort of companionship, partly because some accompanying groups had been either too slow or too fast for me on the road. Two of the lads today were apprentice engineers, perhaps a year older than me, and they regaled me with tales of the shop floor in a big works, suitably embellished, I suspected. They told of Gauleiter foremen who took a micrometer to their test pieces and spat scorn like acid on their best efforts, sent them for left-handed screwdrivers and had them make tea for everyone in sight instead of giving them the all-important experience on the lathes they needed. Even the girlfriend of one of them, who was with us – and keeping up – told of the earthy chitchat of the packing room where she worked and the easy, if very vulgar, camaraderie it engendered. This was a life that I could know nothing of but instinctively recognised that even hearing of it second-hand would be of value to me. It was all part of the escape from the manse.

Almost too quickly, I realised that I was seven days out from my return home from my expedition and had become acutely aware of my shortage of funds. However, I had planned to spend a night with the old aunties in Girvan and therefore would have one less hostel fee and perhaps a few bob from them to tide me over, if necessary. That last week was one of the most enjoyable of all. I was now impressively weather-beaten and well muscled, physically and mentally capable of greater daily distances than I needed to do. In the hostel in Keswick I suddenly discovered myself almost talking down to some whey-faced cyclists who were doing only twenty or thirty miles a day and who looked on me as some sort of 'hard man' who was well into his second thousand miles this trip. That was the antithesis of what I had been like on my own first few days of the expedition so I had to concede to myself that it had been largely successful.

Sunshine and showers greeted me for my peregrination through the Lake District. Windermere, Rydal Water, Grasmere and Thirlmere spun by my left-hand side in quick succession. Naturally I had to stop at Wordsworth's cottage. Amid the bustle within his house, my musings on his Pantheism, and the real quality and nature of his relationships slightly bothered me. On the road again, dodging sheep and walkers, verses drifted in and out of my consciousness as I pedalled along:

> A flock of sheep that leisurely pass by,
> One after one; the sound of rain, and bees
> Murmuring; the fall of rivers, winds and seas,
> Smooth fields, white sheets of water, and pure sky ...
> ('To Sleep', William Wordsworth)

The scale of Lakeland seemed to me substantially less than Scotland, but it is a lovely land, cosier, more circumscribed and less awe inspiring than Scotland with its Torridon, Glencoe or the Black Mount. I was sure I'd be back sooner or later. Meanwhile my target was the hostel at Rockcliffe, near Carlisle, quite a short run, planned to allow me more time in Grasmere and Keswick.

The only sharp memory I have of Rockcliffe was of a flower bedecked little village by the river Eden and the shifting sands of the Solway Firth. There had also been a huge argument in the hostel day-room about whether it was in England or Scotland. To this day I'm not sure. It was certainly the case that I had to cycle a few miles next morning before crossing an iron bridge to reach a large sign saying SCOTLAND. I was surprised by the surge of warm emotion I felt on passing it. This was the land I knew. This was the land I could call my own. Much of what I had seen was interesting, even beautiful, in its own way, but the sense of security and familiarity I felt as I scuttled along the flat road to Annan on my way to Dalry, my next stop, was remarkable.

There was a very merry bunch of young people in the fully-booked hostel at Dalry including Jim Drewery who was, unbeknown to me then, to become a classmate in psychology at Aberdeen University and later a co-professional of some distinction. That evening he was already organising a sing-song as I arrived, a ceilidh which included two Irish girls with excellent voices and a wide repertory, somebody with a guitar and another with a penny whistle. As darkness fell over the Rhinns of Kells the songs and stories became more risqué and laughter echoed around the day-room till the warden came round to chase us off to bed. There was, theoretically, no alcohol allowed in hostels but, next morning, one or two of the lads looked somewhat hang-dog and a number of empty beer tins had to be smuggled out in our saddle bags. It was, nevertheless, one of the best hostel nights of the whole tour. There were at least five nationalities present, including Dutch and French, all intent on fostering an *entente cordiale* with an intensity which reflected the awareness that just two years ago, Europe had been torn apart by war.

Still in an afterglow of hearty internationalism we set out on our various ways in the morning. Nobody, however, was going my way by Dalmellington and then west to Girvan. It was slightly surprising to find out that Dalmellington was a small but fading mining town. It seemed to sit there, run down, uncertain of its future on the edge of the higher lowland moors and the softer, tree girt meadows of lower Ayrshire. The secondary road I was using thereafter passed through villages like Straiton – a sound instruction, I thought – Dailly and Maxwellston, all names I had heard from my father as he reminisced on his own boyhood in these parts. Just after lunchtime I arrived at Kerlaw in Girvan, scene of so many happy holidays in my earlier boyhood. The old aunties, frailer now, had, as usual baked rock cakes and tattie scones for me as they had done a decade ago. They were, I thought, a little put off by my cycling shorts and jersey. They were now remembering who I was and thinking that a minister's son should be a little more formally dressed. But they would never have said that and made me very welcome and wanted to hear my whole story. I also phoned home dutifully to let my parents know where I was. For an hour or so, therefore, I was close to being engulfed again in the old stereotyped image of the minister's son, the very thing that the trip was meant to erode or to erase, at least in its earlier form.

But the old aunts were so touchingly solicitous, ensuring that there was enough hot water for me to have a bath, washing a couple of shirts and socks and so on that I could not but warm to them and slip into the habits of past years while with them. Uncle Hugh had died and they were living not much more than a subsistence life and yet they insisted that I put 10/- in my money belt before I left in the morning. Perhaps the most important thing for me about that episode was that I became more introspective about how relationships change – especially between the old and the very young. My sense of self had grown sufficiently for me to be both more analytic and more tolerant and for me to be comfortable with the thought that I could now take charge of my life. In retrospect, I was, of course wrong. The past month had been formative enough but the ensuing year or two taught me that I still had a lot to learn both about myself and other human relationships.

The next day I followed the coast, looking longingly at the wealth of great golf courses from Turnberry north. One day I'd come back and play them all. By afternoon I had crossed the Clyde and was soon making my way up the western shore of Loch Lomond to the great castle which then formed the youth hostel. It was full of rather intimidating Glasgow lads heading for the hills from the Gorbals and Duke Street. My biggest problem was knowing whether to greet them in King's English or in my native Doric dialect. I went for the safer option of the latter and found some of them to be almost human.

There was still a lot of cloud about when I set off on the long climb to Tyndrum and over the Black Mount to Glencoe. Some of last night's chatter had included a story of a mad stag which had been terrorising walkers, cyclists and even car drivers along the high-level part of the road north of Bridge of Orchy. Apparently it was inclined to charge at any of these, without warning and with potentially serious results. One car was reported damaged and some cyclists had been very scared. The Glasgow boys said that it had been in their papers the day before and averred that they'd shit themselves if it came at them. They were pleased to be going to Oban by a lower route and wished me luck.

This was country I had cycled several times before and I was very familiar with it. Nevertheless, the long hard climb up from Bridge of Orchy to Loch Tulla was done in the stifling damp heat of my rain cape. As usual, the wind was not helpful, there was not much traffic and I imagined a mad stag lurking in every peat hag and round every turn. I was a sitting yellow duck in the cape and began to consider stratagems for my escape. Would I simply turn downhill and run? Could I have time to dismount and climb up on a huge boulder, several of which I eyed prospectively through the heavy drizzle which kept getting in my eyes just enough to blur my outlook? Maybe I would just need to bawl it out as I had done the blackface ram on the Cairn o' Mount. That I discounted as inadequate for this particular crisis. And then I was suddenly shaken out of these gloomy ruminations when I realised that I was now on the flatter road over Rannoch Moor, that the rain had gone off, my cape could be rolled up again and that in the residual fog the chances of being seen by a stag, mad or otherwise, was as slim as the chance of my seeing it.

Through Glencoe, not much of Buachaille Etive Mòr was visible but the waterfall in the gorge was spectacular after the rain. Beinn Fada and the

Sisters on my left and the steep screes and rock faces of Aonach Eagach on the right glowered down at me in their usual oppressive manner, but I was by then rejoicing. No stag, the rain off and it was all downhill now to the village of Glencoe and the ferry at Ballachulish. There was no bridge in those days. Sunshine and showers pursued each other along the length of Loch Linnhe and I pursued all of them as far as Fort William and its youth hostel in Glen Nevis. There, the reason for my relatively unexciting run through from Tyndrum was revealed. The macho stag had decided to fight above its weight and had charged a 30-ton lorry some miles north of Loch Tulla. Head on, it was no match for the lorry and had succumbed with its antlers stuck in the lorry's radiator with sufficient force to make the lorry lose coolant and wait helplessly for a breakdown truck. There was some sympathy for the poor beast having its stamping ground disrupted by noisy and smelly diesels and motor cars racing by all the time. By that time we, the walkers and the cyclists, had begun to forget our trepidation and to assume that it would really never have had a go at us. Unjustified irrationality – but there's a lot of it about!

Two days out from home and I was beginning to regret that my venture was coming to an end. Tomorrow's run was a short one along the three lochs of the Great Glen to a hostel at Alltsaigh, just south of Inverness. That allowed me time for a walk further up Glen Nevis before I left. There was said to be an old lady in a croft up there who had the Second Sight and I was keen to meet her. On that occasion I was unlucky, but some years later I did talk to someone who had done so. He had heard her tell of a 'dream' in which she 'saw' a coffin being carried to the glen graveyard by six pall bearers including her son. They laid it down by the grave and her son left the group to come and tell her something. The vision then faded.

More than a month later one of the glen shepherds was caught in a sudden early winter storm further up the glen near Steall. When he failed to return, searchers went out only to find his body which six of them brought back down the glen on a rough stretcher for him to be buried in that very graveyard. She had demonstrated other episodes of clairvoyance to others but that was the only one told to someone whom I had every reason to trust, a bank manager whom we had met on a holiday in Fort William four years before.

My last day on the road dawned fair and I was up early and through Inverness well within my first hour. This time, the wind was helping, the road was familiar and I cycled more than 80 miles in five hours. The odometer had passed 2,000 miles since leaving home three weeks ago and I had a few coppers left in my pocket. After this circumnavigation of most of Scotland and England, including the unplanned addition of the Isle of Wight, I felt really confident that I could tackle a variety of other challenges that I would have been more hesitant about only a month ago. Nowadays, I suppose such a venture would have been heavily publicised and probably sponsored in aid of some charity or other. Then I was answering a purely personal challenge. As the days and months before university went by I was surer that the adventure had been worthwhile. I still remembered who I was, or rather, who I had been, but I was ready to enter the manse again ready to assert myself more vigorously, to develop my own values and to exert just enough independence of thought and action not to be too trying but also to leave no doubt that I was growing up.

It was disappointing in that early afternoon not to meet any of my school mates or friends of my parents as I cycled along the last half-mile of Castle Street and High Street towards home. It was even more so to find no-one at home when I turned up at the manse – par for the course, I thought – though it was a bit deflating at the time. Then I saw on the hall table a fat letter bearing the stamp of the *République Française* and ran up to my bedroom to devour it. It was, of course, from Marie-Thérèse and did not look as if it had been steamed open, though they must have been sorely tempted.

I enjoyed a much needed bath, made myself a cup of tea and was casually reading the *Press and Journal* when my parents eventually wandered in from the wedding they had been attending. They did seem very pleased to see me and then began the long de-briefing I had expected. Over subsequent weeks the truth was told, if not the whole truth, and I think that both my mother and father were becoming reconciled to the fact that I was a 'virtual adult' and were even a bit proud of me and my achievement. They could not even point to anyone else from the town or in my class who had done what I had in the past three weeks. Maybe we were all learning about each other.

Chapter VII

LIBERATION OF THE SPIRIT

Give me the liberty to know, to utter, and to argue freely according to conscience, above all liberties.' (Milton *Areopagitica*)

In the two months that followed my marathon cycle trip I was still preoccupied with expending physical effort. In August, I entered my first Open 5-day golf tournament at Duff House Royal Golf Club, unexpectedly found myself in the Handicap final (which, in the end, I lost on the last green) and for my efforts was awarded a fine aneroid barometer which continues to grace my hall. The rest of that August and September was spent at Paddocklaw farm, three miles from home, where I harvested and did other jobs to earn something to boost my bursary and grant. In retrospect I can now see that I was displacing effort that should have been intellectual but my immature anxieties about whether I actually had the capacity to do so was driving this.

Plate 22: The author harvesting at Paddocklaw farm

154

It was about this time that the Education Authority for Banffshire noticed that I had been awarded a bursary by the university and penned me a cursory note to say that the grant I had been allocated by them would now be cut by the amount I had won. This hardly seemed to me to encourage mental effort. I might as well, from the monetary point of view, never have tried the Bursary Competition. I reminded myself, however, that I had enjoyed my week in the city and that it had, no doubt, reinforced my claim on a university place in October. That was confirmed in writing a little later.

All this time, the notion of being 'at the university' occupied my mind almost as a state of grace rather than stirring me to appropriate intellectual activity and reading. Somehow I knew that the work I would have to get through as an undergraduate would far exceed anything I had done at school. There I had existed on 'mither wit' as the locals called it, reading only enough to get by and doing the homework that was demanded of me. The glamour of a long, coloured scarf bearing the bold university badge; the prospects of joining a variety of clubs, social, athletic and, less enthusiastically, academic, had engaged me – to the exclusion of serious thought about reading the several books, in English, French and German that I already had bought as specified in the syllabi for the three subjects I would tackle in the first year.

It was a measure of my immaturity that I was simply carrying on as if it would be another year at a stricter school. I had not really explored the other 'non-school subjects' that were available for study – and none of my teachers had suggested before I left school that I should. Psychology, political economy, logic and metaphysics, international relations and so on were all there to be sampled by an enquiring mind, only for me to ignore them. Fundamentally, I was still at the stage of thinking of education as 'lessons' rather than 'learning' and it probably took me a year at university to shake off that misapprehension. The boy at the back of the class who kept his head down and tried to avoid trouble had to become an adult who would have to think independently and accurately, form valid opinions and be prepared to justify them to cleverer people. It was not an easy lesson to learn and, in retrospect, I think I did it the hard way.

That first morning in early October 1947 started with a tolerable breakfast in the digs. We were five, all male and with a span of ages up to twenty-nine. I was the youngest at seventeen and we slowly sussed each other out during the first week. Kenny, by then a second year medical, shared the room with me. Arthur was a shy Shetlander, reading geography, who was constantly yearning to be back in his boat in the Voes. Lawson was a big brash ex-Navy man who had decided to read philosophy and was a bit mad – though not entirely for that reason. Gordon, known as 'Nag' for no good reason we ever found, was also a bit mad, doing physics and had emerged, rather wounded, though in a more complex way than the physical, from a war in which he had (only just) survived two-and-a-half tours of operations as a navigator in

Halifax bombers. He drank copiously but quickly established himself as a brilliant physicist under the aegis of the famous Prof. R. V. Jones, of *Most Secret War* fame, only to pull out of his studies, to the chagrin of the professor, to run off to USA and 'ride the rods' as a hobo, never to be seen again.

Looking back, we should probably have seen something like this coming. Gordon, in his cups, had told us of some of his air experiences under fire over Germany. He had clearly been terribly stressed in combat – crew members next to him on fire and shot to pieces as he watched while he carried all the guilt of surviving. One evening he came back, pretty drunk, and very depressed. We heard some rattling from his room and went up to find Turpie hanging on to one of Gordon's legs and calling for help. Gordon had climbed through the skylight in his room and was hanging head downwards literally, in this case, on the tiles high above the street. He was suicidal and struggling but Turpie and I managed, with great difficulty, because he was struggling against us, to haul him up and back into his room where we held him down and comforted him till he could be got to bed. He never spoke to us about the episode again but it demonstrated to us what were the costs of war that these men bore.

The tramway passed right outside our door and a few pence took us the whole way to Kings College on the other side of town. Rattling and swaying along, I was never quite sure whether it would befit my new role as a student to be seen to be buried in a book or to be studying the rest of the human race which seemed to be scurrying about their business in the streets around us. Since there was a reasonable proportion of pretty typists, shop girls and sixth-year St Margaret's School pupils amongst them, the book notion tended to fall by the wayside.

At King's I seem to remember reporting to the Sacrist, impressive in his tricorne hat and dark blue robe, before wandering like a lost sheep around the quadrangle hunting for the room where I would hear my first lecture. My new, blue, shop clean and brightly badged scarf shouted 'Novice!'. Larger, smarter, higher-browed and clearly more intense and more intelligent young men and women milled around me. Groups of them evinced an easy charm and self-confidence as they chatted. They seemed to have known each other for years – and several had. They had been classmates either at Gordon's College, Aberdeen Grammar School or St Margaret's. My self-esteem, such as it was, took a real battering. How could I possibly compete with this lot?

But such is the resilience of youth that by lunchtime, three lectures later, I had chatted idly with people on each side of me in the class rooms and began to discover that there were others 'in from the sticks' who were feeling just as much out of water as I. Auchterless, Barra, Cornhill, Deskford, Enzie, Fordyce and so on, down the alphabet, had all sent their sons and daughters to try their hands at scaling the academic heights. By the end of the first week, others, perhaps disguising their alienation better, had begun to attach themselves to me. It was then that I began to appreciate the experience of people and elements of a value system which my cycling venture and farm work had supplied me with.

Not all of those who, in these very early days, attached themselves to me, for one reason or another, were, to me, congenial or stimulating. One turned out to be homosexual, who wanted to call me by a pet name and to come and meet some of his small boy friends on Saturdays. He lasted a week. Another spent most of his time in conversation swearing viciously and, worse, inappropriately. He lasted a fortnight. Another, a touchy/feely, fresh in from the outer Isles, clearly wanted to appropriate me entirely and at a pace which frightened me. Because the experience was not entirely unpleasant, she lasted three weeks. In the interim, there were others around me whose goals and personal style were a much better match to my own and in due course I made my own choices, though a sentence or two does not fairly represent the trials and tribulations of that first term before I succeeded in doing so.

My biggest thrill of all, however, was to glance behind me in the French class one morning early in the term to catch a glimpse of the girl with the bouncy hair I had seen at the Bursary Comp. Hardly believing my eyes, I looked again as we left after the lecture. It was really her, but again she was quick out of the traps and away before I could do anything about it. I was terrified she might already have a boyfriend. I needed to know her name but was too shy simply to plan a way of arranging to sit beside her in the class. What I did, however, was to brief one of my new friends to get close enough to her in class in the next week or two to find out her name by reading the front of her notebooks. It was Janet Stephen. At that time we all were the proud possessors of a little green book which contained all the names and addresses of university staff, and of the students. Such things were never considered threatening in those days. That showed that she lived in Andover Hill in Brechin but was in digs in Aberdeen. What I did about it thereafter was up to me – and I'd never even spoken to her. It was all too irrational for words, so all I could do was to worship her from afar.

Plate 23: The crown tower at King's College, Old Aberdeen

What threw me completely in those first weeks was not that many of the classes in French and German were carried out in these languages, but that an English essay had been set for all of the first year, presumably to sort the wheat from the chaff. The subject was

157

'What do you understand by 'culture'?' I looked at the notice board uncomprehendingly, no prefix of agri- or horti- or arbori-, just plain 'culture'. It soon became obvious that many of us had no idea. We knew we had grown up in one, the language, customs, traditions and history of our nation and district. We knew that if someone was said to speak in cultured tones they were toffee-nosed, but we were equally sure that the lecturers wanted more than that. I thought it unlikely that I could simply look up a book for the answer so, immediately, I had to start thinking for myself. The thousand words or so that I came up with were distinctly unmemorable, I am sure, but it was a start to my understanding of learning rather than lessons.

In Jack's Coffee Shop in the High Street of Old Aberdeen, culture really did reign, although I failed to appreciate it at first. There would meet the *cognoscenti* of Honours years in several disciplines, the show-offs (Iain Cuthbertson was a specialist in that, but eventually successfully channelled it into his acting!), the thinkers and big brains like Ronnie Hepburn and Peters, who eventually got a First in Economics in spite of forgetting to turn up for one of the examinations, Jack Tosh and Ralph Dutch in English – and, another, Sandy Fenton, 'a quiet loon fae Auchterless'. Speaking to him then I was reminded of a phrase Geordie Robb, the cattleman at Paddocklaw had been heard to apply to me, 'Aye, he's nae feel a'thegither, that een!' Accolades from such sons of the soil were not bestowed lightly.

Many of us owed much over our four years to the 'crack' in 'Jack's'. The latter was lean, brisk and bird-like behind the counter. His generous aquiline nose struggled to support heavy black framed glasses as he busied himself, the half-smoked fag that hung miraculously from his ever moving lips distributing ash on all the cream buns. But he would get to know us all well with a genial paternalism which only thinly disguised his keen business sense. From time to time members of staff would join us for a coffee for sessions which I am sure they found as informative as we did. Indeed, in my final year Prof. Rex Knight probably held as many seminars in Jack's as he did in the Department of Psychology. In spite of all that, the real benefit of Jack's only accrued to me after my first year had come to an end.

That first year, in spite of the aura of success which surrounded going to a beautiful and ancient university, was crowned by several failures. Apart from breakfast and high tea we lodgers at 339 Holburn Street seldom saw much of each other. Our classes, in different Faculties, seldom coincided and the same was true of our habits outside classes. For myself, formal lectures that year all finished by lunchtime and, because I had not formed good study habits, I was left lonely and at a loose end for the rest of the day. Aberdeen was then a city of many cinemas, in most of which I was to fritter away my hours during the dead period between lunch and tea. I was making up for all the restrictions imposed on me while in the manse, looking at every film, whether worthwhile or not. Similarly, at home, study had been done in the evenings and here I was, still bound into these old habits, reading and checking my notes only after dark – and often breaking the continuity by being too easily led away to the 'chipper' round the corner by my fellow lodgers. Nevertheless, in spite of a curious and unexpected loneliness, I chose never to go home at weekends or mid-term. The struggle for identity had not yet been won.

True, I had joined some of the university clubs, the Football Club, Athletics Club, The Literary Society and the German Club but the sporting ones occupied only Wednesday and Saturday afternoons and the others an evening a fortnight or so. At school I had been a reasonably good footballer but here there were students who had been signed by major league teams together with emergent talents which left me to hack away in the second XI.

In the German Club I was able to star in one Weihnachtsfeier, largely by dint of having taken a leading part in the school Gilbert and Sullivan productions but I still had difficulty learning my words and, worse still, only passing the year's German exam after a re-sit.

The original experience of failure when I scanned the newspaper for the degree exam results at the end of the first year and found my name to be missing from those who had passed first time was devastating. I knew I had been poorly taught at school but I also knew that I had not read enough of the German literature to answer the questions asked of me. I had always been used to success and getting my 'comeuppance' took me hard. Unexpectedly, my parents were, on this occasion, quite supportive and encouraging about my prospects in the re-sit in October. Perhaps they thought it might knock some of the cockiness out of me or perhaps they were just sympathetic and had seen what a blow to my self-confidence it was. My response was simply to ensure that it would never happen again. I would pass the re-sit and work a bit harder to prepare myself before every other exam or similar test in life. Although for a year or more I had been weaning myself from the influences of the manse, I re-valued the situation a bit following that. Strangely, I think my parents did too. They seemed to have become a bit more tolerant and inclined to see me more as a person struggling with adulthood than as a small boy.

Talking to other students illustrated how restricted had been my subject choices after school and had also encouraged me to review my aims to pursue a career in either journalism or the Colonial Service. I was aware that I felt no investment in the subjects I was currently engaged in – with the possible exception of English where I had met, again in Jack's rather than in class, Ken Dron and Ralph Dutch with whom I had felt immediately *en rapport*. That was important to me at that stage because otherwise it had been a somewhat barren and disappointing year. I concluded that a sixth year at Banff Academy would have allowed me to mature a bit longer and to be both emotionally and intellectually better prepared than I had been. Possibly the winning of a bursary when it happened had not been such a good thing. I had accepted it, and the consequences, rather than reject it and perhaps fail to earn one the following year – 'a bird in the hand ... ' had blinded me to my inadequacies.

As usual, I spent my spring and summer vacations working on the farm at Paddocklaw with the Milnes. Here there were no slack afternoons or arguments in Jack's. Now I rose at six, made my own breakfast and cycled the three miles to start at 6.45 a.m. Topping and tailing 'neeps' often came first when the ground was rock hard with frost and the rime melted off in your frozen hand as you wielded the machine-like blade. First the tail (root) off, then the stalk, and on to the next, back breaking and unending. Then the neeps were flung into the cart and away. If the year had been snowy and the ploughing late, I might also have to help 'Ca'in dung' out to the fields, digging it out of the midden with a graip as my back muscles cracked and strained with the effort. Now, machines, driven by one man do the whole job in hours that took us a week. Not only did we have to dig out the dung and straw mix, we also had to cart it to the fields and spread it, flinging it around us with a graip, spattering the stubble till the plough turned it in. Sweat stung the eyes and a damp shirt stuck to your back. Muscles ached and hands grew blistered, and later, calloused. Not many of the finer points of philosophy were discussed. Nobody whistled a few bars of Mozart. A few curses were muttered at nobody in particular or Geordie would pause, take out his fob watch, and with due deliberation, announce that, 'It's nae lowsin' time yet, loons.!' At 6 p.m. I'd cycle back home, run a bath and soak away the pain before bed.

Harvest time was easier, and warmer. Unfortunately, Alan, the farmer's son, with whom I worked, was inclined to be competitive with the neighbouring farms about how quickly we could either stook or 'lead' 10 or 12 acres of corn. The former skill took me longer to master than the latter for I would have difficulty getting the first four sheaves to stand properly before setting the other four against them. Thistles seemed always to work their way to the outside of the sheaf out of the binder and from there into my fingers, under my nails and against my legs. The others had hands like leather but in spite of that we would all spend a good part of our break for lunch (or dinner, as it was called) picking out bits of thistle from our hands and fingers. A stout needle became a prize possession.

When it came to leading in the dry sheaves, we developed a technique whereby little Johnnie (aged twelve or thereabouts) would steer the 'Fergie' (Ferguson tractor), in low gear, but never stopping, up the middle of two lines of stooks, while Alan, on one side of the cart, and I, on the other, would heave up the stooks, four sheaves at a time with our twin tined forks, to the 'bigger' (builder) on top of the load. It was his job to arrange the sheaves in an orderly, mutually supporting pattern around the edges of the cart, oats or barley heads inwards, then filling in the centre space. This ensured that all would be safely transported to the stack yard. The 'forkers' and the 'bigger' would rotate every few cart loads.

Once, for a bet of 10/- (50p), I said I'd 'big' a few loads of barley while

Plate 24: Paddocklaw staff, 1949 or 1950. Alan Milne, Flo Milne, Mr Milne, Robbie, Geordie, wee Johnnie Milne and Mrs Milne

wearing my kilt. I did, but it was a hard-earned 10/- because the 'barley yaavins' – the tails on the corn heads, found their way into parts of my anatomy I scarcely knew about and I spent the whole evening in the bath soothing the after effects. I worked for three years and a bit with the Milnes and it was good for me. At first I was sure that Mr Milne had taken me on just to please the minister, but when, after a year's work, he said, 'It'd be fine if ye could work for us neist year an' a'!', I began to feel that I was really worth my hire. I certainly knew by then that I had bulked out with muscle and was as physically strong as I'd ever be. Even that contributed to my growing self-confidence.

A little episode at the summertime funfair that usually planted itself down at the Greenbanks in Banff endorsed this nicely. Alan and I had decided to try our luck at the shooting stalls and roll-a-penny booths one Saturday night. We turned up rather sharply dressed, at least, we thought so, I in a new sports jacket, flannel slacks and fawn suede shoes. There was one of these 'trial of strength' machines where one is invited to strike down on a block with a 16 lb sledge hammer, thus sending a metal bolt up a slotted vertical pole far enough to ring a bell at the top. Several of the local lads, including some who had left school with me and several other 'fairm chiels' were standing around having failed to ring the bell. Alan was first to go. A strong six-footer, he gave me his jacket to hold, spat on his hands in the time-honoured fashion, swung the mallet and rang the bell straight away. 'Your turn noo, Davie!' he said as he donned his jacket again. A few of the rural bystanders paid a little more attention as this apparently effete young student hefted the hammer determinedly but fractionally more apprehensively. Fortunately, my timing and strength combined to send the bolt rocketing up against the bell which gave out a comforting 'boing'. As Alan passed me my jacket again, we heard one querulous country voice ask, 'Fa's yon bugger wi' the flannel sheen?' Alan promptly answered, 'If ye wint tae tak' on Puddockla' ony time, ye'll seen fin' oot!'

The work on the land had a rhythm of its own. The season and the weather determined the day's activities so that a combination of opportunism and planning had to be employed. During my first year with Mr Milne, I would be sent back home if the weather precluded harvesting, but in subsequent years I was kept on whatever the weather and other jobs were found for me. Sawing logs, helping to mend a cart or taking the cattle in from the fields to the byre or vice versa.

There was a counterpoint within each day created by the calculated breaks for tea and a 'piece' at mid-morning and mid-afternoon and the longer rest at dinner time. We would start at 6.45, work till about 9.00 when Mrs Milne or one of the girls would bring out flasks and bread sandwiches to the field. Then, at 11.45 a.m. we stopped until 1.00 p.m. – a long break in which we ate dinner in the farmhouse kitchen. If our boots were 'afa sharny' we would leave them at the door and sup our soup in stocking soles. The broth was always augmented with a few freshly boiled tatties, the rest of which came with some boiled beef or a stew or roast pheasant, all with plenty oatcakes which Mrs Milne would be baking on a griddle over the fire at the time. Hot, and with fresh butter, they were a feast for kings. No wonder we got stronger and tougher.

We then 'flapped' in the hay for a snooze, picked out thistles in our hands, or got up to some mischief about the steading. From time to time we would get out the farmer's .22 rifles, take a tractor down to the foot of one of the fields where we knew there was game and try to shoot a pheasant or two, a rabbit, or even a roe deer for the pot. The game were not disturbed as we approached because the tractor outline disguised our human predator shapes and we could therefore get close enough to use a rifle rather than a shotgun. Our afternoon break came at about 3 p.m. or 3.30 p.m. and was probably even more welcome than the morning one because of our growing fatigue.

Those I worked with on the land had a kind of placidity which I did not find elsewhere. They worked exceedingly hard but it was at a steady, even tempo in which there was always some kind of conversation amongst those working closest to one. It might often be banter or leg-pulling but might just as easily range widely over national or international affairs, developments in agricultural engineering, or a cutting, and generally accurate analysis of people we all knew. Rank was a reality but understated. The grieve was just under the 'mannie', the farmer. Then came the cattleman, or baillie, the horseman, the orraman or loon, like me. All worked hard and together, but in arguments or decision making, there was due deference to the higher rank.

My time there showed me the value as well as the quality of the hard physical work then required of the 'primary producers'. It showed me the risk the farmer took with timing his crops and breeding cycles, his need to understand the weather and his dependence on the loyalty of his workers. It also showed me that loyalty in action and even induced it in me. I watched the effects of good everyday practical reasoning and judgment and I grew in strength with them. The whole experience every year was a necessary and useful counteraction to any tendency the university might have created in me to become an aesthete or intellectual snob or to any tendency to harbour or develop ideas devoid of practicality or operational value.

Within a week of my return to university, my second year got off to a completely new start. I heard I had passed my re-sit but decided that my plans for the future required some reconsideration. French and German were to be subjects of the past and I would try Advanced English (since I had got a Distinction Certificate in the first year (Ordinary) class) but take Psychology and Education as ancillary subjects. At last I was trying to tackle some of these non-school subjects that had intrigued me earlier. It turned out to be a wise move.

Along with the new subjects which demanded that I do the necessary reading, there was scope for me to form new concepts, think independently along lines that I would never have developed otherwise and talk with a completely new bunch of lecturers and students. Many of the latter in the Education (Theory and History) class were graduates who were sitting the subject for an M.Ed degree (or Ed.B as it then was) and contained a proportion of ex-servicemen and women who had a much wider experience of life than I. This too was recognised by the teaching staff, the quietly erudite John Nisbet (later to become Professor) and a suave, witty and entertaining lecturer called Roderick McLean. In breaks from expositions of the writings of Plato, Rousseau and Dewey, our seminar sessions were lively and ranged widely over more contemporary issues in education generally. Now I was beginning to understand what 'culture' meant.

Two *obiter dicta* regarding Mr McLean spring to mind. He moved to a Readership, I think, at St Andrews University at the end of my year and by chance was the person to put me up there, some months later, after my involvement with the university athletics team on a Field Day between the two universities. A charming host, he plied me with a dram or two and introduced to me the piano music of, among others, 'Fats' Waller which he played with verve and enthusiasm. More 'culture'! Over twenty years later I discovered that the editor of AUP who decided to publish my first book was, I think, a relative of his, possibly a brother, one Colin MacLean, equally academically distinguished and a delightful, slightly larger than life personality to boot.

The psychology class was huge, by the standards of those days. Not long appointed to be the Anderson Professor of Psychology, Rex Knight was a charismatic figure rapidly acquiring a reputation as the most lucid, persuasive and entertaining lecturer in the university. Students, like me, would take the subject simply to hear him perform – for that is what every lecture was – a performance. There were even students who sneaked in from other Faculties without being registered for the class. I was completely hooked by the subject, never even considered missing a lecture, by whichever member of the staff, and worked through the reading list effortlessly.

The key item in the latter was what Rex would announce as 'our little red book' It was disconcerting for me to hear him say this the first time. I gloomily thought it was his 'little read book', *A Modern Introduction to Psychology* by Rex and Margaret Knight, first published that very year (1948). I need not have been so apprehensive. The book mirrored their lectures in style and topic and careful reading of that book alone could almost guarantee a pass at the end of the year. It still graces my bookcase. Rex, working with others such as the novelist Nigel Balchin, had been occupied in the Department of Psychological Warfare during the war and had a wealth of stories about propaganda techniques of both sides in the conflict, processes of 'misinformation', counter-intelligence and the use of psychological techniques to enhance instrumentation in aircraft cockpits and submarines to facilitate good decision making and the assimilation of new information. He was even using these on us every day he lectured.

Objectively, Rex was not that impressive. A smallish, stocky Australian, balding, with a slight divergent squint and some exophthalmia, he would not have been especially noticed in the street by the layman. In the university, he had a stature and reputation envied by other professors and lecturers and delighted in by his students. Those who went on to the Advanced and Honours classes with him generated an intense loyalty and affection for him which was fully reciprocated. He had no children of his own. Years after I had graduated, I and others would drop in on him at Kings. He would inevitably greet us warmly, enquire as to what we were up to personally and professionally and pump us as to what other members of the Honours classes that he had not heard from were doing. He kept a file of our post-university progress and would often extract it from the cabinet to say something like 'Drewery's doing clinical work at the Crichton Royal you know' or 'Have you heard from Ferries – I believe he's somewhere near Birmingham', or 'I was speaking to Elizabeth Brown recently' and so on.

My first sight of him was in the first psychology class I took that year.

Plate 25: The late Professor Rex Knight

Perhaps 130 of us were crowding the lecture room at Marischal College and there was a good deal of anticipatory noise and chatter. Enter right: a slight, buff overalled figure, stooping, but peremptory in style. This was Stubbs, Rex's departmental porter and factotum. 'Quieten down, you lot,' he intoned to us rowdies, gesturing with his hands. We didn't quite know what to make of Stubbs. Was he an incubus from Middle Earth, a 'familiar' who was seeking a new witch, or just another admirer of the great man? He turned and left the stage. A moment later he reappeared, seeming to have gained a little in stature, preceding the Prof, who followed two yards in his wake, to the lectern on which Stubbs would place a volume or two and the lecture notes for the day, stand to one side to let Rex take the podium, and then scuttle back into the shadows from whence he came. The parallel between this little pantomime and my memories of father and the beadle in procession to the pulpit in Banff St Mary's Church was almost uncanny.

The subsequent hour, however, could not have been more different. Here all was rationality, the measured presentation of hard data and empirically established fact, the adjuration to us all to question, to seek experimental confirmation, and, in general, to immerse ourselves in the hypothetico-deductive method, the cornerstone of all science. This offered me all the structure I needed, not only to adopt (though not recognised at the time) a new ego-ideal in the form of Prof. Knight, but also to guide my thinking and understanding of so much in the world that I had yet to experience. A year later, I was even reconstructing my signature to assume the broad general form of that used by Rex when he signed papers, and so it has remained to this day.

All of that, of course could not happen within a few weeks or months. The process developed over the next three years. Nor was I then fully conscious of what was happening to me. In Advanced English, while, in spite of all her erudition, I would squirm with boredom in Dr Jane Robertson's lectures in and on Old English, even when old Beowulf was up to his more violent tricks, the essays I produced and the analyses I made of the literary works we were adjured to engage with confirmed to me that I was by temperament more Classicist than Romantic. The ideas in I. A. Richards' *Principles of Literary Criticism* gave me opportunities to combine what I was learning about human physiology and psychology with one approach to literary analysis much more than did Prof. Bickersteth's insistence, for example, on the role of post-

Medieval 'courtly love' in understanding much of English literature.

Curiously, the approach I then adopted in which I used psychological knowledge and principles to illumine and explain authors and their works also seemed to intrigue my tutors in English whose familiarity with this new science of psychology was limited to a cursory awareness of Freud and psychoanalysis, early experiments in perception of j.n.d.s (just noticeable differences) and possibly a little of Piaget's work with children. But I seem to have leapt ahead rather too precipitately.

Mentally, I came awake in my second year at university. My study habits improved and I spent much more time in the library reading and annotating. This was mainly because I was much more invested in the subjects I was then studying and also because I had had the good fortune to meet Ralph Dutch both in English and as a member of the Harriers Club which I had joined in place of soccer. Ralph, his pal Ken Dron from Stonehaven and Ralph's girl friend from his schooldays, Mary, later his wife, and myself seemed to find each other not only congenial but also capable of being a bit disputatious with each other without inducing rancour. All were witty and Ralph in particular is one of the most intelligent, humane and perceptive people I have ever met. I hoped some of it would rub off. Long sessions doing (fairly simple) experimental work in the Psychology Laboratory also filled the afternoons when, a year ago, I would have frittered away the time. Even statistics, with its parametric and non-parametric tests of significance and so on was a subject I could get by in, even if it seemed to be anathema to most of the class. The reduction of, or rather the measurement, of chance suited my analytic turn of mind.

Another of the features of my second year was that, not being a Bajan (freshman) any more, I was inclined to mix in a bit more with students, including some of the ex-service ones who were nearly ten years my senior. This was especially true of those I met on the athletics field or on cross-country training runs. Geologists, medics, historians, foresters and mathematicians were all flung together on the sports field and in the changing rooms. Amongst the former were war heroes like Dick Kendall, captain of the Harriers, who taught me so much about distance running and training methods. He had been awarded the DCM for his bravery on midget submarines against the *Tirpitz*. A very genial divinity student with whom I occasionally had a hand of bridge in the Pavilion turned out to have won a DFC after piloting bombers on numerous, and some near fatal raids over Germany. Another, from the Western Isles, had a badly twisted shoulder, the legacy of his being a gunner in a tank in the Western Desert when a German Panzer 88 mm shell penetrated the armour of his tank's gun turret, decapitated his loader and shattered his shoulder.

It was little wonder that I was finding all manner of models for my behaviour and attitudes as a young adult. The switch from manse life, with very few friends, all immature, to this busy, goal-filled academic and social environment was dramatic and enriching in a way that I could never have anticipated. Although the proportion of older students among the females was quite different, Ralph, Ken and I were among the ten percent or so of students in that year who were not ex-servicemen. The latter had quite different attitudes to the educational process and environment from ours. They were impatient either to complete degrees they had started before the war or to gain a degree now and the work it was then thought it would guarantee after all the wasted years of conflict. They did not stand in awe of their lecturers as we tended to do. They had seen enough men of straw in the previous five years to recognise another when they saw him. A boring or ill-prepared lecture would be summarily dismissed by these chaps by stamping and/or an obvious walk-out. Meanwhile, we school leavers would just thole it and write our notes, such as they were. But it did keep most of our mentors up to scratch and we benefited from their boldness.

Interestingly, these signs of disapproval were only seen by me to occur in the larger English classes, often where evaluations were, at the end of the day, a matter of opinion. In Education the class was much smaller and the relationship between student and lecturer more personal, so simple absence from class was about the strongest protest one might ever see. In Psychology we were mostly all assimilating a completely new body of knowledge, heavily based on observation and experiment. Opinion was not something we were entitled to until a couple of years' assimilation of the necessary concepts and data might justify it.

One of the most fascinating features of the psychology we were taught then was the way it touched on and overlapped with both neurophysiology and philosophy. Its early history as a subject at Aberdeen had, of course, been largely associated with the latter. Perhaps most influential of all in establishing the general tenor of psychological teaching at Aberdeen University was that of Alexander Bain, a true polymath and 'lad o' pairts' as they are called in Northeast Scotland. He was appointed as professor of Logic and Rhetoric at Aberdeen in 1860 having earlier come under the influence of the thinking of Hume and, even more so, Locke. Bain's father, a weaver, made sure that the boy had some elementary education in a Dame School. Another teacher found that Bain had a great facility for arithmetic and algebra. Then Bain met two sons of a well-read blacksmith and was introduced to the writings of Berkeley and Kant. By the age of seventeen Bain had met a local minister who encouraged him to study at university and to win a bursary but he had not learned enough Latin to succeed in that endeavour. However, a Dr Cruickshank at Marischal College obtained some cash aid in the form of a lapsed bursary for him and Bain set about studying physics and chemistry there, simultaneously becoming interested in and studying moral philosophy in 1840 to prizeman level.

I could not but help seeing a parallel with my own situation at that stage of my own university career, in that Bain, through all his varied studies, could never come to terms with his father's devout Christian faith. He felt that all he was learning and discovering about the world was incompatible with the religious outlook. Bain actually held the post of Professor of Mathematics at Glasgow University for a year but found that little to his liking and then found he was often turned down for jobs because of his lack of religious faith.

Bain then spent time in London with John Stuart Mill until in 1860 the two colleges in Aberdeen, Marischal and Kings, were united into one university and Bain was appointed as Professor of Logic and Rhetoric. Amid many other writings, Professor Bain produced two important textbooks of the day in *Mind and Body* (1872) and *Education as a Science* (1879). He was also the founder of the famous Journal *Mind* which, although primarily a journal on philosophy, was the only vehicle for psychological studies at that time. Rex Knight saw Bain as the first true psychologist and wrote of him 'It was in psychology, which he did much to free from metaphysical speculation and to establish as a positive observational science, that he achieved his international reputation. Bain laid the foundations of physiological psychology.'

My own further introduction to psychology was in the form, in this instance, of Mrs Margaret Knight, Rex's wife. This charming but incisive lecturer on these topics also introduced me to the concepts of epiphenomenalism, interactionism and behaviourism. She too broke new ground for me in the philosophy of science. Epiphenomenalism, of course, takes the view, broadly speaking, that all mental events are caused by bodily processes, largely, but not exclusively in the nervous system, and no mental events are caused by mental processes. Mental events then are by-products of bodily processes. The term interactionism is perhaps closer to the layman's view that holds that some mental events are caused by physical events and some bodily events are caused by mental events. Of course, the extreme behaviourist view would be that only physical or neurological events have any reality and that mental events are simply our consciousness of the bodily events occurring.

Now this is not the place to go into the various arguments for and against these positions. Suffice it to say that, like Bain, I was for the first time learning about the anatomy and physiology of the nervous system and linking my knowledge of that to my understanding of how people 'worked' and related to each other and the wider world. It was a huge adventure and I launched myself into it with enthusiasm. The laboratory sessions on perception, reaction times, autonomic responses, attitude change and so on gave substance to the notion that behaviour and consciousness could be made amenable to scientific examination and analysis and that experiment and observation was the cornerstone of further understanding.

Not so much in that second year, but progressively in subsequent years of study, I was engaged in trying to develop similar enthusiasm for my studies in literature. Disillusionment about how great literature could enrich one's understanding of life generally set in with my greater understanding of concepts from psychoanalysis and psychopathology. It became increasingly obvious that much of fictional writing had to be about people who were essentially abnormal or at least maladjusted to get themselves into the scrapes and associations with difficult people they did. On top of that I formed the view that many writers, myself included, might have been using their writing to resolve personal conflicts which might have been better and more efficiently resolved in other ways. However, I have reluctantly concluded that a world of balanced, well-adjusted and phlegmatically successful problem solvers might be a duller, if safer, place.

What happened in that second year was that I had suddenly been afforded a way of getting direction into my mental life and simultaneously getting strength and confidence in my physical activities. One element which contributed largely to the latter was that I learned to swim.

Pete Lane, Ralph, Hamish Robertson, one of the Harriers, and Jimmie MacPherson, who had been just a year ahead of me in school at Banff and was already well on the way to being awarded a swimming 'blue', all advocated the value of a swim after hard training on the field to relax tired muscles and generally refresh. When, in my shame, for I had not told them about my near-drowning at Girvan years before, I said I could not swim, they all agreed to help me that very day. Although I was needlessly sceptical, they also agreed not to scare me in the process. None of them did, and by the time I had a week's lessons from some or all of them, I swam a length of the university pool and rapidly improved. It was rather like these signal episodes in life when one learns to whistle for the first time, or to ride a bike. I whistled first just outside the primary school and kept it going all the way home in case I lost the knack. The first solo effort on my first bike, in 1938, I think, was not dissimilar, except that I had not then really mastered what to do to effect a dignified halt. So I fell off. Later on, passing my driving test first time was another confidence booster which, like the other events above, seemed to generalise to my whole life situation and bolster my self-assurance in many unrelated areas.

At the end of that eventful and busy second year came another climactic moment. The guilt of a manse background flooded my consciousness when, just the day before I was due to return home for the summer vacation, Rex Knight's secretary, left a message with the Sacrist to the effect that the Prof. wanted to see me in his office that afternoon. I had sat the Ordinary year degree exam. but did not yet have the result. Foreboding hung heavily on my shoulders as I sipped coffee in Jack's till 2.00 p.m. – the allotted hour.

'Ah, come in, Clark! Nice to see you. I expect you're looking forward to a welcome break.' He was positively genial, so I relaxed a bit.

'I've noticed, Clark', he said, 'that you're aiming for an Honours English degree.' I concurred. 'Well, I've also noticed that, without appearing to work unduly hard you have done extremely well in psychology this year. You have, by the way, not only passed the exam but have a 1st class Merit Certificate. It'll be posted on the notice board and in the paper shortly.' My relief was palpable.

He went on to say that he would like me to undertake a two-hour battery of psychological tests there and then so that he could better advise me. He thought I might be interested in their content anyway. So I did, and with a stopwatch ticking away in his hand, Rex plied me with intelligence, aptitude and personality tests one after the other.

'Thank you, Clark. I'll telephone you at home in the course of the next day or two to talk to you about this. I think it's important.'

Two days later he called me to say that I should call up my grant awarding body, Banffshire County Council, and tell them that I was being advised by himself to change to a joint Honours degree in English and Psychology. There was no stand-alone psychology degree at that time though there was a year later. He went on to say that he thought that, in spite of its incurring a huge amount of work, I was capable of doing both the Advanced class and the Junior Honours class in psychology simultaneously, so would still finish my degree within the four years.

'Let me know by the end of the week, Clark. Talk it over with your parents and see what you think yourself. I think you have a future in the subject and there will be more and more jobs in the field in the next couple of decades.' One man's unsolicited advice – and my whole career future, to say nothing of my fundamental attitudes, was changed.

At home, my parents were mystified. They saw my proposed change of degree as preparing me for something between alchemy and charlatanism. 'You'll never get a job with that, boy!' declared my father. 'What's wrong with journalism or the Civil Service?' asked my mother, knowing nothing about either. In my own head, however, I was sure that the change was right and said so. They retreated with a great shaking of heads. Only when I telephoned Rex and gave him my decision did I begin to grasp what I had let myself in for – an Advanced course plus two Junior Honours courses, English and Psychology in the same year! It would be no pushover. But, the decision was mine and one more step in my weaning from the influence of the manse had been taken.

Even the summer holiday was hectic that year. Before the harvest had ripened and I was needed at Paddocklaw I cycled in to Aberdeen to buy or borrow from the library some of the books I'd need next session. There was not going to be enough time to read them all from October onwards.

More cycling was entailed in exploring where Janet lived – though I had as yet no invitation to do so. By this time, though with some difficulty because she tended to go home at weekends and could seldom be found at the student dances, I had found a way of being introduced to her and having a chat after lectures. She was no doubt a bit wary of this young whippersnapper trying to prise her away from her friend Jeannie (later our bridesmaid) but at least it was a start. I thought that if I were to bike over the Cairn o' Mount and stay at the Youth Hostel at Phesdo during the holidays I might wander about in Brechin and thus meet her on her own. To my chagrin, I did not and had to bike all the way back, so to speak, empty-handed.

Happily, things improved by the following year and my journeys became more rewarding. As is the way with students, we both had brief friendships with other students from time to time but as far as I was concerned, there was really only one in the running. My friends Ralph and Mary, secure in their own relationship, felt sorry for me not having a permanent girl friend and kindly arranged a 'blind date' one weekend with a perfectly pleasant girl. It was a disaster. We bored each other stupid for a couple of hours until by mutual consent we went our own ways. It was never tried again.

My third year at university was possibly one of the best years of my life. It did not have the quiet desperation of the final Honours year when all was geared to 'not getting a Third!' and in spite of being a time when I was working extremely hard intellectually, putting in time in the lab., reading compendiously and talking, talking and arguing in seminars, talking with my colleagues and talking endlessly in Jack's with anybody prepared to listen, I was also trying to cut down my times in the mile (to get nearer to the magic 4 minutes) and three miles on the track and in the six miles over the country in winter. I was by this time running for the university and it became a matter of honour not to be a total flop. It also meant that if I made the team then Field Days at other Universities became possible. These were great jollies where we were deadly serious during the event but had a great time with our 'enemies' afterwards in the bar. A phenomenon reported by all students engaged in these was that whereby every student visiting our university expressed the view that we had some cracking girls among our students, so also did we find other universities to be populated by far prettier girls than we could find at home. I have heard that that is still the case.

The only setback I had in athletics that year derived from the ill-founded notion on the part of Colonel Brocks, our Director of Sport, that, apart from my track running, I might make a pole vaulter. In those days the pole was a simple twelve foot bamboo with a bit of string whipped round it here and there. The landing area was a patch of sand about an inch deep and the run-up was on frequently damp and slippery grass. He had me down in the gym at Marischal swinging weights to build up my shoulders and thighs etc. and was timing my sprint run-ups with the greatest assiduousness. When I asked around why old Brocks should pick on me for this arduous event, wiser heads would nod and little aphorisms would be muttered like, "Cos it's too bloody dangerous for anybody else' or 'You've got to be daft to take that on!' I struggled on for a couple of months reaching only around 11 feet (though that could get you a few pretty heavy landings) until one afternoon I was at the apex of my vault, just approaching the point where you heave your body vertical on the pole to clear the bar when there was the most horrendous crack and the pole broke in two. Luckily, the sharp end of the bottom half just missed spearing my torso on the way down as I suffered a bruising landing half on the sand and half on the 'box', the wooden hollow into which one plunged the pole on take-off.

Back on the track I trained a great deal with Pete Lane who was a reasonable half miler and of course met several other students from all Faculties who were taking part in the other field events. Duncan MacPherson, J. G. Munro and A. O. Robertson, our captain (later to become Chaplain to the University) were sprinters. Pete Lane and J. A. Russell were on the longer sprints and I remember one, Sandy Gall, later to gain fame on radio and television as a world-wandering reporter. I think, though I am unsure of this, he threw the discus.

There was enormous companionship among all whom I met in university sport throughout the Scottish universities and frequent competition made us familiar with names later to become household words in National and Commonwealth athletics. Joe McGhee of Glasgow springs to mind for his later winning exploits at that level in the 6,000 metres and Marathon. Dick Kendall, Ralph and I often chased him on winter cross-country races, getting mud in our eyes from his running shoes until he stretched the distance from us so far that we couldn't see him – and it was not just the mud!

By this time, my life was being lived at a very high level of intensity. New knowledge, new ideas, new relationships with friends, including girl friends and even members of the lecturing staff, high physical fitness and readiness to meet any challenge meant that my severance from the restraints of manse life was becoming a reality – although at the time I do not think I recognised that process for what it was.

Since the end of the first year I had changed digs twice. This was yet another example of my growing sense of autonomy. Mrs Stuart at Holburn Street wanted another half-crown a week and I had other 'roadies' for my money. Consequently, Lawson Turpie, the philosopher, and I left the others to find a delightful youngish childless widow in Ashley Park South who had never taken in students before but was prepared to give us bed, breakfast and an evening meal for £2.5s.. We saw nothing ominous in the fact that her husband had recently committed suicide since the description of his last days she gave us in due course was that of a poor man with severe cycloid depression. We devised the most ridiculous stratagems to arrange to be at

Opposite. Plate 26: Aberdeen University Athletics Team 1950 – some members were absent from this photograph

Back Row (l. to r.): J. Philips (Coach), P. Fuglestvded, J. G. C. Munro, G. L. Simpson, H. A. Gall, J. A. S. McPherson, A. I. Cheyne, N. F. Stewart, A. I. Littlejohn, A. W. H. Smith, Col. A. W. Brocks (Director of P.T.).

Middle Row (l. to r.): P. H. Lane, Miss J. Pringle, R. A. K. Long (Secy.), A. O. Robertson (Capt.), Miss Q. Shivas (Women's Capt.), J. A. Russell (Vice-Capt.), F. G. Thomson.

Front Row (l. to r.): D. F. Clark, A. W. Clubb, D. J. McPherson, Miss S. S. Cameron, Miss J. Davie, Miss D. Ferguson, J. V. Watt, D. C. M. Corbett, T. G. Scott.

home with her when the other was away – most of which failed, but for a year we enjoyed sheer luxury, a blazing fire in the sitting room to study at if we chose, excellent meals and strong lines in suggestive badinage which she made a play of discouraging. All good things come to an end, however, and she decided to emigrate to New Zealand the following year. There were, in due course, a few letters to us from New Zealand (where she remarried), by far the most to my student housemate – so you can draw your own conclusions.

Before she went abroad, our landlady did, however, arrange for a more elderly friend of hers in Union Grove, 'Ma' Gordon, to take in the two of us till our graduation. She was a character. Stiffly corseted, she creaked like a black-sailed galleon in the wind as she bore down on us.

'Now you loons! Here's a key the piece. Ye can come in ony time ye like if ye come in an' dinna mak' a noise but ye hiv t'be in yer beds tae get up in the mornin'. Nae bidin' oot a' nicht! Nae smokin' in yer rooms, (only Turpie smoked) an' if I win on the pools on a Saiterday ye'll baith get a bottle o' beer tae yer supper'. This was not the manse we were in now!

As it happened, we were treated to a bottle most Saturday evenings, either IPA or Guinness, for she seemed to have amazing luck with 'Ten Results', her favourite bet. She did it with a pin over the newspaper programme of games for the day and with her eyes closed. At least the beer compensated slightly for her more insalubrious habit of frying every meal she gave us, usually in the same fat she'd used for the previous one. Little frizzled bits of bacon shared a bed with little frizzled bits of haddock, egg, sausage or kipper. Time after time we'd try to help her wash up so that we could scrub out the frying pan but she always intervened, 'Na, na loons, Ah'm nae wastin' gweed fat by poorin' it doon the drain wi' a' that soapy watter. Jist pit it back on the cooker till mornin',' and we would be shoo'ed away. We had a better chance of success every fourth Saturday when she would don her finery and sally out to one of her friends (all sturdy widows) for an evening's whist. There was a regular circuit of their four houses for this ritual. When it was in Union Grove it was in the best room (to which we were never admitted) and it soon became apparent that they were not teetotal!

Basically kind hearted, she allowed us enormous freedom in most things except getting up in the morning. Breakfast was at 8 a.m. except on Sundays when it was at 9 a.m. Strangely, for my contemporary habits would really have worried her, I rose reasonably reliably then. Turpie was the recalcitrant. I would be leaving for Kings when Ma would bawl, 'Davie Clark, c'm'ere an gie me a han' tae get this big lazy bugger Turpie oot o' 'is bed!' Back up the stair to his room and there she was, having already pulled off his pyjama trousers, hauling vigorously at one of his legs while he desperately hung on to the rails at the head of the bed. 'Just leave me alone!' was his plaintive cry, but that cut no ice with Ma and she would not rest till we had him lying naked on the floor. She was not a shy lady.

For me, over the two years I lived at 255 Union Grove, it was just a room and two meals. I spent all my time at Kings, mostly taking a tram there and walking back. As an Honours student I had a personal carrel in the library where I could leave books and notes I was working on and where it was known by my friends I could be easily disturbed for a whispered chat and then whisked off to Jack's. After all, there's not a lot of point in temptation if one doesn't yield to it once in a while.

The main social event for most students in these days was the Saturday night dance, usually held in the magnificent Mitchell Hall at Marischal College – impudence within dignity, I often thought. It was, apart from the various athletics and sports occasions, the only opportunity for students of all the Faculties to mix and get to know each other. The members of different faculties tended to carry certain reputations in the eyes of others, mostly undeserved but oft repeated. The Medics were reputed to be a bit clannish and inward looking, not inclined to mix much with the Arts or Sciences people. The latter were reputed to be a bit more brash and insensitive than the Arts lot and the Foresters were the coarsest of all. Strangely, the foresters I got to know were all total gentlemen in every respect and also included a high proportion of ex-servicemen.

But, make no mistake, it was the girls we were there for and in their cases their Faculties were of no import, only their other faculties, and where their digs were! All of us were never without our little green books of names and addresses. If one were to make so bold as to ask to escort a girl home to her digs then the geographical position of these mattered a great deal. None of us could afford taxis, and anyway, the whole point was to allow of protracted, if somewhat directionless conversation on the way. Lodged where I was, not that far from Bridge of Dee, there would be a certain reluctance to escort home a lass who was from the Hilton hostel of the Teachers' Training College or from Bridge of Don – not that she didn't deserve an escort. It was simply because a five or six-mile-walk after midnight did not appeal to those of us who were worn out by dancing and football or running all afternoon. There were, of course, exceptional cases. Ideally, one might find a girl whose digs were near one's own. Then, there might be a chance to loiter with intent along the banks of the Dee or elsewhere.

Many of the ex-servicemen eschewed the dances in favour of the bars. Some of them preferred simply to go home to their wives. Some did grace the dance floor, however, and we immature little school leavers had our noses rubbed in our terpsichorean and other inadequacies by their self-assurance and élan on the boards. When we did summon enough courage to ask a girl to dance to the rhythmic beat of Wee Georgie Wood and His Orchestra, the conversation would quickly exhaust our store of the usual clichés and then the trick was to find out both a bit more about the girl and especially where she lived. The girls knew this perfectly well and could string along a dozen blokes all night without really revealing very much. But it was great game, and there was occasional pay-off!

Entertainments available to us students were very limited compared to the present day. Some might have had a wireless (seldom called a radio) in the digs which they would be allowed to listen to during specified hours, because the set would be in either the dining room where we ate or in the landlady's front room. Almost no student had her or his own. There was, of course, no such thing as television anywhere and the computer had not then been invented. So many books had to be read for academic purposes that most of us seldom read light literature except during the vacations. Consequently only the cinemas, of which there were an unnaturally large number in Aberdeen then, provided us with comfort, warmth and relaxation, with or without a friend or partner.

Many of us, especially those in digs for the duration of term, went for long walks during the weekends – round Hazlehead, along the long sandy beaches north of the Don, down by Fittie and along to the Brig o' Balgownie and so on. These became, for me, occasions for discussion of topics we were studying and general chat about the lives and background of those who accompanied me. Landladies were not keen on 'stewdies' who hung about their houses during the day.

There was no actual examination at the end of the Junior Honours year, only continuous assessment on the basis of essays, seminar performance and laboratory projects, but I did have to sit the Advanced Psychology examination like everyone else doing that class. Much of my early reading in psychology had included most of the work of Freud, Jung and Adler, but their 'dynamic' psychology was facing severe assaults from the new 'learning theory', hard-nosed, behaviourist psychologists like Skinner in America and Eysenck at the Maudsley in London. The two 'models' for the understanding, prediction and control of behaviour hardly seemed compatible to me and I was impressed by Eysenck's description of the former as *Verstehende Psychologie* as against the *Erklärende Psychologie* of the latter. However, although my intellectual predilections were clearly toward the 'learning theorists', I never did completely discard the other models. Much later, my experience as a clinical psychologist and psychotherapist demonstrated that it was often a case of finding the best model to construe the difficulties and solve the problems that particular patients presented. By my postgraduate years I had found several more such theoretical models and used them all.

That eventful year, however, ended on a high – perhaps even a number of highs. In spite of a temporary fling with Margaret, a girl from Turriff who later became my friend, Jim Drewery's, wife, I had managed to ingratiate myself sufficiently enough with Janet from Brechin, my original wonder-girl from the Bursary Comp., to take her out fairly regularly, though to nothing very expensive. Occasional cinema visits, a coffee and a walk was as much as any of us could afford in these straitened days. To me, however, that was real progress. I am sure she was less impressed with me than I was with her – but she has always been fairly discriminating. Ralph and Mary were my constant companions both for discussion of topics in English, and sometimes psychology too. Both of them had very sharp intellects and neither would let any of us away with loose thinking or over-extravagant flourishes in our written work. But the arguments cemented our friendship (really the first lasting friendship, other than with Janet, I'd ever experienced during my life in the manse and subsequently) and I learned a lot from both of them.

At the end of that extraordinarily busy year too, Rex Knight's predictions that I'd feel comfortable in my changed academic direction was borne out. From every class, including Junior Honours English, I was lucky enough to emerge with a 1st class Distinction Certificate and to my considerable surprise was also awarded the Henry Prize as the best student in the Psychology department for that year. At the time I was highly delighted with my success and even my parents, seeing it all recorded in the august pages of the *Press and Journal*, offered their congratulations, not quite so grudgingly as in times past. Later in life, I was sometimes dogged with the unworthy notion that Rex had boosted my marks simply to confirm his test predictions. Shame on me! I should have realised that he himself marked only one paper from several. Theoretically, the money which went with the award was expected to be spent on books. I succeeded in spending about a quarter of it thus but used the rest to fund a golfing holiday over several of the Ayrshire courses that I'd surveyed so briefly on my cycle exploration three years previously. I rationalised that it did me and my golf good and that I could always borrow books from the library anyway.

At home during the holidays in the summer preceding my final year at university I again smelled the freedom of the stubble parks at Paddocklaw, forked the sheaves and biggit the corn stacks that would shelter and feed hundreds of mice over the coming winter. High cirrus stretching itself gently over a lavender and purple late evening sky reflected the last pink rays of sun as I cycled home. I was calm and at one with myself.

For a year or two I had engaged with my father in discussions about the nature and aims of religion and Christianity in particular. My mother found such episodes unsettling and would usually leave the room, saying sniffily that she had better things to do. This time I had decided that it was completely inappropriate for me to continue as a communicant member of his parish church. I had become one, almost unwittingly, after regular attendance at Bible Class (taken by my father) over the years at home in Banff before I went off to university. Now I was utterly and completely irreligious and could find no place for the God concept in my understanding of the world. Perhaps my parents had seen this coming, perhaps not, but sheer inertia had prevented me from doing anything formal about it until now. So I decided that I would hand back my Communicant's Card to my father and tell him that I could no longer be a Christian in the formal sense or a member of his congregation.

I had plenty of time for many of the Christian values and well understood some of the beneficent effect Christianity had had on learning and the Western world generally, but the acceptance of dogma that had no foundation in publicly verifiable experience was beyond me. It had seemed to me for a year or two that man had made God in his image rather than vice versa and that many people were happy to accept religion as a way of explaining to themselves the world and its events by dint of a kind of laziness about rationalising their own conscious awareness of the world, using concepts which applied in all other spheres of their intellectual and emotional experience.

Most of all, I tried to explain that I saw religion, as my father and mother practised it, as being a damaging generator of unnecessary guilt, something that I was now in the process of shrugging off. The idea of original sin seemed to be particularly damaging. Babies did not come into the world containing essential badness within themselves. Most humans learned to behave badly just as many learned to behave well. In both instances, other people taught them and taught them within the cultural parameters of where in the world they lived. Hard-wired neurophysiological characteristics might well determine, for example, how easy or how hard it might be to learn and what levels of anxiety might be experienced under varying circumstances, but the idea that a baby, a monkey or a spider came into the world with an inbuilt store of 'badness' did not seem to me to be tenable.

I tried to explain that I simply couldn't see what God was for. If He was there to offer me 'salvation' then I needed to have some evidence about what I was to be saved from. I had seen none. In any case, I thought, rather flippantly, He was said to be both all-forgiving and omnipotent so I'd let Him get on with it without my interfering too much. There was nothing in my experience that could not be understood without the God concept, so I was discarding it, just as I had discarded phlogiston and the theory of a flat earth.

My father heard me out and finally concluded that, unlike him, I had no faith to support any understanding of the Scriptures which he had had me read in their entirety years before. That being so, he felt he could say nothing to make me change my mind, took my card and said I'd be taken off the Church Roll. I've been off it ever since.

Long after that trying conversation I've been aware that I can know things and I can be ignorant but I will not fill the intervening space with belief. Neither of these conditions of knowledge or ignorance is permanent, both wax and wane, but I see that attempts to fill the gulf between these with belief has caused nothing but harm and strife in the world, whether these beliefs are religious, political or commercial. If people could simply rest happily, saying either 'I know' in the sense that what they know is publicly and experimentally verifiable, or that they don't know but will try very hard to find out, then we might have some chance of perpetuating the species. It is the role of the imagination to offer the chance of extending knowledge either by creating new hypotheses to be tested and refuted if found wanting in the sciences or by creating novel moods and ideas through literature, poetry, and music in the arts. But these are media to extend our understanding of the world and to enrich our spiritual awareness, not gods to be worshipped or the creators of beliefs the content of which can be neither refuted nor confirmed.

My mother was more distressed by my rejection of religion than was my father, who had, previous to his 'conversion' to the church, not been particularly religious and, I think, was not totally immune to periods of doubt himself. As a minister he would have been described as liberal. He enjoyed sherry after a sermon and a dram at any time and many of his parishioners would indulge him. He had no objections to his flock playing golf on a Sunday provided that they went to church also. My mother had, however, all her life soaked up everything associated with what was then thought to characterise a God-fearing member of the Church and her family had reinforced this. She was a bigoted believer who could imagine no state of unbelief and thought that I was destined for Hell right away. It would have been asking too much of her to undertake any revaluation of her deeper ideas at that time of her life so I simply re-assured her that we agreed to differ on such matters and that was the end of it. She wrongly predicted that, later in life, I'd be sorry I'd done what I had.

I remember going off to the farm next day with a new lightness of heart in that I was free of the sense of hypocrisy that I had harboured about being a Church member and yet knowing myself to be so arrant an unbeliever. It was like coming out of a shower and donning a fresh clean shirt after a long hard, dirty and sweaty day's work.

Apart from my golfing break, I was at home in the manse for four or five weeks before going back to university in October. My young brother Tom had left school and was by then away in Aberdeen himself at the start of an apprenticeship in a surveyor's office. His absence, as the youngest of the family, seemed quite suddenly to have brought it home to our parents that we were fleeing the nest to seek an independent life. We each had our own set of friends and interests. In fact Tom and I saw little of each other in the city and our parents became intermediaries whereby I found out what Tom was up to and he learned about me. My father was then approaching seventy and although he was then still relatively fit I am sure he was suddenly aware that both of us were now young men and ready to tackle life's exigencies in our own ways. They had always been a bit more protective toward Tom, partly because he challenged them less and partly because he had been slightly less successful at school than I. Additionally, at that stage, he was not introducing a girl into their lives.

Janet and I had been, in the parlance of those days, 'going steady' for several months and I had already cycled down to Brechin and met her parents. To balance things up I felt that my parents should meet her too and she came up that winter to spend a few days in the manse. It was, I think, so trying for her that our affair nearly foundered there and then. She felt, probably rightly, that she would find it very difficult to get on with my mother, who still harboured notions that whoever I brought into the house I 'could have done better for myself'. Although my father did his very best to compensate for mother's coolness, he was torn in his loyalties between those toward his son and those toward his wife. I fought my corner as best I could, especially trying to reassure my girl that she was the one for me in spite of the storm clouds that hung over the manse. After Janet had gone home, I sat up late with my parents and explained that they should try to be pleased that I was happy in my relationship, that I had met and valued Janet's family. It was obvious to me that they had given her and her brother a good home, that they valued their home life and that, so far, they had not expressed any antipathy to myself. On the contrary, they had welcomed me into their home – as they always did as long as they lived. My father rounded up our discussion with, 'Well, if that's what you want, boy, so be it!' Thus was I declaring a shift in my emotional priorities. Another tie to the manse had been severed.

The final year of my undergraduate course left me almost nothing to remember but unremitting preparation for the final ten hours of Honours degree examinations. I still ran cross-country in the winter, swam and played table tennis for general fitness but there would be no athletics season in the coming summer. I expected, all going well, that I'd be away from university by then. The climate of attitudes and expectations within the university at that time was relatively serious. In this small university of about 2,000 students in all Faculties many of us knew students from these as well as from our own immediate circle. As I have remarked above, only a small proportion of the males were school leavers so that the influences, good and bad, of the ex-servicemen were significant. They, and we, saw our degrees as almost a guarantee of work after graduation because, in the aftermath of war, jobs were there to be filled. None of us wanted to waste our time. Our tutors came to know us rather well and the whole ethos surrounding us was that we should do as well as we could and see our university not just as a higher technical college but as a widely enriching experience which prepared us better in a wide range of ways for life in whichever community we might settle. We were expected to emerge as reasonably clever, cultured, tolerant and thinking people whether we were engineers, writers, doctors, foresters or whatever, and perhaps to feel a lifelong loyalty to the institution that had made us thus.

The closer to Finals I came, my world became more restricted to my relationships with Janet, Ralph and Mary. Janet had by this time completed her own degree and was at the College of Education busying herself with, but not particularly liking, her postgraduate teacher training – though she loved teaching. We were able to see each other only in the evenings when I fear I burdened her with my apprehensiveness about the outcome of the Finals and with my need to learn up many suitable quotations from the books of the external examiners. Along the banks of the Dee she heard not 'sweet nothings' in her ears but a host of boring quotations from textbooks. Mary, on the other hand, was a year behind Ralph and me in her degree course so she was under slightly less pressure than we were. Jim Drewery was my main discussant for matters in psychology and Ralph in English. We would talk about the various essays and projects set us by our tutors and I can remember often writing the final sentences of an essay on his front door as I waited for John Lothian (my English Tutor) to let me into his house where the tutorials were held. Rex Knight, Betty Fraser (later Professor) and Freddie Smith (later Professor at Durham) were my Tutors in psychology but they heard my material in the Department or in Jack's!

Getting hold of the right books toward the end of the session was a real difficulty because everybody wanted them urgently – especially those which, in psychology in particular, had just been published. I eventually bought Hilgard's *Theories of Learning* which purported to bring a new kind of scientific analysis to models of human and animal learning, simply because there was so little time to assimilate its contents (which we were sure would come up in one of the examination papers) and there were only one or two copies in the library, borrowed almost continually by staff. There was similar trouble getting hold of one of Maurice Bowra's books of literary criticism.

John Lothian was a quiet and charming tutor who listened to my essays with a whimsical smile when I was 'pushing the boat out' a bit provocatively. 'Very interesting, very interesting!' he would murmur, and then quietly draw my attention to another author's quite different analysis of the topic. His great strength as a tutor, to me at least, was that he had the knack of giving his students enough slack to stretch their own ideas, while at the same time making sure that they had a grasp of the more orthodox point of view. And it was all done in a relaxed and very 'homely' way. I enjoyed my times with him and he nearly always managed to stretch the allotted hour to twenty minutes more.

In psychology, especially with Rex, everything was much tougher. He would set out experimental scenarios which might or might not have a flaw in them and then test out his students to see whether they had enough grasp of principle to find that flaw – or not. His own grasp of the literature was compendious and he could actually quote the page and even paragraph of a book (without reference to the actual book) which would illustrate or refer to the point being pursued in our discussions. On other occasions, after a specially tough tutorial, he would propose we all went down to Jack's for coffee and would indulge us with a relaxed and cheerful series of anecdotes about his war work or about ex colleagues such as Prof. Alec Rodger or Bill Belson, Head of Audience Research at the BBC, both of whom he had previously invited to visit the department and lecture to us. In my later professional career as a psychologist, I was to become an acolyte of the same Alec Rodger, another charismatic figure in the discipline.

As is so often the case, May, the last month before Finals, was filled with romantic sunny days when we could lie on the grass outside the Elphinstone Hall and English Department (Psychology just had tarmac!) and read or talk between lectures. It was far from conducive, however, to systematic study. Thoughts and scrutiny of our girl friends – and the girl friends of others – were too tempting and with the sap rising in every other growing thing, we just had to retreat to the library for peace of mind.

My first Finals paper was scheduled for 30 May, my 21st birthday! *Quelle joie!* We were all revising four years' material with a kind of hectic desperation, reading through previous Honours exam papers to see if we could spot likely questions or establish that certain topics were more than likely to turn up in this year's question papers. These, however, could not be depended upon so we could still be found reading the most recent texts and debating the best line to take should these be the basis for a major question.

In my case, there were ten three-hour papers with two quite often taking place on the same day. Occasionally there would be the bliss of a day or two free of papers and as we chalked off the topics covered in papers already completed the revision became more limited in scope but more concentrated in topic. Janet and I would walk for a mile or more along the banks of the Dee while she 'heard' an even greater stock of suitable quotations I had prepared myself to incorporate in answers to certain papers. Jack's was open a bit later at this time and there we would talk through matters to do with the remaining papers with any post-graduates or other Senior Honours students we considered brighter than ourselves. Looking around our fellow examinees it was easy to believe that nearly all of them were better prepared, more intelligent and better read than we were – especially those with English accents. Among the latter were several who had been at Public Schools and who affected such an air of intellectual and social superiority that we would assume they had brain power to match. As it turned out, we were quite wrong in this and we allowed ourselves the occasional quiet smirk of gratification when we found in the end that all of us 'teuchters' had outdone them in terms of final results.

The night before, and, on the first day, waiting for the examination hall doors to be flung open were terrible. My anxiety could be assuaged only by reading some relevant book right up to the very moment when we had to enter the hall and leave the book in the cloakroom. At least two years earlier I had learned a psychological principle, the Yerkes-Dodson law which stated that, while some degree of anxiety could aid learning or performance up to a certain point, were the anxiety to continue to increase, then learning and performance would be adversely affected. Each time I waited for the examination room door to be opened, I wondered where on the graph of anxiety/performance I was then placed.

Before entering the examination room I was weak with anxiety, but strangely, as soon as I saw the papers and read the questions the anxiety just seemed to evaporate and I would tackle the paper with determination and even verve. I did seem to have a knack for drawing on information and ideas from widely different sources whichever paper I was dealing with and making them seem entirely relevant to the thesis I was pursuing. My micrographic hand meant that I put a lot of words into a page but it also meant that I could review what I had already written without having to refer to too many pages and I could consequently keep the 'flow' of my presentation going evenly. To that extent, I think I was lucky to be a 'good examinee'. Perhaps the best confidence booster of all was when I found one of the subjects in the first Essay paper to be very close in content to a project I had undertaken for one of my tutors only six months before. It was on a theory of comedy, and even if I was not quite in the mood to tell all the best illustrative jokes, at least I had read some very useful books, including Koestler, on the topic.

The first two weeks of a sunny June saw us all returning day after day to the examination hall, become more washed out and zombie-like as we tired. It is the case that not only I, but many others, found those two weeks or so of highly concentrated mental effort among the hardest of our lives. A few, including myself, when perhaps more anxious than usual in later life, still report dreams in which they are having to sit these exams again and have not read the books or done the work and there's only a day to go etc. etc. We all expected to go on a monumental booze-up right after the last paper but in the event were so flaked out that we simply went to our digs and slept.

Some days later, Ralph, Mary, Janet and I treated ourselves to a picnic below the cliffs at Muchalls and wallowed in the freedom from swotting. Both Ralph and I had had our commitment to National Service deferred while we completed our degree courses but we knew that a buff envelope was likely to fall through the letterbox any day inviting us to report for duty at some military base or other. Some months before, I had done tests for the RAF and subsequently was sent to an airfield and medical centre near London for even more giving of samples, being centrifuged (me, not the samples!) and blowing up mercury in a tube. This was some sort of service pre-selection which I promptly forgot about under the then greater pressure of academic work. The sequel to all that became the substance of my book *Stand By Your Beds!*.

I went home to Banff and there passed a few weeks until the results came out. These weeks seemed endless. My moods and anticipations would swing from the deepest depression to moderate confidence that I'd avoided a third class Honours degree. I never knew why we so scorned 'a Third'. After all it

Plate 27: The author and Janet. Plate 28: Their friends, Ralph and Mary taken at the post-Finals picnic near Muchalls, 1951

was a degree of some kind and better than none at all.

Notices were by custom displayed with the results on the Quadrangle notice boards and the next day in the local press. Desperate to get into Aberdeen to scan the notice boards, I wangled a seat on a Women's Guild bus trip to see Harry Gordon at the Beach Pavilion on the Friday night I thought the results must come through. Manfully I sat through the first half of the very funny show – and even laughed in a rather uptight kind of way until I could stand the tension no longer and left the theatre telling my parents that I was going up to Marischal College and would join them before the bus left again for home. I practically ran all the way up to the town, entered the quadrangle to see only one solitary student scanning the notices. I was by this time so ambivalent about looking for the results that I could hardly read the notices already there. 'History' – no, 'Mathematics' – no, 'Engineering' – no, 'Logic and Metaphysics' – no, then there it was, posted only an hour or so before,

'Psychology and English'. At first glance I failed to see my name at all. We were only a class of twenty-three in Senior Honours and there were only twenty-two names! Someone had failed totally. I scanned them again, from the bottom upwards. There were some 'Thirds', no Clark there. Then the 'Seconds (Upper and Lower)', no Clark there, then I saw the two 'Firsts', Elizabeth Brown and David F. Clark. It seemed hardly credible. The other student beside me in the quadrangle had been doing pure 'English'. I asked him to check the list. 'Yep. That's you, alright. Congratulations! What about a pint?' He too had just seen that he had got a 'First' as well so we popped round the corner and drank each other's health.

On the journey home I was full of beer and euphoria. To give them their due, the Women's Guild offered me sweets and congratulations. My parents thought I should really wait until the results came out in the paper. The authority of the *Press and Journal* seemed in their eyes to exceed that of a simple notice on university paper. The final accolade was when Rex Knight telephoned me at home a few days later to tell me that I had also won a scholarship to do research at one of three USA universities – if the military authorities would give me further deferment. Unfortunately, they did not, and the scholarship went to the next student in line, a woman who did not have to do National Service.

Rex and Margaret Knight both congratulated me on the degree result but Rex went on to say that he thought I would be better advised to look for work or further study in the field of applied psychology rather than settle for an academic career. Having taken his advice to good effect once already I was disposed to take it again. My father's comment was 'Well, if you think you can earn a living in that sort of field go ahead but I have my doubts!' I had my own but I was certainly not going to let on to him. Later that week I heard that Ralph had also got a First in 'pure' English and a gold medal in addition. Mary got the same a year later. Surely we could not all have

Plate 29: Rev. Dr D. Findlay Clark congratulates the author on the occasion of his graduation in July 1951

wasted our time in the previous years!

Just before my own graduation ceremony in Aberdeen, my father got news that he had been awarded the Honorary Degree of Doctor of Divinity by his last *alma mater*, Edinburgh University, for his work in Christian ministry over so many years. He was delighted about my degree and I about his. We had come to a reconciliation about the divergence in the paths of our personal philosophies. My mother still found that difficult, but both of my parents had now come to the view that the bonds the manse had once wound round me had loosened and that I had to 'dree ma ain weird' (pursue my own destiny), take what life threw at me on my own and use my own best judgment in selecting a mate, hopefully for life. For myself, I felt a new confidence in my own ability to do all of these. It was far from obvious what the next step along that path would hold, but nothing was now going to deflect me from a career in applied psychology. Rex Knight had got it right. Although I had no idea when, there would be a chance to undertake the research I had wanted to do in America, or something similar, at a later time.

There was no doubt in my mind that university life, in all its aspects, had been a crucial, and on the whole, enjoyable phase of my life. I had found out for myself who I was and what I could and could not do. I had found good friends and colleagues who reciprocated the sense of value in which I held them. Importantly, I was able to argue my secular corner while not scorning the moral principles that a Christian upbringing had taught me (often harshly). I was able to take a wider conspectus of other value systems and kinds of knowledge, and most of all, I had found the girl I would marry.

***

I had finally grown out of the manse. I was no longer its captive.

Plate 30: The author with Janet on his graduation day, 1951

Chapter VIII

POSTSCRIPT

'Better is the end of a thing than the beginning thereof.'
(Holy Bible, Ecclesiastes, 7:8)

Those readers who just wanted to read my story should stop here. For the more doggedly persistent, however, I should explain that in a conversation about what I was writing before this book was completed, Sandy Fenton, one of my fellow students at Aberdeen and now Professor and Director of the European Ethological Research Centre in Edinburgh, and a prolific writer himself, suggested that it might cast some light both on the style and content if I were to write a brief chapter indicating to the reader how my life subsequent to the first twenty-one years, which the foregoing chapters have covered, finally evolved. Knowledgeable as he is about such things, he thought it would be informative for me to comment on the extent to which the nature of my professional training, development and habits might have determined the way in which I have recounted the story of my earlier life.

My ready response to his suggestion was perhaps a bit hasty. When I reviewed the rest of my life to isolate the factors which have determined the style of my writing (at least in an autobiographical context) I have finished up less sure than I was when I started. Certainly the fact that I went on to become a professional psychologist, university clinical senior lecturer and researcher made me well aware of the need to be able to stand back and review as dispassionately as possible those influences and events which seemed to have had the greatest effects on me.

The reader then will need to know that, after two years of National Service in the RAF immediately following university, which is reported in my book *Stand By Your Beds!*, I did postgraduate training first as an industrial

Plate 31: The author's younger brother, Tom, at the Manse, on leave from National Service, 1950

psychologist and subsequently as a clinical psychologist working in hospitals in the UK and abroad both with the mentally and the physically ill. Professor Rex Knight was correct in his predictions that I would enjoy my professional life and progress rapidly to Consultant grade in the work into which he had guided me. One of the most important aspects of that work was to be both a sympathetic and yet detached observer of the people one dealt with – and I don't always mean the patients! Looking, listening and interpreting behaviour became my stock in trade. That had to be detailed and persistent but it was important if correct analyses of the patients' problems was to lead to accurate diagnosis and treatment programmes. That behavioural scientist's habit of being a participant observer and looking for cause and effect must have carried over into the writing of this autobiography. If I had written about these years just after I had lived them, rather than now when I am well past middle life, I am sure there would have been a more bitter taste to my commentary. I would not then have seen the gradual development of both process and personality in myself which has given me a secure platform from which I can now look back, not in anger, but in acceptance – 'emotion recollected in tranquillity' as Wordsworth would have it.

Part of my work in associated university appointments also involved lecturing to undergraduate and post graduate students. All of these activities were bound to influence both the style and content of my writing. All of that material had to be written in a relatively flat, unemotional style befitting the academic. In consequence, it is difficult for me to write 'purple prose' full of rich description and high-flying metaphor. Temperamentally, I am also a fairly phlegmatic sort of person disinclined to exaggerate emotional responses though I can recognise drama when it occurs. In a sense, I have been writing a psychological report on myself – just a bit fuller than the many thousands of reports I have written on patients for consultants in other specialties or for the courts. The main problem is that, because of my job, I know that there will be errors of perception and interpretation in my story, for I know that I could not be an unbiased observer within my own family. I have tried to be such, but only the reader will be able to assess how far I have been successful.

In the first chapter I think I indicated some of the determinants of what memories might be available to an autobiographer. As a psychologist, I have been all too aware first, that many of these, especially earlier ones, have been episodic and lacking in continuity. Second, there must be many which have disappeared irretrievably but yet might have had significance at certain times in my life. Thirdly, I may have repressed some memories so deeply that I have never been conscious of having experienced the events or feelings which they comprise, and finally, there will be some which, quite deliberately, I have consciously chosen not to reveal. It would be fair to say, however, that none of the latter would, had they been revealed, have altered the structure of my general thesis which deals with the peculiar features that can limit the development of a small boy by being brought up in a Scottish early twentieth century manse and his gradual weaning himself away from these.

It is important for me to stress that my experience of growing up in a manse should not be generalised to all children with that background at that point in history. I am sure there will have been many whose story would be quite different. What I am sure of is that there would be fewer differences between the life experience through childhood and adolescence between the children of, say, several carpenters or engineers or fishermen or farmers than between the children of several Scottish Presbyterian ministers. Nevertheless, what I have written will, I am sure, ring bells with many of the latter and illustrate to many of the 'lay public' the peculiar difficulties which accrue to children of the manse.

In early life, the associated emotional context of memories was bound to play a major part in a way which would not be characteristic of later adolescent or near-adult memories. As one grows older, one constructs a self-image which, more and more, selects those memories which can be effectively rationalised into the life pattern one seeks for oneself. It is as if early 'chunks' of memory stand out like landmarks in an alien country. They can only be fitted in to a broader picture when, so to speak, experience allows a map to be formed around them in which they come to take their place. There will be times when the scale of that map is small and only the most salient 'landmarks' stand out, and others, when the scale is greater and more of the surrounding detail can be included. The map is drawn under the conspectus of the passing years whereby the data of memory are riddled through many sizes of grid. What falls through is then ordered and placed on the map with reference to one's maturing attitudes and changing values.

There is a constant hazard of egocentricity in the writing of an autobiography which is exceedingly hard to combat. One of the toughest skills to master for the maturing individual is that of being able to cultivate the habit of listening to that little voice of that monkey on your shoulder, that homunculus, 'your better self', which will advise you not to be so daft, so impulsive, such a prig or so arrogant or boring as you might tend to become. Selecting what might be interesting to a reader rather than what is interesting to oneself is far from easy when one knows that everyone else's life will have its own pattern and structure making them more ready to assimilate and understand what fits in to their view of themselves and the world rather than what does not.

The early years of my life were seen through a child's eyes with a child's understanding, expectations and assumptions. Then, I had no idea how I was supposed to think or react. It was always more difficult for me to compare what happened to me with what happened to other kids. These early childhood perceptions are therefore different from my observations of the events and people around me in adolescence when I would have talked to my fellow adolescents and read more about how teachers, other adolescents and other adults usually tried to understand them.

Later still, at university, I would have begun to read and be taught about the characteristics of normal and abnormal human development and family life, the importance of mutual affection, contact and continuity within families and so on. Having experienced a lack of almost all of these as a young child, I could see that the generations tend to recapitulate their own earlier experiences. In some ways my parents were simply living out their own experiences with their parents and others and I have to fight with myself sometimes not to act out with my immediate descendants habits and attitudes unconsciously learned from my recent ancestors. I am not always successful in this but much of what I have learned in my work has helped to supply checks and balances which have been helpful.

Finally, the experience of marriage and of my own children, and now, grandchildren, has given me an infinitely deeper understanding of what I have read professionally about relationships and family rearing practices in the course of learning my trade. The one illuminated the other. I looked back at my own childhood experiences and determined not to make the mistakes I saw my parents make. I had learned better ways of doing things, though as with most parents, I will only have had partial success. On the other hand, I hung on to a great deal of the set of values my parents, as Christians, had indoctrinated me with. As a scientific humanist I see the sanctions for such a system not in terms of the 'given word' but in terms of what seems to contribute to a happier, more tolerant and cooperative way of living together – in short, the fostering of behaviours which seem to contribute to the continuance of the species rather than the destruction of it.

According to W. H. Auden, 'Man is a history making creature who can neither repeat his past nor leave it behind.' I know that the past has permanence and cannot be changed, but that memory of the past is a variable dependent on many factors. The present is evanescent and the future is in our

heads, but reminiscence, our own 'history making', can inform and encourage us to get to grips with understanding and enjoying our pasts and the pasts of others, each and all in our own very personal present. Martial, in his *Epigrams* in the first century AD, was wise enough to declare that, 'to be able to enjoy one's past life is to live twice'.

Plate 32: The author with Ralph and Mary
as final year undergraduates, 1951

Epilogue

David Steel (The Rt Hon The Lord Steel of Aikwood KT KBE DL)

I have written many forewords in my time, but never an epilogue. What is one supposed to say on the assumption that by the time they reach this page the readers will have read the book for themselves?

I have three reflections to offer:

First, I am impressed – indeed astounded – at Dr Clark's capacity for clear recall of events in his early life. Having tackled my own autobiography I found this much more difficult than he. The clarity and vividness of his prose also impress.

Second, with the exception of his later rejection of religion, I was struck by the remarkable similarities of our manse life experience. Let me list these:

'Cold and cavernous' houses. Until a new manse was built at my father's last parish long after I was away and married in the late sixties, central heating was an unknown joy.

A grandfather smelling permanently of old tobacco with a huge collection of pipes.

His father's first parish being in the Fife coalfield.

The highly visible Sunday morning march down the church aisle to the manse pew in the front row.

The rigid family discipline – we were not allowed to play on our bikes in the street on Sundays.

The near drowning experience pursuing a model yacht – him on a boating pond and me in the river Clyde.

Children kept out of the way when visitors came to meals.

Father's study in the manse treated as the holy of holies – rarely to be entered by children.

The row of bells in the kitchen.
The Boys' Brigade as an approved outlet for youthful activities.

The war-time clothes – we had the added indignity of wearing smelly leather mittens made from the imperfectly cured skins of the rabbits kept in an outbuilding for food.

Tattie howking to earn some extra pocket money.

The bicycle tour with brother in youth hostels (though ours was limited to a few days in Scotland.)

The pressure to do well academically, and the persuasion to learn ancient Greek (which I rather enjoyed).

And of course 'Remember who you are'.

Third, he mentions how his upbringing influenced his choice of career and how manse life tended to steer towards the helping professions. Certainly my parents were proud of the fact that all five of their children entered such: parliament, medicine, nursing, occupational therapy, and the police. I have heard Gordon Brown acknowledge the same legacy.

That perhaps is the most significant lesson of this fascinating book.

David Steel, February 2007